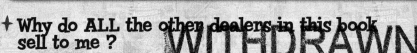

LIGHTS! CAMERA! ACTION!

The Overstreet® Guide To Collecting Movie Posters
takes our "How To" series to the cinema to explore the history and artistry
of movie posters, old and new, American and foreign, across the genres of
horror, Disney, adventure, comedy and many more...

Full color, filled with plenty of visual examples
and all the basics of grading, preservation and storage.

www.gemstonepub.com

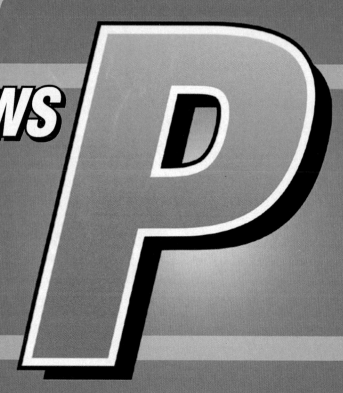

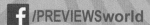 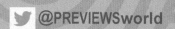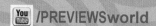

STEPHEN A. GEPPI PRESENTS

THE OVERSTREET® PRICE GUIDE TO
STAR WARS
COLLECTIBLES

BY AMANDA SHERIFF
AND ROBERT M. OVERSTREET

JON STEFFENS, J.C. VAUGHN,
AND CARRIE WOOD
CONTRIBUTING WRITERS

MARK HUESMAN
LAYOUT & DESIGN

BRAELYNN BOWERSOX
MARK HUESMAN
AMANDA SHERIFF
J.C. VAUGHN
AND CARRIE WOOD
EDITORS

TOM GAREY, KATHY WEAVER, BRETT CANBY,
AND ANGELA PHILLIPS-MILLS
ACCOUNTING SERVICES

SPECIAL THANKS TO
MIKE BOLLINGER, ERIC BRADLEY, RUSSELL BRANTON,
JOE FIORE, JAMES GALLO, STEVE GEPPI, HAKE'S AUCTIONS,
HERITAGE AUCTIONS, KURT KALATA, TERENCE KEAN,
KELLY MCCLAIN, ALEX NYC, BRIAN RACHFAL, ROBERT SIMONS,
JESSE CEDAR SOBERMAN, JON STEFFENS, CHAD THOMPSON,
PAUL WILSON, AND ALEX WINTER

GEMSTONE PUBLISHING • HUNT VALLEY, MARYLAND
WWW.GEMSTONEPUB.COM

FROM THE PUBLISHER

It seems hard to imagine that all of this – a multi-billion-dollar industry – was spawned by a film that was originally touted as "From the director of *American Graffiti...*"

Sure, George Lucas' 1973 offering of *American Graffiti* was a hit at theaters and its soundtrack sold well in record stores. And likewise, it definitely preformed far better for Universal Studios than *THX-1138* did in 1971 for Warner Brothers.

But it wasn't in the same league as what would follow.

In fact, it's not in the same galaxy.

To be more specific, it's not even in a *nearby* galaxy.

Perhaps *American Graffiti's* powerful combination of visuals and music tipped his hand just a bit, but it's truly safe to say that *no one* saw all of this coming.

From the moment that the first scenes of *Star Wars* – now known as *Episode IV – A New Hope* – debuted on the big screen in May 1977, the world of popular culture was irrevocably changed. The movie and its sequels, prequels, and spin-offs have become the stuff of legend.

If one looks at the comic book world, one will note that *Star Wars* collecting began a month earlier with the release of the first of six issues from Marvel Comics adapting the original film. If one turns to the novels, it seems clear that it actually began with Ballantine Books' mid-November 1976 release of the novelization, predating the movie's release by half a year.

The action figures, vehicles, playsets, pop-up books, one-sheets, three-sheets, original novels, cartoons, and so many other products were barely even dreams at that point, if they'd been conceived of at all.

From one-of-a-kind, set-used props to the most common of mass-produced items, however one defines *Star Wars* collecting, there are so many niches that there's practically something for everyone. In the end, we have to say this multi-generational adventure has turned into a compelling way to spend quality time with family and friends.

Bob

Robert M. Overstreet
Publisher

THE OVERSTREET PRICE GUIDE TO STAR WARS COLLECTIBLES. NOVEMBER 2018. ISBN: 978-1-60360-228-0. PUBLISHED BY GEMSTONE PUBLISHING, INC., 10150 YORK RD., SUITE 300, HUNT VALLEY, MD 21030. CONTENTS ©2018 GEMSTONE PUBLISHING AND RESPECTIVE COPYRIGHT HOLDERS. STAR WARS® IS A REGISTERED TRADEMARK OF LUCASFILM, LTD. OVERSTREET® IS A REGISTERED TRADEMARK OF GEMSTONE PUBLISHING, INC. ALL RIGHTS RESERVED. PRINTED IN THE UNITED STATES OF AMERICA.

TABLE OF CONTENTS

INTRODUCTION

Cue the John Williams Score...

From the start, George Lucas' *Star Wars* story was a grand scope idea of multiple worlds, sentient alien species, advanced technology, large scale battles, and a tyrannical government. But at its center, its most basic level, *Star Wars* is simply about good overcoming evil and normal people becoming extraordinary heroes.

Based on that concept, *Star Wars* became a vast mosaic built on the foundation of George Lucas that strengthened and grew for over 40 years. His movie became a trilogy that added two more trilogies, along with standalone, made for TV, and animated movies. There are TV specials and animated shows, and hundreds of comic books and novels with their own compelling story arcs. Worlds of video games and tabletop games introduce fans to immersive experiences where they can enter *Star Wars* to fight for the Light or the Dark Side.

Thousands of writers, artists, game designers, prop makers, musicians, toy makers, and others have been a part of this massive series. All of these entertainment opportunities created by Lucas and other contributors has fostered a fiercely loyal fanbase.

With those hundreds of titles and that loyal fanbase comes the desire to collect.

In this book, we bring together our uninhibited love of *Star Wars* with the inherent joy of collecting. Topics of toys, comic books, and movie posters anchor the book, with a deep look into their respective histories, detailed pricing on the secondary market, and tons of full-color images. They are surrounded by content on novels, video games, trading cards, Halloween costumes, screen-used material, theme park exclusives, and more, with background information, market perspectives, and prices.

Additional content includes interviews with a *Star Wars* collector whose toy collection has made international news, a collectibles dealer and expert, and the CEO of Action Figure Authority. The book opens by recounting the history of the series, followed by tips on understanding canon and story eras. Readers will also find features on individuals like Charles Lippincott and Ralph McQuarrie, among others, as well as an exploration on the complicated process of pricing certain collectibles.

The story of *Star Wars* is brimming with adventure, imaginative worlds, stalwart heroes, and nefarious villains. It's a place where we become enraptured by the fantasy and collect toys, books, posters, and games to retain a piece of that feeling.

A long time ago in a galaxy far, far away...

Chronicling the History of a Galaxy Far, Far Away

Over the past century, the entertainment industry has grown into a thriving circulatory system of creation and consumption. The most successful movies, TV shows, books, and games expand to sustain fans, branching into other entertainment mediums, making advertising deals, and creating merchandise. And then, there is *Star Wars*.

STAR WARS TIMELINE

May 14, 1944 – *Star Wars* creator George Lucas was born

March 1971 – *THX 1138*, Lucas' first feature length film, was released

August 1973 – Lucas' second film, *American Graffiti*, was released

December 1976 – *Star Wars: From the Adventures of Luke Skywalker* was published

The style C one-sheet for *A New Hope* depicts the primary cast, both good and evil.

Few series and franchises come close to the popularity of *Star Wars*. The underdog story about a group of rebels fighting an empire, quickly earned fans not just of science fiction but of adventure, drama, and even romance. It may have begun as a genre film, but 40 years of build-up in the pop culture zeitgeist has turned it into an entertainment juggernaut.

Star Wars grew into books, comics, radio, television, and games, plus several more

April 1977 – The first *Star Wars* comic was published by Marvel

May 1977 – *Star Wars: Episode IV – A New Hope* hit theaters

December 1977 – Kenner issues Early Bird Certificate Packages for action figures

November 1978 – *The Star Wars Holiday Special* aired on CBS

films – both sequential and standalone. Merchandizing took hold of fans by providing action figures and toys, costumes, posters, and just about anything that could display the iconic title. What began with a little known director, buckets of imagination, and innovative special effects has grown into a beloved multi-billion dollar series.

Star Wars was created by George Lucas, a man with two passions. Before his love of film came his love of fast cars. As a child, he aspired to be a race car driver, but after surviving a near fatal car accident in high school he changed his mind. His appreciation of cinematography and clever camera tricks began while attending community college. It bloomed into career aspirations when he transferred to the University of Southern California's filmmaking school. His film career began in the mid-1960s, working in the sound department, as a camera operator, production assistant, cinematographer, and editor.

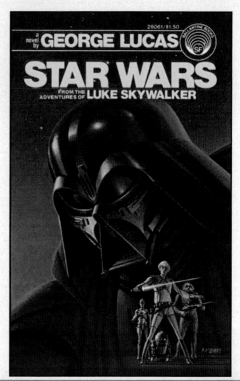

Before the film was released, the *Star Wars: From the Adventures of Luke Skywalker* novel was published.

Though his first feature film, *THX-1138*, was considered a flop by its studio, his second one, *American Graffiti*, did quite well. The teen movie about a group of friends spending a final night together after graduation was released in 1973. Boasting the young talents of Ron Howard, Richard Dreyfuss, Candy Clark, and a kid named Harrison Ford, it was filled with nostalgia, love of beautiful cars, and music. Co-written and directed by Lucas, it earned five Academy Award nominations, including Best Original Screenplay, Best Director, and Best Picture.

Lucas wanted his next project to be the modern equivalent of a Saturday morning children's program, combining fairy tale elements with fantasy and adventure, set in space. It evolved into the feature length *Star Wars*, that eventually became titled *Star Wars: Episode IV – A New Hope*, which he wrote and directed.

When it was released in 1977, the movie mesmerized audiences with its unique blend of special effects, characters – both human and otherwise – and exotic settings. The story begins 19 years after the formation of the evil Empire with the galaxy in a state of turmoil as a rebel faction tries to fight back. The Empire is ruled by a vicious emperor and overseen by his number one apprentice, Darth Vader (David Prowse, voiced by James Earl Jones). Princess Leia (Carrie Fisher) is among the rebels trying to save the galaxy through subterfuge and cunning. Luke Skywalker (Mark Hamill) is a young farmer bucking to be free, and who begins training in the ways of the Force by Jedi Obi-Wan Kenobi (Alec Guinness),

April 1980 – *The Empire Strikes Back* novel was published

June 1980 – *Star Wars: Episode V – The Empire Strikes Back* was released

March 1981 – *A New Hope* radio dramatization aired on National Public Radio

May 1982 – The first series video game, *The Empire Strikes Back*, was released on Atari 2600

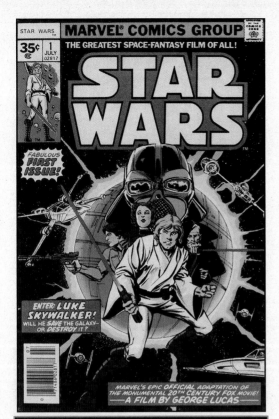

STAR WARS TM

MARVEL® COMICS GROUP

35¢ 1 JULY 02817

THE GREATEST SPACE-FANTASY FILM OF ALL!

STAR WARS

FABULOUS FIRST ISSUE!

ENTER: LUKE SKYWALKER! WILL HE *SAVE* THE GALAXY— OR *DESTROY* IT?

MARVEL'S EPIC OFFICIAL ADAPTATION OF THE MONUMENTAL 20TH CENTURY FOX MOVIE! —A FILM BY GEORGE LUCAS

Marvel published the first *Star Wars* comics, beginning in 1977 and running until 1986.

Star Wars comics have been produced by multiple publishers over the years. Marvel was the first to secure the rights, starting with a six-issue adaptation of the film. Publication began in April 1977, a month before the movie was released; it was written by Roy Thomas with art by Howard Chaykin (who also created the first movie poster). That series went on for 107 issues and 3 annuals through 1986. It was a high selling comic in the late '70s, which also included adaptations of *The Empire Strikes Back* and *Return of the Jedi* as well as other stories.

Over the years, *Star Wars* became one of the most merchandized franchises in all of pop culture, beginning with the beloved Kenner line. The toy company picked up the license for the action figure and toy line in '76, though figures weren't available for several months. Kenner wasn't prepared for the unprecedented level of consumer interest in *Star Wars* toys during the '77 holiday season. To compensate for not fulfilling the immediate high demand, Kenner issued Early Bird Certificate Packages that could be mailed away for the actual figures in early '78. From that point through 1985, Kenner produced tons of action figures, playsets, and vehicles. Toys featured different versions of characters, multi-pack examples, and card-back variations that both kids and adults consumed with voracious appetites.

and Han Solo (Ford) is a smuggler scoundrel who reluctantly joins the fight with his Wookie co-pilot, Chewbacca (Peter Mayhew). During its initial release, *Star Wars* earned over $307 million at the box office.

The first novel based on the series was published in December 1976, six months before the movie was released. *Star Wars: From the Adventures of Luke Skywalker* is a novelization of *A New Hope*, credited to Lucas, but ghostwritten by Alan Foster. The book does feature some differences from the film, which is likely due to editing processes for both versions. It was followed by film novelizations of *The Empire Strikes Back* by Donald F. Glut (1980) and *Return of the Jedi* by James Kahn (1983).

A year after the first movie was released, CBS aired *The Star Wars Holiday Special*. In the special, Chewbacca goes back to his home planet Kashyyyk to enjoy Life Day with his family. Celebrities who appeared in skits and musical numbers during the special included Bea Arthur and Jefferson Starship. While the special was a bankable idea, given the popularity of the series, it had a notoriously nega-

February 1983 – *The Empire Strikes Back* radio dramatization aired

May 1983 – *Return of the Jedi* novel was published

May 1983 – *Star Wars: Episode VI – Return of the Jedi* debuted in theaters

November 1984 – *Caravan of Courage: An Ewok Adventure* TV movie aired on ABC

Kenner secured the toy license for *Star Wars*, creating toys through the mid-1980s.

Some of Kenner's toys, like this vinyl cape Jawa, are more popular with collectors based on rarity and variations.

tive reception. Lucas famously hated the special and blocked it from airing again or being distributed on home video. There's an 11-minute animated portion with Boba Fett (who was not in the first film) that is largely considered the redeeming segment of the special.

In 1980, the film story continued in *The Empire Strikes Back* with Luke journeying to the planet Dagobah to be trained by Jedi Master Yoda. Leia and Han flee the Imperial forces after an attack on their rebel base and end up in the Cloud City of Bespin with Han's former friend Lando Calrissian (Billy Dee Williams), where Darth Vader has set a trap for young Luke. Despite warnings from Yoda and the now-ghostly Obi-Wan to stay on Dagobah, Luke takes the bait and leaves to save his friends, while promising to return and finish his training. During a dramatic duel that cost Luke his hand,

Darth Vader drops the ultimate movie bombshell, revealing to young Luke that he is his father, Anakin Skywalker. Directed by Irvin Kershner, with story by Lucas and screenplay by Leigh Brackett and Lawrence Kasdan, the worldwide box office totaled beyond $530 million.

A year after the second film was released, National Public Radio aired a 13-episode radio dramatization of *A New Hope*. Written by author Brian Daley and directed by John Madden, it included original score by John Williams and sound design by Ben Burtt. National Public Radio aired *The Empire Strikes Back* in 10 episodes in '83 and HighBridge Audio released *Return of the Jedi* as 6 episodes in '96. Though several characters were voiced by different actors, series stars Hamill, Anthony Daniels, and Billy Dee Williams reprised their roles for the radio productions.

September 1985 – *Star Wars: Droids* and *Ewoks* animated TV shows debuted on ABC

November 1985 – *Ewoks: The Battle for Endor* TV movie aired on ABC

January 1987 – Star Tours, the first amusement park ride, opened at Disneyland in California

May 1987 – Starlog Salutes Star Wars 10th anniversary convention was held

In 1982 *Star Wars* entered the realm of video games with this *Empire Strikes Back* shooter game.

THE SAGA CONTINUES.

STAR WARS
REVENGE OF THE JEDI

Coming May 25, 1983 to your galaxy.

Return of the Jedi was originally titled *Revenge of the Jedi* making the advance one-sheet highly collectible.

Star Wars reached into a new entertainment medium in 1982 with the first licensed video game, *Star Wars: The Empire Strikes Back*. The scrolling shooter game was published by Parker Brothers for the Atari 2600. As Luke, the player is situated in a Snowspeeder with the objective to shoot AT-AT walkers on the frozen planet Hoth. After Atari, it was released for Intellivision in 1983.

The final episode of the original trilogy came out in 1983, directed by Richard Marquand, written by Kasdan and Lucas. *Return of the Jedi* sees the Empire working on a more powerful Death Star while the Rebels plan their most ambitious attack. Before joining the fight, Luke learns that Leia is his twin sister and shares the news with her on the Forest Moon of Endor. After the fighting ends she put a nervous Han at ease, explaining that her love for Luke is familial and the pair begin their relation-

ship in earnest. When faced with killing his son or the Emperor (Ian McDiarmid), Darth Vader chooses to save his son at the last minute, costing him his life. In the end, the Empire fell at the hands of the Rebels, led by a young farmer, princess, scruffy looking nerf herder, a Wookie, an old smoothie, and a couple of droids. The final piece in Lucas' first trilogy made over $570 million.

Audiences were introduced to the furry little forest-dwelling Ewoks in *Return of the Jedi*, who went on to star in two movies of their own. The TV movie *Caravan of Courage: An Ewok Adventure* aired on ABC during Thanksgiving weekend in 1984. Wicket the Ewok from *Return of the Jedi* (with

May 1991 – The first in the *Thrawn* trilogy novels was published

December 1991 – Dark Horse Comics published their first *Star Wars* comics

February 1995 – The *Star Wars: Jedi Knight* video game series began with *Dark Forces*

August 1996 – *Return of the Jedi* radio dramatization was released

Warwick Davis reprising the role) helps two kids find and save their parents from a giant. Lucas provided the story and Bob Carrau wrote the screenplay, which was directed by John Korty.

A year later in the sequel *Ewoks: The Battle for Endor*, Wicket and Cindel (from *Caravan of Courage*) face an evil witch and meet a hermit who might be able to save the Ewok village from raiders. Once again Lucas provided the story, which was written and directed by Jim and Ken Wheat.

The first two animated *Star Wars* TV series began in 1985, both produced by Nelvana, the studio that created the animated portion of the *Holiday Special*. *Star Wars: Droids* ran through 1986, chronicling early adventures of R2-D2 and C-3PO (with Daniels voicing Threepio). *Ewoks* ran from '85 to '87 telling stories about young Wicket.

In conjunction with the 10th anniversary, Star Tours became the first live attraction for the series. The motion simulator debuted at Disneyland in

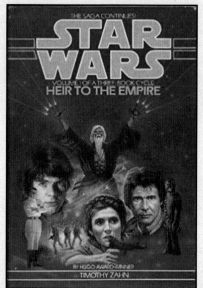

Timothy Zahn's *Thrawn* book trilogy, beginning with *Heir to the Empire*, is considered one of the best companions to the movie series.

Tales of the Jedi was a notable comic series that was published by Dark Horse.

California in 1987. Piloted by a droid named Captain Rex (voiced by Paul Reubens), it took guests on a trip to Endor to encounter the Rebel Alliance and Empire. It opened in Disney's Florida, Tokyo, and Paris parks by 1992.

To commemorate a decade of *Star Wars*, a 10th anniversary convention was held in 1987. Officially called Starlog Salutes Star Wars, the event was hosted by *Starlog Magazine* in Los Angeles. Lucas was a celebrity guest, along with Daniels, Mayhew, Billy Dee Williams, and concept artist Ralph McQuarrie.

From 1991 to 1993, Timothy Zahn wrote the bestselling *Thrawn* trilogy, which is considered to be one of the best companion series. Also known as the *Heir to the Empire* trilogy, it introduced popular characters like Imperial military commander Grand Admiral Thrawn, Mara Jade (Luke Skywalker's wife), and smuggler Talon Karrde. Set in the expanded universe about five years after *Return of the Jedi*, the Rebellion is now known as the New Republic, trying to defeat the last of the Imperial

February 1997 – Star Wars Weekends annual festival debuted at Disney's Hollywood Studios

December 1998 – *Star Wars: Rogue Squadron* video game was released

April 1999 – The first Star Wars Celebration was held

May 1999 – *Star Wars: Episode I – The Phantom Menace*, the first in the prequel trilogy was released in theaters

resistance, while creating a new government structure. At the edges of the galaxy Grand Admirals are working together to attack the New Republic.

Beginning in '91, Dark Horse Comics published the limited comic series *Star Wars: Dark Empire*. They published dozens of *Star Wars* comics through 2014, including a bunch of series within the franchise, like *Tales of the Jedi*, *Star Wars: Republic*, and *Knights of the Old Republic*. In '99, Dark Horse published a prequel for *The Phantom Menace* along with adaptations of that film, *Attack of the Clones*, and *Revenge of the Sith*, as well as *The Thrawn Trilogy* book series.

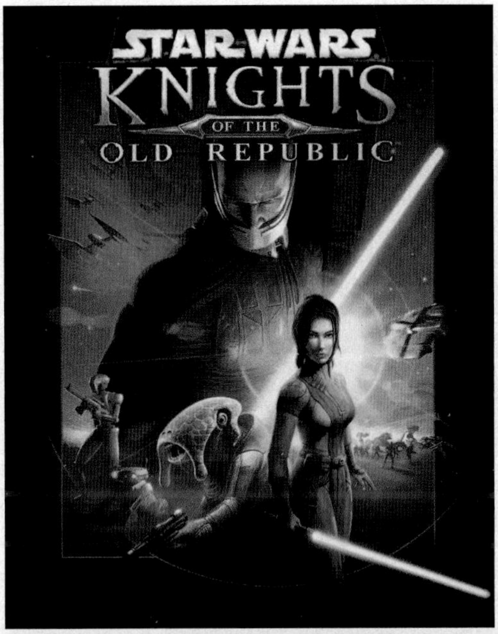

The *Knights of the Old Republic* roleplaying video game takes place 4,000 years before the Galactic Empire.

The *Star Wars: Jedi Knight* video game series began in 1995 with *Dark Forces*. This first- and third-person shooter was developed and published by LucasArts. It primarily focuses on Kyle Katarn, a former Imperial officer who became a Jedi and instructs at the Jedi Academy.

From 1997 to 2015, Star Wars Weekends, the annual festival at Disney's Hollywood Studios, celebrated the series with a plethora of events. Cast and crew members would meet fans, Disney characters would dress up in *Star Wars* garb, and there were fireworks displays, Jedi training, live shows, interactive events, and parades.

The *Star Wars: Rogue Squadron* video game series began in 1998. This arcade-style action game was jointly developed by LucasArts and Factor 5 for Nintendo. It is set during the original trilogy with the Rogue Squadron unit using starfighters to battle the Empire.

By the late 1990s special effects technology had made significant leaps forward and Lucas decided it was time to continue his *Star Wars* film saga with the prequel trilogy. Released in 1999, written and directed by Lucas, *The Phantom Menace* focuses on Darth Vader as a child and a young Jedi Obi-Wan Kenobi (Ewan McGregor). Jedi Master Qui-Gon Jinn (Liam Neeson) recognizes the potential in young Anakin Skywalker (Jake Lloyd), deciding to train him in the ways of the Force, while Queen Amidala (Natalie Portman) leads the people of Naboo against invasion.

The movie made $1 billion worldwide, but fans were divided regarding the movie's success. Many longtime *Star Wars* fans felt that it was bogged down by politics, they didn't connect with some new characters, and the tone was more like a family film. This critique is due in part to the immense pressure older fans put on the new movie, with 16 years' worth of love and loyalty. Younger fans, or those new to the series,

October 1999 – *The New Jedi Order* novel series kicked off with *Vector Prime*

May 2002 – *Star Wars: Episode II – Attack of the Clones* premiered in theaters

July 2003 – *Star Wars: Knights of the Old Republic* video game was released

November 2003 – *Star Wars: Clone Wars* animated TV show debuted on Cartoon Network

loved Darth Maul (Ray Park), from his weapon to his striking appearance and physicality.

Special effects were also a point of disagreement. No one could argue that the new effects had no boundaries, prompting huge battles, gleaming new ships, and impressive creatures, but some fans preferred the practical effects of the original over the computer effects of the new.
Star Wars Celebration began in 1999, with the inaugural event held in Denver to celebrate the release of *The Phantom Menace*.

Subsequent Celebrations were held for the releases of *Attack of the Clones* and *Revenge of the Sith*. It has since been held every few years, primarily in the U.S. with some installments hosted internationally.

Del Rey started publishing *The New Jedi Order* novel series in 1999. Set 25 to 30 years after the original series, it introduced the alien race Yuuzhan Vong's attempt to conquer the galaxy. From 2006 to 2008, Del Rey published the *Legacy of the Force* series, telling the story of Jacen Solo, Han and Leia's son who turns to the Dark Side of the Force – a storyline that would later be adapted in *The Force Awakens*.

Released in 2002, *Attack of the Clones* picks up ten years after *Phantom Menace* with Anakin (Hayden Christensen) training to be a Jedi, taught by Obi-Wan while Padmé Amidala has become a senator of the Galactic Republic. Obi-Wan traces the location of an assassin to a remote region of the galaxy where a clone army has been building, using the DNA of bounty hunter Jango Fett (Temuera Morrison). Anakin swears to protect Padmé and the pair fall in love on the beautiful planet of Naboo. Visions of his mother in distress prompt Anakin to go home to learn that she has been kidnapped. He finds her as she's dying and he subsequently slaughters a party of Tusken Raiders, well on his way to the Dark Side. It ends with the Jedi in aggressive negotiations with Count Dooku and the separatists. Lucas directed this one and co-wrote it with Jonathan Hales. *Attack of the Clones* reached over $649 million at the box office worldwide.

Released in 2005, *Revenge of the Sith* was the final installment in the prequel trilogy that shows the rise of Darth Vader.

September 2004 – *Star Wars: Battlefront* video game was released

May 2005 – *Star Wars: Episode III – Revenge of the Sith* premiered in theaters

May 2006 – *Legacy of the Force* novel series began with *Betrayal*

August 2008 – *Star Wars: The Clone Wars* animated TV series began with a movie

In 2003 the roleplaying game *Star Wars: Knights of the Old Republic* was released on Xbox and PC. Developed by BioWare and published by LucasArts, it takes place 4,000 years before the Galactic Empire. The role-playing game remains a standout among both BioWare and *Star Wars* video games.

The *Star Wars: Clone Wars* animated show ran on Cartoon Network from 2003 to 2005. Sandwiched between releases of *Attack of the Clones* and *Revenge of the Sith*, the show featured events from both movies.

Pandemic Studios developed and LucasArts published the first in the *Star Wars: Battlefront* game series in 2004. The first- and third-person shooter faces warring groups against each other, such as the Galactic Republic vs. Confederacy of Independent Systems, or Galactic Empire vs. Rebel Alliance, or First Order vs. the Resistance. Though the game featured a lengthy single player campaign, it was particularly praised for the online multiplayer battles.

Following the Republic's fight against the Separatists, *The Clone Wars* was introduced as a film, then ran as a TV show.

Lucas wrote and directed the final install-ment of his second trilogy. *Revenge of the Sith* was released in 2005 with the Jedi leading the clone army in a battle against the Separatists. Supreme Chancellor Palpatine continues his political maneu-vers to gain more power while whisper-ing into the increasingly receptive ear of Anakin Skywalker. After having a vision that Padmé will die in childbirth he makes the ultimate choice, pledging himself to the Emperor and his burgeoning Galactic Empire. As the Jedi are being exterminated across the galaxy, Master Yoda and a few others are forced into hiding. Upon discov-ering Anakin's betrayal, Obi-Wan battles his former Padawan, leaving Anakin for dead, but he is saved by the Emperor and becomes Darth Vader, while Padmé gives birth to Leia and Luke. *Revenge of the Sith* totaled almost $849 million at the box office worldwide.

Lucasfilm's Animation division produced the CGI animated series *Star Wars: The Clone Wars* from 2008 to 2014. Despite being set during the previous *Clone Wars* show, this iteration didn't recognize the predecessor. The adventures of Obi-Wan, Anakin, Yoda, and Mace Windu are shown

September 2008 – *Star Wars: The Force Unleashed* video game was released

October 2012 – The Walt Disney Company acquired Lucasfilm

May 2011 – *Star Tours – The Adventures Continue* attraction opened first at Disney's Hollywood Studios

September 2014 – *Star Wars: Rebels* animated TV show began airing on Disney XD

SABINE WREN
STAR WARS REBELS

A NEW HOPE?

Topps has been issuing *Star Wars* trading cards since the first film debuted. In 2015, the company issued their first series based on the *Star Wars Rebels* animated show.

as they lead the Republic against the droid army of the Separatists. Unlike previous television programs, Lucasfilm accepted the show and originating film as canon.

LucasArts released the action-adventure game *Star Wars: The Force Unleashed* in 2008. Set between the original and pre-quel trilogies, the game follows Starkiller, Darth Vader's secret apprentice, who hunts down the Jedi. It is part of a larger interconnected multimedia series that includes a sequel video game, tie-in novel,

Marvel Comics began publishing new ongoing *Star Wars* comics in March 2015. The series published the first 50 issues by the summer of 2018.

comic book, action figures, and roleplaying game supplement.

In 2011 *Star Tours* was reinvigorated with *Star Tours – The Adventures Continue*, updating all previous iterations of the ride at Disney parks around the world. The 3-D motion simulator takes attendees through the galaxy with C-3PO. *The Adventure Continues* encourages multiple rides, as any given tour is randomized with different scenes, plus Disney has updated the ride with each new film, adding even more scenes for a variety of experiences. At this book's publication date, all locations were still active.

On October 30, 2012, it was announced that The Walt Disney Company had acquired Lucasfilm for $4 billion, making George Lucas, with 40 million Disney shares, the company's second-largest non-institutional shareholder, following the trust of Steve Jobs, the late Apple co-founder. In the time since, Disney announced a full slate of new Star Wars film projects and expansions to both Disneyland and Walt Disney World.

The *Star Wars: Rebels* CGI-animated TV show began in 2014. Set between *Revenge of the Sith* and *A New Hope*, it tells the adventures of a group of Rebels resisting the Empire's tightening hold on the galaxy. The visual

January 2015 – After regaining the license, Marvel began publishing *Star Wars* comics

November 2015 – Electronic Arts released the *Star Wars Battlefront* video game series reboot

December 2015 – *Star Wars: Episode VII – The Force Awakens*, the first in the third trilogy hits theaters

August 2016 – R2-D2 performer Kenny Baker passed away at age 81.

style was inspired by McQuarrie's concept art for the original films, with some characters inspired by early versions of established characters. The series follows popular characters Ezra Bridger, Kanan Jarrus, Hera Syndulla, Sabine Wren, and Zeb Orrelios.

In addition to purchasing Lucasfilm, Walt Disney had bought Marvel Entertainment in 2009. Six years later, Marvel regained the license to Star Wars comics and began publishing with ongoing series for *Star Wars* and *Darth Vader*. They also created miniseries for characters across all three trilogies, including Princess Leia, Lando Calrissian, Mace Windu, and Captain Phasma.

The film series began a new trilogy in 2015 with *The Force Awakens*. Set about 30 years after *Return of the Jedi*, the militant First Order has been built from the ashes of the fallen Galactic Empire while the Resistance has picked up the mantle of the Rebellion. The Resistance is trying to find a map that will lead to Luke Skywalker's location while the First Order is situated on the Starkiller Base – a planet that's been converted into a catastrophically powerful weapon.

New characters include Rey (Daisy Ridley), a scavenger who turns out to be powerful with the Force; Kylo Ren (Adam Driver), a formidable member of the First Order; Finn (John Boyega), a Stormtrooper reluctant to follow the First Order's creed; Resistance pilot Poe Dameron (Oscar Isaac) and his quirky, comical droid BB-8; and Captain Phasma (Gwendoline Christie), a high-ranking Stormtrooper who became very popular despite limited screen time. But the big news was the return of series leads Princess Leia, Han Solo with Chewbacca,

and Luke Skywalker. Princess Leia has become General Leia and is still a leader in the Resistance, Han and Chewie have returned to their smuggling days, and Luke appears only briefly as a secluded hermit.

The film was directed by J.J. Abrams (who had seen recent success directing *Star Trek* films), co-written by Kasdan, Abrams, and Michael Arndt. It was a huge success, clearing over $2 billion at the global box office and had the largest opening weekend ever with $529 million (a record that stood for nearly two years), and fastest film to hit $1 billion, which was done in just 12 days.

In 2015, *The Force Awakens* began the third trilogy with many new characters and the return of Han, Leia, and Luke.

December 2016 – *Rogue One: A Star Wars Story*, the first standalone film, was released

December 27, 2016 – Princess Leia actress Carrie Fisher passed away at age 60.

December 2017 – *Star Wars: Episode VIII – The Last Jedi* debuted in theaters

May 2018 – *Solo: A Star Wars Story*, the second standalone movie, was released

Hasbro has released a number of toys in their Star Wars The Black Series line, including 6" action figures for the third trilogy of films.

Rogue One: A Star Wars Story became the first standalone film in the series.

A year later, *Rogue One: A Star Wars Story* became the series' first standalone feature length film. It is set before the first trilogy when scientist Galen Erso (Mads Mikkelsen) has been pressed to create a super-weapon, capable of destroying planets, i.e. the Death Star. Galen refuses the assignment and his wife is killed, though his daughter survives and is rescued by Rebel extremist Saw Gerrera (Forest Whitaker). Years later Bodhi (Riz Ahmed), a cargo pilot who defected from the Empire plans to share a message from Galen with the Rebels. Galen's now-adult daughter Jyn (Felicity Jones) meets Rebel intelligence officer Cassian (Diego Luna) and joins their cause. After witnessing a test run of the weapon that destroys a city, a group of Rebels led by Jyn and Cassian head to the Imperial data bank to steal the Death Star's schematics and reveal its weakness to the Alliance. Directed by Gareth Edwards, co-written by Chris Weitz and Tony Gilroy, the movie made over $1 billion during the theatrical run.

The Last Jedi, the second installment in the third trilogy, broke from the traditional three-year release schedule to hit theaters in 2017. Written and directed by Rian Johnson, it opens with the First Order fleet finding the Resistance forces led by General Leia, and stalks them through space. Rey has found Luke Skywalker and tries to convince him to join the Resistance and teach her about the Force. Once Luke sees her raw talent, similar to that of his nephew Ben – now Kylo Ren – he is frightened of her power. While on the island, Rey begins communicating with Kylo through visions as he deals with his own uncertainties regarding his place in the First Order. Poe disagrees with the new Vice Admiral Holdo (Laura Dern), sending Finn and mechanic Rose Tico (Kelly Marie Tran) on their own mission to disable a tracking device attached

Turmoil and danger abound in 2017's *The Last Jedi*, which cleared over $1 billion globally during its theatrical run.

and they embark on a mission to steal a very profitable, very volatile substance wanted by the whole galaxy. Directed by Ron Howard and written by Kasdan and his son, Jonathan Kasdan, *Solo* filled in some of Han's notorious history, including his first meetings with Chewbacca (now played by Joonas Suotamo) and Lando as well as the famous Kessel run.

A dramatic amount of pressure was on Ehrenreich and Glover as they were stepping into the beloved roles played by Ford and Billy Dee Williams. Though the prequels did cast younger versions of established characters – Obi-Wan and Anakin – they were supporting characters in the original series, whereas Han was one of the three main leads. Its worldwide box office total was $392 million.

Star Wars long ago became a global sensation and what began as a science fiction film expanded into every major form of entertainment and facet of pop culture. From media saturation over new movie releases, through periods of limited new content, the fans of *Star Wars* endure and continue to grow. We are consistently reminded that it can bring down the house with a screen shot, a line of dialogue, or a few notes of the score.

to the Resistance's fleet. Audiences flocked to theaters to see *The Last Jedi*, giving it the second largest opening weekend to date, behind *The Force Awakens*. It debuted with $220 million at the box office and has since grossed over $1 billion worldwide.

Solo: A Star Wars Story, released in 2018, became the second standalone film and first one centered around one character. It opens on Corellia where Han (Alden Ehrenreich) and his girlfriend Qi'ra (Emilia Clarke) are trying to escape a local gang. He makes it out, she doesn't. Years later, he is an Imperial soldier who wanted to become a pilot to find a way back to her, but is quite unhappy with the state of his life. So, he seizes the opportunity to flee by joining a crew of thieves, led by a man called Beckett (Woody Harrelson). Their first job together is a catastrophe, putting them in a dangerous position with crime boss Dryden Vos (Paul Bettany), who happens to employ a wiser, more refined Qi'ra. She joins their job, leads them to Lando Calrissian (Donald Glover) to seek a ship,

Solo: A Star Wars Story cast younger versions of established film series characters, including Donald Glover as Lando Calrissian. His performance was well received by fans and the Funko Pop! Vinyl collectible of his interpretation is popular with collectors.

UNDERSTANDING CONTINUITY

Collectively, *Star Wars* encompasses hundreds of stories told on film, TV, in comics, games, and books, which makes understanding and defining continuity pivotal to the franchise. The issue of continuity has been a topic of serious debate among fans and collectors for years, which led to decisions by George Lucas and Lucasfilm to categorize the content.

During and after the original trilogy took off, *Star Wars* extended into licensed comics, books (non-film adaptations), TV, and games. While they may have had guidance from the film team, they were telling original stories, which coined the Expanded Universe (commonly abbreviated as EU). Through the EU the world of *Star Wars* went back over 36,000 years before *The Phantom Menace* and around 100 years after the third film trilogy. Many other planets, people, and species are also housed there, including some of whom are closely associated with canon characters and storylines. For many years canonicity was defined, though in several groupings.

What we have today is Star Wars Canon and Star Wars Legends.

Canon is the distinction given to any title/series/event that is considered part of the official *Star Wars* story. This encompasses the feature film series and certain other material, like *Star Wars: The Clone Wars* animated TV series and movie, and *Star Wars Rebels* animated TV show.

Star Wars Legends, formerly known as the Expanded Universe, is all of the officially licensed material (books, comics, games, TV shows, and TV movies) outside of the film series.

On April 25, 2014, Lucasfilm announced that the Expanded Universe was going to be reorganized under the non-canon heading of Star Wars Legends. This was done in part as preparation for the third film trilogy. New material released since that date is generally considered as Canon.

Some new material continues as Star Wars Legends, including the comic series *Star Wars: Legacy Vol. 2*, the *Star Wars: Rebel Heist* mini-series, and the U.K. comic strip. As of 2017 the only new Legends media still being released is in the form of updates for the *Star Wars: The Old Republic* online video game. To keep the designation clear, this material is created under the Legends banner. When material from the former EU is reprinted, for instance new editions of the older novels, they are also stamped with the Legends banner.

EXPANDED UNIVERSE CANON LEVELS

In 2000 Lucas Licensing created a database to track continuity, called the Holocron. Letters were assigned to represent levels of canonicity based on the content available at that point, and updated to reflect new material until the 2014 transition. While this is no longer the accurate way of tracking content, its use is still found in *Star Wars* collecting circles and auctions where collectibles can be procured.

The Expanded Universe canon level distinctions are G-canon, T-canon, C-canon, S-canon, N-canon, and D-canon.

G-canon is George Lucas Canon
Comprised of the film series and any decrees by George Lucas.

T-canon is Television Canon
This is mainly the *Star Wars: The Clone Wars* TV show and animated series.

C-canon is Continuity Canon
More recent works across books, comics, games, and animation, among some other material.

S-canon is Secondary Canon
Mostly older non-film series material, like the first volume of comics. The "secondary" distinction means that it could be used or ignored by writers.

N-canon is Non-Canon
This is anything that contradicts the movies, any "what if" stories.

D-canon is Detours Canon
Material used in *Star Wars Detours*.

DEFINING THE STORY ERAS OF STAR WARS LEGENDS

From the movies to the books, games, and comics, *Star Wars* has a rich, detailed history that unfolds over thousands of years. Beyond the beloved core stories of the Rebels and the Empire, there are further adventures of film characters, other brave heroes and powerful villains, political conflicts, and alliances. With such a lengthy, complicated web of stories, it's imperative that eras are distinguished, ensuring that fans will know where each story fits into the larger landscape of the series.

The eras of Star Wars Legends are situated around the first major event of the film series – the Battle of Yavin. This fight between the Rebellion and the Empire saw the moment when Luke Skywalker destroyed the first Death Star in *A New Hope*. As such, the calendar eras are designated as BBY (Before the Battle of Yavin) and ABY (After the Battle of Yavin).

The eras are defined below, however, it's important to note that changes and additions can steadily occur as new stories are being added to the Legends banner. While the Legends banner includes the original trilogy's Battle of Yavin and surrounding events, it does differ from some other canonical content. One such example is the Jacen Solo storyline of the Legacy Era that differs from the events of the third film trilogy.

The Star Wars Legends story eras begin thousands of years before the Battle of Yavin, telling origin stories that lay the groundwork for the Jedi, Republic, and the Empire. They continue into the not too distant future after Yavin to watch Luke Skywalker reestablish the Jedi and see the galaxy threatened by a foreboding enemy.

Before the Republic (37,000 BBY - 25,000 BBY)
Before the Galactic Republic, the Je'daii Order discover the Force on Tython.

The Old Republic (25,000 BBY - 1,000 BBY)
The Old Republic government unites the galaxy through the Galactic Senate with Jedi protecting peace and justice from the Sith.

The Rise of the Empire (1,000 BBY - 0 BBY)
As the senate is embroiled in corruption and bogged down by bureaucracy, governing becomes futile. Senator Palpatine, the Dark Lord of the Sith, maneuvers into the position of Supreme Chancellor and Anakin Skywalker becomes Darth Vader. This is the era of the prequel trilogy.

The Rebellion (0 BBY - 5 ABY)
Resistance spreads throughout the galaxy, leading to the Galactic Civil War. This era starts when the Rebellion acquires the Death Star plans, sees the Battle of Yavin, Retreat from Hoth, and ends after the Emperor's death. This is the period of the original trilogy.

The New Republic (5 ABY - 25 ABY)
The Rebel Alliance must create a functioning government, deal with the remaining leaders of the Empire and other enemies. Luke Skywalker begins training new apprentices, establishing the New Jedi Order.

The New Jedi Order (25 ABY - 37 ABY)
The New Republic and remaining Imperial loyalists have signed a peace treaty, and the Jedi Knights have redeveloped. It's a time of peace until the Yuuzhan Vong alien regime from beyond known space invades and later the New Jedi face a hive-minded species.

Legacy (40 ABY -)
The newly formed Galactic Federation of Free Alliance is struggling to maintain a single government with threats that include the remains of the Dark Side. Jacen Solo (Han and Leia's son) has become a powerful Jedi, falls to the Dark Side, and attempts to create a new Empire.

Star Wars Books

–

A Novel Collectible

One of the most versatile, affordable, and bountiful ways to collect *Star Wars* is in the vast array of novels. The dynamic quantity of *Star Wars* novels numbers into the hundreds of titles. They are set across a wide swath of time in familiar and foreign territories throughout the galaxy. Novels are geared toward adults, young adults, and kids providing entertainment for all audiences.

Most of the books are the non-canon Star Wars Legends brand (formerly known as the Expanded Universe), though a few of the books are canon. The large catalog of books includes movie adaptations, several standalone adventures, and multi-book series.

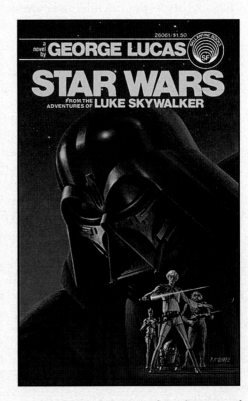

Star Wars: From the Adventures of Luke Skywalker sells in a wide range of $12 to $1,100 depending on edition, condition, and whether or not it is autographed.

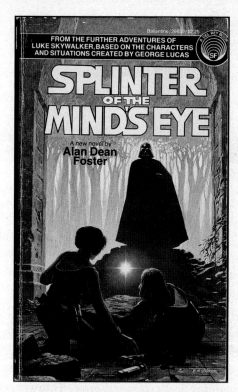

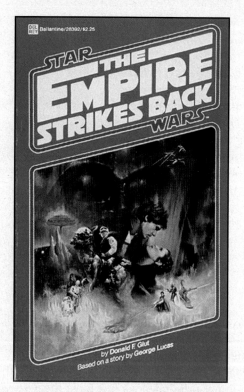

The second series novel, *Splinter of the Mind's Eye*, realizes $5 to $50.

The *Empire Strikes Back* novelization first edition averages $5 to $50.

The framework and anchor of *Star Wars* is the film series, but before movie audiences even saw a glimpse of Luke Skywalker, they had the chance to read the novelization. The first novel based on the film series was *Star Wars: From the Adventures of Luke Skywalker* (Ballantine Books), which was published in 1976, months before the movie premiered in theaters. Though it was a novelization of the movie, there are some minor differences between the two. Authorship was credited to George Lucas, but it was ghost written by Alan Dean Foster, who used the script and concept art to write the book. Collector's note: after the first printing, later editions included full color photos from the movie and some used the episodic retitling as *A New Hope: From the Adventures of Luke Skywalker* and *Star Wars Episode IV: A New Hope*.

Two years later, Foster wrote *Splinter of the Mind's Eye* (Ballantine Books), a sequel to the first book. Foster was commissioned to write a story that could be realized on film at a lower budget than the original, in case the first movie wasn't a grand success. In it,

Luke and Leia go on a mission and he finds the Kyber crystal (identified as Kaiburr in this book) that can give great power over the Force to whoever possesses it. Since the first movie was a success this wasn't transitioned on film so it's considered as a further adventure set between *A New Hope* and *The Empire Strikes Back*.

The smuggler starred in his own trilogy from 1979 to 1980 in *The Han Solo Adventures* (Del Rey). Set before *A New Hope*, it recounts the exploits of Han and Chewbacca smuggling and having misadventures across the galaxy with daring escapes, complicated deals, and treasure hunts. Individually titled *Han Solo at Stars' End*, *Han Solo's Revenge*, and *Han Solo and the Lost Legacy*, the books were written by Brian Daley.

The Empire Strikes Back (Del Rey) novelization was published in 1980, a few months before the movie premiered. Written by Donald F. Glut, this adaptation, similar to the first one, contains some scenes and details that are different from the movie.

It was originally released in two forms – the standard edition and a special *Young Readers Edition*, which was shortened – but both contain pages of color photos in the center of the book. Collectors note: the original printing does not have the *Episode V* title on the cover.

The *Return of the Jedi* (Del Rey) novelization was published just days before the film saw release in 1983. Written by James Kahn, like its predecessors, the book contains differences from the movie including more character exposition. Collectors note: the original printing does not have the *Episode VI* title on the cover.

Also that year, the old smoothie was given the spotlight in *The Lando Calrissian Adventures* trilogy (Del Rey) by L. Neil Smith. The books are set before he was introduced in *The Empire Strikes Back*, chronicling his experiences when he was still captain of the Millennium Falcon. The individual titles are *Lando Calrissian and the Mindharp of Sharu*, *Lando Calrissian and the Flamewind of Oseon*, and *Lando*

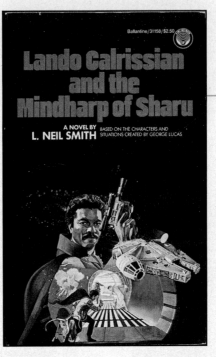

Lando Calrissian and the Mindharp of Sharu, the first book in the Lando Calrissian trilogy, averages $3 to $15.

Calrissian and the Starcave of ThonBoka.

The *Thrawn* trilogy (Bantam Spectra) by Timothy Zahn is considered to be among the best entries within *Star Wars* books. Also known as the *Heir to the Empire* trilogy, the books are set five years after *Return of the Jedi* as the Rebellion is trying to set up a new government and continue fighting the remaining Imperial resistance. Thrawn and other grand admirals of the Empire try to retaliate and regain control. The series is well known for introducing Imperial military commander Grand Admiral Thrawn, Luke Skywalker's wife Mara Jade, smuggler Talon Karrde, and Imperial officer Gilad Pellaeon. The trilogy's individual titles, which were published in 1991-1993, are *Heir to the Empire*, *Dark Force Rising*, and *The Last Command*. A few years later, Zahn followed up with the two-book series *The Hand of Thrawn* in 1997-1998.

Each first edition hardcover in the *Thrawn* trilogy sells for about $3 to $35.

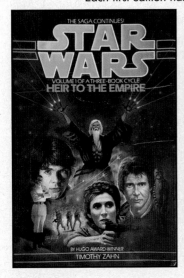
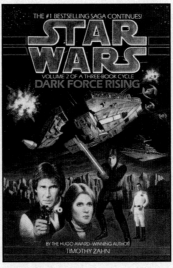
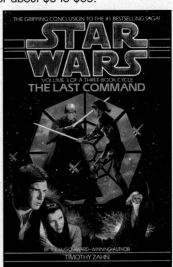

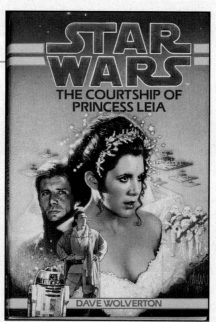

In 1994 the leading lady of the galaxy's recalcitrant love life was the center of Dave Wolverton's *The Courtship of Princess Leia* (Bantam Spectra). Things were looking good for Leia and Han after the Battle of Endor, but when the Rebel Alliance searches for a powerful ally, they learn that it may come in the Hapes Consortium – if Princess Leia will marry Prince Isolder. Han, unhappy with the scenario, tries to change Leia's mind, while Luke becomes friends with the jilted prince and tries to find his now-missing friends.

Also published that year, was the *Jedi Academy* trilogy (Bantam Spectra) by Kevin J. Anderson. Individually titled *Jedi Search*, *Dark Apprentice*, and *Champions of the Force*, the story takes place about seven years after *Return of the Jedi*. Luke Skywalker devotes himself to rebuilding the Jedi Order by setting up an academy and the New Republic deals with a new catastrophic weapon.

The 14-book *Young Jedi Knights* series (Boulevard and Berkley Jam) by Anderson and Rebecca Moesta was published in 1995-1998. The popular young adult series centers around the Jedi training of teenaged Jacen and Jaina Solo, the twin children of Leia and Han Solo.

Shadows of the Empire (Bantam Books) by Steve Perry was included in an ambitious multimedia project. The book debuted in 1996 as part of a cross-platform series that comprised this novel, a comic miniseries, video game, trading cards, roleplaying game, and other related merchandise. The main plot of the project unfolds in the book, which is set between *Empire Strikes Back* and *Return of the Jedi* – a point rarely utilized in the expanded universe. It introduces Prince Xizor, who runs the largest criminal group in the galaxy and wishes to take Vader's place as Emperor Palpatine's second in command.

The *X-Wing* series (Bantam Spectra and Del Rey) recounts missions of Rogue Squadron and Wraith Squadron, formed by Wedge Antilles after the Battle of Yavin. Their adventures involve trying to regain ground for the New Republic, defeating an Imperial warlord, the Republic seeking alliances, and launching important investigations. Michael A. Stackpole and Aaron Allston wrote the 10-book series in 1996-2012. Books 1-4 are a complete story, 5-7 complete another arc, book 8 mostly refers to the first story, book 9 is considered a standalone, and book 10 connects back to the second arc.

The *Jedi Apprentice* series (Scholastic) was among the first to tell stories set in the prequel timeframe once *Phantom Menace* was released in theaters. Comprising 18 books for young readers, they tell the adventures of Master Jedi Qui-Gon Jinn and young Jedi Obi-Wan Kenobi before *Episode I*. The series starts with Obi-Wan trying to become an apprentice, loyalties are challenged, remote planets explored, a scientist experiments with the Force, and there are political struggles, all the while Obi-Wan comes of age during their missions. Published in 1999-2002, the first book was written by Wolverton and the rest were written by Jude Watson.

Jedi-focused series were predominate during the years of the prequel films, including *The New Jedi Order* (Del Rey), which unfolded in 1999-2003. Various authors contributed to the 19-book series, which

Part of a multimedia project, the *Shadows of the Empire* hardcover averages $5 to $25.

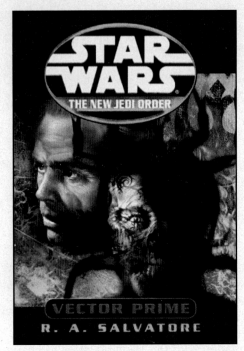

Books in *The New Jedi Order* series are very affordable at $1 to $7.

was set two decades after *Return of the Jedi*. The New Republic, what was the Rebel Alliance, is dealing with internal conflict. From even farther away comes the Yuuzhan Vong, who invade the galaxy, destroying and occupying portions in an effort to conquer.

The 11-book *Jedi Quest* (Scholastic) by Watson was another series for young readers. Published in 2001-2004, their protagonists were Obi-Wan and his apprentice Anakin Skywalker in the time between *The Phantom Menace* and *Attack of the Clones*. In the books, Anakin completes tasks in his Jedi training, they investigate a variety of situations on several planets, and the tension between the Master and Padawan becomes evident.

Obi-Wan Kenobi held the spotlight as a solo act in *The Last of the Jedi* young adult series (Scholastic) in 2005-2008. Written by Watson, the 10-book series follows Obi-Wan Kenobi after *Revenge of the Sith* when he's in exile on Tatooine. Obi-Wan adjusts to solitary life, protects baby Luke, laments what happened with Anakin, and mourns the loss of the Jedi – then finds out that Jedi

apprentice Ferus Olin is alive and decides to help the vulnerable fugitive.

Legacy of the Force (Del Rey) is a series set about 40 years following the events of *A New Hope*. After the Corellian system plans to leave the New Republic's Galactic Alliance, other systems start to follow suit. Jedi Knight Jacen Solo believes that he can defeat the potential threat and bring the galaxy back together, but his methods cause concern with his uncle Luke Skywalker. Authors Allston, Karen Traviss, and Troy Denning shared writing duties on the nine-book series, which was published in 2006-2008.

These are some of the popular entries in the world of *Star Wars* novels, but there are many more that collectors can seek like a bounty hunter hired by Jabba the Hutt. Some other notable standalone books are *Star Wars: Darth Plagueis, Darth Maul: Shadow Hunter, Star Wars: Kenobi, The Truce at Bakura, Death Troopers, Bloodline, Ahsoka, Catalyst: A Rogue One Novel, Battlefront: Twilight Company, Lost Stars, Tarkin, Dark Disciple*, and *Heir to the Jedi*.

Additional series worth checking out are *Lost Tribe of the Sith, Tales of the Jedi, The Old Republic, Darth Bane, Boba Fett, Republic Commando, The Clone Wars, Galaxy of Fear, The Bounty Hunter Wars, The Corellian, The Black Fleet Crisis,* and *Aftermath*.

Pricing Star Wars Novels

Collecting *Star Wars* novels is a great hobby for several reasons. It's the kind of collectible that can be enjoyed hands-on, rather than a boxed item that would be devalued by opening. There are hundreds of books in the series, providing many, many collecting opportunities. On the secondary market, *Star Wars* novels are priced in a wide range, making them accessible for collectors at any level.

The titles featured in this article are presented here with prices that reflect a range of conditions from those in Poor or Good to those in Very Good or Near Mint. First editions are mentioned for key titles as they will fetch higher prices than later editions; while some titles, particularly those published in later years, sell for the same averages, regardless of edition number. Cover type is also specified if it differentiates the first edition or value.

Star Wars: From the Adventures of Luke Skywalker
1976; Ballantine Books
By George Lucas, ghost written by Alan Dean Foster
1976 paperback
$12 Poor
$90 Good
$150 Near Mint

1977 hardcover
$8 Poor
$56 Good
$130 Near Mint

1977 hardcover autographed
$30 Poor
$360 Good
$660 Very Good
$1,100 Near Mint

Splinter of the Mind's Eye
1978; Ballantine Books
By Alan Dean Foster
First edition hardcover
$5 Good
$17 Very Good
$50 Near Mint

The Han Solo Adventures trilogy
Individual titles: *Han Solo at Stars' End, Han Solo's Revenge,* and *Han Solo and the Lost Legacy*
1979-1980; Del Rey
By Brian Daley
First edition paperback (for each book)
$4 Good
$13 Very Good
$20 Near Mint

The Empire Strikes Back
1980; Del Rey
By Donald F. Glut
First edition paperback
$5 Good
$25 Very Good
$50 Near Mint

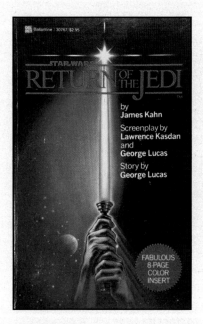

Return of the Jedi
1983; Del Rey
By James Kahn
First edition paperback
$7 Good
$15 Very Good
$20 Near Mint

The Lando Calrissian Adventures trilogy
Individual titles: *Lando Calrissian and the Mindharp of Sharu*, *Lando Calrissian and the Flamewind of Oseon*, and *Lando Calrissian and the Starcave of ThonBoka*
1983; Del Rey
By L. Neil Smith
First edition paperback (for each book)
$3 to $15

Thrawn trilogy
Individual titles: *Heir to the Empire*, *Dark Force Rising*, and *The Last Command*
1991-1993; Bantam Spectra
By Timothy Zahn
First edition hardcover (for each book)
$3 to $35

The Courtship of Princess Leia
1994; Bantam Spectra
By Dave Wolverton
Hardcover: $4 to $20

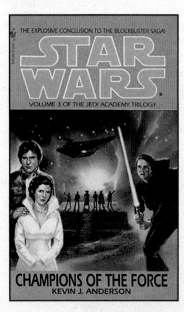

Jedi Academy trilogy
Individual titles: *Jedi Search*, *Dark Apprentice*, and *Champions of the Force*
1994; Bantam Spectra
By Kevin J. Anderson
$1 to $5

Young Jedi Knights series (14 books)
1995-1998; Boulevard and Berkley Jam
By Kevin J. Anderson and Rebecca Moesta
$1 to $8

Shadows of the Empire
1996; Bantam Books
By Steve Perry
Hardcover: $5 to $25

X-Wing series (10 books)
1996-2012; Bantam Spectra and Del Rey
By Michael A. Stackpole and Aaron Allston
$1 to $6 each

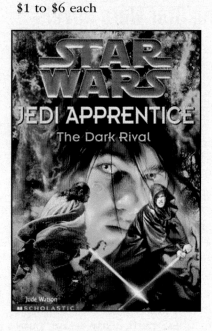

Jedi Apprentice series (18 books)
1999-2002; Scholastic
By Dave Wolverton and Jude Watson
$1 to $5

The New Jedi Order (19 books)
1999-2003; Del Rey
Several authors
$1 to $7

Jedi Quest (11 books)
2001-2004; Scholastic
By Jude Watson
$1 to $5

The Last of the Jedi (10 books)
2005-2008; Scholastic
By Jude Watson
$1 to $4

Legacy of the Force (9 books)
2006-2008; Del Rey
By Aaron Allston, Karen Traviss, and Troy Denning
$1 to $10

STAR WARS BIG LITTLE BOOKS

Big Little Books became a popular storytelling format beginning in the 1930s, a compact illustrated children's novel in a small block-shaped book for 10¢. Adventures with Disney characters, cowboys, space heroes and lawmen charmed young readers through the format's heyday of the '30s and '40s.

Starting in 1999, Chronicle Books produced these film adaptations in the classic format as hardcovers with a 4-1/2" tall by 3-5/8" wide page size, with text pages next to illustrated pages as was done about 60 years earlier. **Note:** There was no edition created for *Episode 3 - Revenge of the Sith*.

Three prices listed are for Good (2.0), Fine (6.0) and Near Mint- (9.2) conditions.

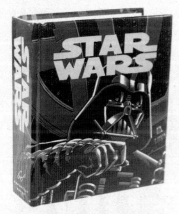  

STAR WARS – A NEW HOPE
1997, CHRONICLE BOOKS
320 PGS. 1-COLOR (BLUE) ILLOS.
$3.00 $7.50 $20.00

STAR WARS – THE EMPIRE STRIKES BACK
1997, CHRONICLE BOOKS
296 PGS. 1-COLOR (BLUE) ILLOS.
$3.00 $7.50 $20.00

STAR WARS – RETURN OF THE JEDI
1997, CHRONICLE BOOKS
312 PGS. 1-COLOR (BLUE) ILLOS.
$3.00 $7.50 $20.00

 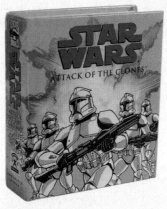

STAR WARS EPISODE 1 – THE PHANTOM MENACE
1999, CHRONICLE BOOKS
(LUCAS BOOKS/MIGHTY CHRONICLES/
FIRST STREET FILMS), 344 PGS. 1-COLOR (BLUE) ILLOS.
$1.00 $2.50 $9.00

STAR WARS EPISODE 2 – ATTACK OF THE CLONES
2002, CHRONICLE BOOKS
(LUCAS BOOKS/MIGHTY CHRONICLES/
FIRST STREET FILMS), 340 PGS. 1-COLOR (BLUE) ILLOS.
$1.00 $2.50 $9.00

THESE ARE THE TOYS YOU'RE LOOKING FOR

At some point in their lives, typically the early portion of it, just about everyone is a toy collector. While many people leave the hobby as they transition into their teen years, some remain stalwart or return to their beloved toys during adulthood. *Star Wars* is perhaps the definitive example of how toy collecting transcends the toy box to be situated in display cases.

The success of *Star Wars* toys in the collecting market is simultaneously measured by nostalgia and investment potential. Lots of passionate collectors fondly remember playing with the toys as children and find that owning the toys as adults is a cathartic reignition of their imaginations and reminder of an emotionally simpler time. Fitting into any collector's budget, the toys can be purchased for as little as a few dollars to a handful of items that are now worth five figures. With so many variants and rarities, they are also desirable items for collectors that enjoy treasure hunting. Regardless of the motivation, *Star Wars* toy collecting is a very entertaining hobby enjoyed by passionate collectors.

ACTION FIGURES
KENNER'S ORIGINAL LINES OF STAR WARS TO POWER OF THE FORCE

Star Wars toys had a major impact on movie tie-ins, movie marketing campaigns, and the toy industry at large. George Lucas and 20th Century Fox had an ambitious marketing plan for the film to ensure interest before the movie was even released in theaters. In 1976 the *Star Wars* toy license was offered to the Mego Corporation, the leading action figure producer of the 1970s, but they turned it down.

After being shopped around, the license went to Kenner, a subsidiary of General Mills. Movie toy licenses hadn't been very successful as films were considered too fleeting to sustain and build sales. Kenner had established themselves as savvy handlers of licensed material on their license for *The Six Million Dollar Man* based on the TV show. Kenner President Bernie Loomis also saw it as an opportunity to make good toys in the new 3-3/4" scale, which would be cheaper to produce than the larger figures that were popular at the time.

Kenner received massive interest in *Star Wars* toys and the company had a short amount of time to design, test, produce, and package the figures. Because they weren't able to build stock before the holiday season of 1977, they sold an "Early Bird Certificate Package." It included a cardboard display stand featuring the characters and a certificate that could be mailed to Kenner and redeemed for the first four figures of Luke Skywalker, Princess Leia, Chewbacca, and R2-D2. The box also had a diorama display stand, stickers, and fan club membership card. By the time figures were in stores, C-3PO, Darth Vader, Stormtrooper, Ben Kenobi, Han Solo, Jawa, Sand People, and Death Squad Commander were added to the line, for a total of 12 figures.

Luke, Leia, Chewbacca, and R2-D2 were the first figures in the series.

The original line of figures would've been
incomplete without the roguish smuggler Han Solo
and the film's villain Darth Vader.

Throughout the run of *Star Wars* action figures, the toys would be known for having variations that include re-sculpts, different accessories, paint details (like the color of hair and clothing), or sculpting material. These differences can lead to higher values on the secondary market due to their rarity.

Some of the most valuable variations of the original 12 are the Luke, Obi-Wan, and Darth Vader double telescoping figures. The "double telescoping" term is used to describe the lightsabers, which have double action telescoping, meaning the main portion of the lightsaber slides out of the figure's arm and then has a small tip that slides out from within the lightsaber. Not many carded double telescoping figures remain, because Kenner switched the lightsabers early in the process, suggesting that

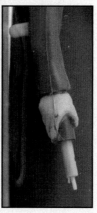

This Obi-Wan Kenobi 12-back with
double-telescoping lightsaber is one of the
most valuable *Star Wars* action figures.

The vinyl cape Jawa is another
popular rarity due to the different
design of its outerwear.

few were made and even fewer were put on the card. Typically, Luke is the easiest to find because he was part of the Early Bird Kit mail-away promotion.

Another popular variant is the early vinyl cape Jawa figure. When it was originally designed, it had a plastic cape like the other figures. However, because it was so much smaller, it had a lower perceived value, but carried the same sale price. As a solution to add some value to the figure, Kenner removed the small vinyl cape and replaced it with a cloth fabric tunic that pulled over the top of the figure. Production of the figure was pulled when they had barely hit shelves. Often a mid-production run change like that can add a lot of value to the first version of the toy.

Some of the subtler variations include Luke's hair color, which ranges from blond to brown and Obi-Wan's hair that is white or grey. The early Han Solo had a smaller head sculpt that was later replaced with a larger one with a somewhat better resemblance to Harrison Ford.

The next wave began with four figures from a Cantina Adventure playset (more on that later) that were then made available for individual sale. These were followed by four more figures – three droids and another Luke – coming to a new total of 20 by 1979.

Preparing for *The Empire Strikes Back*, Kenner did a mail-in promotion in which four proof of purchases could be redeemed for a rocket-firing Boba Fett action figure. But, the rocket-firing toy was pulled from the line, as it was deemed a safety hazard for children. Those who sent in their proof of purchases for the toy would receive the version without the rocket-firing ability and a letter apologizing for the change. Some action figure cards had already been produced so stickers were placed over the image of the rocket-firing mechanism on the back.

The prototype was on display at the 1979 Toy Fair in New York City, but since the figure never went into production, the prototypes in circulation now are almost all unpainted, blue figures. The original rocket-firing versions are known as L-slot or J-slot, referencing the shape of the firing mechanism on the figure's back.

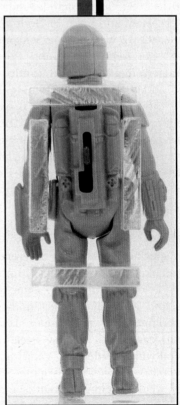

The rocket-firing Boba Fett was pulled from production because it was a safety hazard, making prototypes very rare.

Lando Calrissian and Yoda, who were introduced in *The Empire Strikes Back*, joined the line of figures.

In conjunction with *The Empire Strikes Back*, Kenner produced over 30 more figures from 1980 to 1982. They included new versions of Leia, Han, and Luke in Hoth and Bespin outfits. R2-D2 was given a Sensorscope and C-3PO got removable limbs. Popular new characters like Yoda and Lando Calrissian were added to the line. Joining Boba Fett were other bounty hunters Bossk, IG-88, Dengar, 4-LOM, and Zuckuss. The addition of the giant AT-ATs warranted figures of the driver and the commander. They also added Rebel and Imperial soldiers in Hoth battle gear, commanders, Cloud City resident Lobot, and a few more droids.

Variations in the *ESB* line were similar to the first, specifically coloring differences. Once again Luke (Bespin Fatigues) came with different colored hair. Lando came with dark eyes and no smile while another version had brighter eyes and a smile. Leia (Bespin Gown) came with a crew neck or a rarer version with a turtleneck. Yoda had different skin colors, as well as his gimer stick and a snake that was either brown or orange.

From '82 to '84, Kenner produced over 30 more action figures for *Return of the Jedi*. New versions of the main characters were Luke as a Jedi Knight, Leia in Boushh disguise and combat poncho, Han in trench coat,

and Lando in Skiff Guard disguise. Rebel additions were Admiral Ackbar, General Madine, Nien Nunb, and Prune Face. Ewoks were represented by Chief Chirpa, Logray, Wicket, and Teebo. Characters from scenes with Jabba the Hutt like the Gamorrean Guard, Klaatu, Weequay, Squid Head, Bib Fortuna, Ree-Yees, and the Rancor Keeper were added. Finally, the Emperor himself became a figure, along with the Emperor's Royal Guard.

The *Return of the Jedi* line added the powerful, intimidating Emperor figure.

Variations in the *ROTJ* line included Luke with a blue lightsaber instead of a green one, his cape either sewn shut or with a snap, and different hair colors. Han's Endor trench coat comes with plain lapels or camo lapels and the Ewoks can have different shades of their fur.

Since no more films were in the works, Kenner rebranded the line with the name Power of the Force, in 1985. The line contained what collectors call "The Last 17" figures, which were packaged with aluminum character coins. Some new figures include Han in Carbonite, Lando as the general pilot, Luke in the Stormtrooper outfit and one in the poncho, R2-D2 with the pop-up lightsaber, Anakin Skywalker, the EV-9D9 droid, and a few more Ewoks, among others. Yak Face was not available in the U.S., making that figure harder to find and more valuable. Power of the Force also reissued several figures from the original product line with the new packaging logo.

The new and reissued figures were not enough to reinvigorate interest in the toys, so Kenner discontinued the line. It ended with a total of 92 figures released in the U.S.

The cards on which figures were packaged are important pieces to identifying where they fit into the full series. From 1977 to mid-1984 the cards depicted film

After being unmasked at the end of *Return of the Jedi,* Anakin Skywalker was issued a figure in the new Power of the Force line.

titles close to each movie's release, finishing with the Power of the Force. As the number of figures increased, their images were added to the card-back design, which became the way to designate cards. So, the first range of figures features the original 12, known as 12-back, then after the next eight were released it increased to the 20-back, and so on to the 92-back. The fronts also had variations with different illustrations and promotional stickers. In

Star Wars action figures are designated in order by the number of toys depicted on the card-back.

addition to the number designation, cards are categorized with letters that denote changes on the card that show the same number of figures on the back.

DROIDS AND EWOKS LINES

Two more collections of figures were released for the animated series *Star Wars: Droids* and *Star Wars: Ewoks*, which were aimed at a younger audience. They included brightly colored packaging images of the characters accompanying the figure on the card. A short character biography appeared on the back of the card and, similar to the Power of the Force figures, they also came with a collectible coin.

The Droids line was led by R2-D2 with a pop-up lightsaber and C-3PO with removable limbs, along with characters like Kea Moll and Thall Joben. The figures came with extra accessories and weapons and the *Droids* line also included the ships ATL Interceptor, Side Gunner, and A-wing Starfighter. The *Ewoks* line began with Wicket, Logray, King Gorneesh, and a few Duloks.

Both lines saw domestic and foreign releases. The Brazilian Glasslite company created *Droids* figures and vehicles, which were sold on different cards than in the U.S.

They included characters from the U.S. line, as well as the henchman Vlix, who was not issued in other countries. Kenner made a prototype figure of Vlix for U.S. distribution, but it never went beyond a mock up, which makes it one of the rarest *Star Wars* action figures.

FOREIGN RELEASE

Licenses were issued to several countries for production outside of the U.S., many of which were subsidiaries of General Mills. Around the world, licenses were held in the U.K., Spain, France, Germany, Italy, Japan, Mexico, and Brazil, among other countries. Some of the non-U.S. release versions had some variations from the ones Kenner produced, which included re-sculpts, different paint details, and different fabric accessories.

In 1984, near the end of the run, the European market issued cards with the logos in English, French, and Spanish that became known as tri-logo. This was done as a way to cut costs by using multiple languages for easier distribution. Most figures in the line were put on the tri-logo cards, with card-backs that featured 70 characters. These tri-logo examples are popular with collectors, specifically Yak Face, who had only been issued in Canada and Australia.

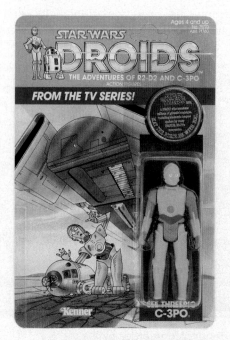 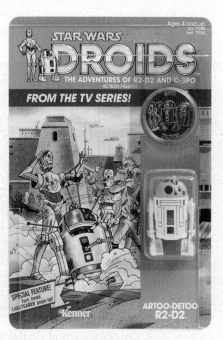

———————— Naturally, the Droids toy line was led by C-3PO and R2-D2. ————————

MULTI-PACKS, 12" FIGURES, PROOF CARDS

The standard single 3-3/4" action figures dominate Kenner's *Star Wars* line, but they aren't the only toys sought by collectors. To keep the market thriving, Kenner produced several multi-pack sets and an assortment of 12" figures. These, along with production proof cards, have found a robust home on the collecting market.

Kenner created 16 three-pack special action figure sets with the *Star Wars* or *ESB* logo. The sets are predominately themed by character type, status, and geographic location, including packs of creatures, heroes, Rebels, Imperials, droids, villains, Hoth, and Bespin.

The six-packs are much rarer, consisting of only two varieties, both featuring *The Empire Strikes Back* logo. Boxed rather than carded, each figure came sealed in an individual plastic bag. The very rare six-packs are often referred to by their yellow or red backgrounds on the box art.

The 12" figures, marketed as large size action figures, were released around the time of the first two movies. Most of the main characters, plus a few secondary, were produced in the line and sold in window boxes. Larger figures had been the standard size of most action figures before Kenner introduced the 3-3/4" *Star Wars* line, but these new larger figures weren't as popular, possibly because the smaller ones had more options for vehicles, playsets, and accessories.

Marketed as "large scale action figures," the 12" series towered over the regular line.

A popular facet of the toy collecting is in the proof cards, which were printing production samples made to finalize the card designs that would provide backing to the action figures. Because of that, only a small number have survived.

Cards with the *Revenge of the Jedi* title are among the most popular. Though the *Revenge* title wasn't used, the proofs were printed, along with other packaging and posters. After the title was changed and all merchandise depicted the *Return of the Jedi* title, those cards became the closest collectors can get to *Revenge of the Jedi* action figures.

PLAYSETS

In 1978, vehicles and playset accessories were added to Kenner's action figure toy line. The 3-3/4" action figures created more opportunities for companion vehicles and playsets at reasonable prices, far more so than would have been afforded to 8" or 12" figures.

An easy choice for a marketable playset was the Death Star Space Station. It was among the first releases and was beloved by kids. The large scale toy is 20" tall, housing four floors of activity space, an elevator, trash compactor, and a Laser Cannon.

The Sears exclusive Cantina Adventure Set came with figures of Snaggletooth, Walrus Man, Hammerhead, and Greedo with a cardboard backdrop and base of Mos Eisley. Though the set was fairly basic, it's known for having the Snaggletooth figure with a blue outfit and silver boots. It was then updated to make it match the movie more closely, re-sculpted as a shorter figure, barefoot, and in a red outfit. Only the "Red Snaggletooth" was released on card, making the "Blue Snaggletooth" a rare, desirable figure.

The Imperial Attack Base set is a curious piece. It has a cool design, set on Hoth, atop icy cliffs with a collapsible bridge. But per the box art and set name, it sug-

Proof cards, which are printing production samples, with the *Revenge of the Jedi* title are rare collectibles.

The Cantina Adventure Set is known for housing the Blue Snaggletooth figure, which was never released on card.

Another interesting set is the Ewok Village Action Playset, which was sold near the end of the series.

gests that the Empire is defending an attack from the Rebels – a stark contrast to Hoth scenes in the movie.

One of the last in the series was the Ewok Village Action Playset. It came with large plastic trees that hold a central platform and play area. The set has lots of details, including a hut, an escape passageway, a working elevator, and a net underneath the main square.

Star Wars is such fertile ground for fun toys like playsets and Kenner created lots of good examples that also included a Droid Factory, Hoth Ice Planet, Cloud City, Star Destroyer, Dagobah, Jabba the Hutt Dungeon, among several others.

The Micro Collection launched in 1982, features playsets for different scenes from the movies with small die-cast figurines. They comprised sets for the Death Star, Hoth, and Bespin with each made to connect with others in the series. Individual sets were also sold together as world sets.

VEHICLES

In space and on land, *Star Wars* has some very creative vehicle designs, which kids were itching to pilot themselves. Kenner produced a variety of vehicle toys in a large range of sizes for the smallest to biggest hands. Die-cast and plastic vehicles were created for specific vehicles like the Land Speeder and Slave I, down to fleet vehicles like the Speeder Bike and Imperial Shuttle.

One of the most memorable is the J.C. Penney's exclusive Sonic Controlled Land Speeder, which had a sound activated mechanism that paired with an R2-D2 remote control clicker. This toy could be ordered through the store's catalog, starting in 1978, and is among the most popular vehicles with collectors.

Naturally, the Millennium Falcon was one of the first vehicles made, seeing release in '79. The large toy is about 21" long and stands on three landing gears and has a removable canopy. The cockpit could hold two figures and it has a large living area where figures could be positioned.

The Imperial Troop Transporter was released in 1979 before it was seen on film. This toy gained popularity for its six side compartments to carry Stormtroopers, gun turret, and ability to make sounds from the movie. It came with a booklet that explained how the Empire used it while searching for C-3PO and R2-D2.

Slave I Boba Fett's Spaceship was available in 1981, featuring a Han Solo in Carbonite figure. It had gravity operated wings, a clicking moveable cannon, a removable side panel, and opening rear ramp.

Mini-Rigs began hitting store shelves in the spring of '81. These were small size vehicles that began with the MLC-3 (Mobile Laser Cannon), MTV-7 (Multi-Terrain Vehicle), and

The Sonic Controlled Land Speeder, available through J.C. Penney, is a popular vehicle with collectors.

No. 40010   Ages 4 and up

STAR WARS THE EMPIRE STRIKES BACK

MTV-7
Multi-Terrain Vehicle

ACTION FIGURES SOLD SEPARATELY

Kenner

Meets or exceeds all safety requirements of Product Standard 72-76

Contents: One vehicle with spring-loaded legs and movable cannon.

This MTV-7 was part of the line of Mini-Rigs that were available starting in 1981.

PDT-8 (Personnel Deployment Transport). They were followed by similar vehicles like the Endor Forest Ranger and Desert Sail Skiff, housed in *ROTJ* packaging.

After the Mini-Rigs, Kenner released a line of Body-Rigs, which were even more compact. More focused on the person connected to the rig rather than the vehicle, they included the Security Scout, Sand Skimmer, and Imperial Sniper.

In addition to playsets, the Micro Collection also included small scale vehicles like the X-wing and TIE Fighter, plus a Millennium Falcon Sears exclusive and a Snowspeeder available through J.C. Penney. A mail-away promotion was available with a Build Your Armies set of Hoth Rebel Soldiers and Snowtroopers.

OTHER KENNER TOYS

Kenner created a haberdashery of other *Star Wars* toys, including toy weapons that were similar to those seen on film. They made a Laser Pistol with packaging for all three original movies, three-position rifle for the first movie, and Biker Scout Laser Pistol from *ROTJ*.

An inflatable lightsaber was available in '78, then a solid tube design for *ESB*, available in yellow and red, followed by a green

one for *ROTJ*. A battery-operated lightsaber with an extendable piece released with the *Droids* line.

Other Kenner toys included a Darth Vader and a C-3PO Collector Case, Radio Controlled R2-D2, Luke Skywalker AM Headset Radio, hand puppets, bop bags (basically, inflatable punching bags), modeling set, Ewok plush stuffed animals, and others.

TOY RESURGENCE – 1990s TO NOW

In the mid-1990s, George Lucas announced that he was planning to create new *Star Wars* movies and the original trilogy was being remastered to return to theaters. Kenner was now owned by Hasbro, but the new toys were published under the Kenner name to connect to the original line. The new line was successful, though it wasn't as popular with fans of the original toys.

The toys were dubbed the "Hero Age" sculpts and were overly muscular with a wide-legged stance that was incompatible with vehicles. Plus, Leia had a notoriously bad face sculpt. But, thanks to the special edition releases, the toys were popular for a new generation.

Hasbro started adding to the line, even including Expanded Universe elements like using the names of Yak Face and Hammerhead (Saelt-Marae and Momaw Nadon), which were given in the EU, as well as characters from the novels and video games like Mara Jade.

A focused transition to *The Phantom Menace* gave potential audiences a significant look at the new characters who would be introduced in the prequel trilogy. They were no longer done in the Hero Age sculpts, creating more natural stances. The toys also came with a voice chip accessory that could be used with a toy based on Qui-Gon Jinn's communicator to play dialogue.

In the *Attack of the Clones* line, the toys were given more articulation, which continued with additional toys in the *Revenge of the Sith* line. Hasbro started making new figures for characters from the original trilogy and was bolstered by the *Clone Wars* animated series.

In 2013 they announced The Black Series of 6" figures with better details, aimed at the collecting market in sleek, black packaging. These were initially centered on variations of characters from the original trilogy and some from the prequels, then refocused on characters in current films and TV shows. There have also been 3-3/4" figures and vehicles in varying sizes and full-size lightsabers. Some are exclusively available at certain stores, conventions, or events, and a 40th anniversary collection was produced – all adding to price increases on the secondary market.

Funko, one of the dominate forces in the current collecting market, has also created a large number of *Star Wars* items in their various lines of collectibles. They feature characters from throughout the series with special attention paid to those introduced in the new films. they have included Pop! Vinyl toys and deluxe figures, plush toys and keychains, Mystery Minis, backpacks, coin bags, wallets, shirts, pen toppers, lanyards, mugs, and party lights, among others.

Vintage or modern, action figures or vehicles, there is a plethora of *Star Wars* toys to satisfy collectors. The volume of vintage and newer material is so vast that years could be spent on the hunt for these beloved toys. With hundreds of options across a wide spectrum of price ranges, they can be a part of any *Star Wars* fan's collection.

This die-cast Phasma figure is from the Disney Store-exclusive line, the *Star Wars* Elite Series. As a die-cast, it is much heavier than many other similarly-sized figures.

This Kylo Ren Funko Pop! bobblehead figure was released in conjunction with the debut of *The Force Awakens*.

ACTION FIGURE PRICES

The subject of *Star Wars* action figures is both vast and complex, with a standard list of figures, plus characters with simple to major variations and characters that are reissued on different card-backs. To provide accurate and easy to follow values, the following price list was collated based on prices of graded, carded figures achieved in auctions over the last few years. Values represent the first release of the figure and variations are only noted if they represent a noteworthy discrepancy in price. The list is organized first by card-back number, then in alphabetical order. The values listed are based on figures graded in conditions of Poor/Good, Very Good/Excellent, and Near Mint/Mint.

STAR WARS 12-BACKS

	PR/GD	VG/EX	NM/MT
Ben Kenobi (double telescoping)	$10,000	$43,000	$76,700
Ben Kenobi	$200	$1,155	$2,115
C-3PO	$340	$1,350	$2,390
Chewbacca	$390	$2,400	$4,450
Darth Vader (double telescoping)	$9,000	$37,000	$64,900
Darth Vader	$500	$10,000	$19,500
Death Squad Commander	$430	$1,500	$2,625
Han Solo	$385	$2,400	$4,750
Jawa (vinyl cape)	$10,065	$15,500	$21,600
Jawa (cloth cape)	$305	$1,850	$3,350
Luke Skywalker (double telescoping)	$7,000	$10,000	$17,000
Luke Skywalker	$5,000	$25,000	$50,000
Princess Leia	$2,000	$15,000	$29,500
R2-D2	$300	$1,400	$2,750
Sand People (Tusken Raider)	$100	$730	$1,275
Stormtrooper	$200	$2,400	$4,050

STAR WARS

TM *TM* TRADEMARKS OF TWENTIETH CENTURY FOX FILM CORP.*

Start your own collection of STAR WARS Action Figures and Space Vehicles!

12 authentically designed figures in realistic STAR WARS costumes. All have movable parts, scaled to fit inside STAR WARS Space Vehicles.

- **Sand People**™ (3¾") in sand fighter costume with Gaderffii Stick.™
- **See-Threepio**™ (3¾") in shining gold finish.
- **Death Squad Commander**™ (3¾") with Laser Rifle.™
- **Han Solo**™ (3¾") with Laser Pistol.™
- **Chewbacca**™ (4¼") with Laser Rifle.™
- **Princess Leia Organa**™ (3½") has a removable cape and Laser Pistol.™
- **Luke Skywalker**™ (3¾") with action Light Saber.™
- **Artoo-Detoo**™ (2¼") with movable legs and head that "clicks".
- **Darth Vader**™ (4¼") with action Light Saber™ and removable cape.
- **Stormtrooper**™ (3¾") with Laser Rifle.™
- **Ben (Obi-Wan) Kenobi**™ (3¾") with action Light Saber™ and removable cape.
- **Jawa**™ (2¼") with shining eyes and Laser Gun.™

All 12 STAR WARS Action Figures may not be available in your store at the same time.

How to work Light Saber™

When in closed position, tip of saber sticks out slightly.

Pull Saber out by tip or push Saber out using slide lever.

Tie Fighter™ with fly-off solar panels; Laser Light™ and sound.

X-Wing Fighter™ with retractable wings; Laser Light™ and sound.

Land Speeder™ with "floating" motion.

STAR WARS ACTION FIGURES NOT INCLUDED WITH COLLECTOR'S ACTION STAND.

STAR WARS
Action Collector's Stand

Display all 12 figures on this colorful STAR WARS galaxy stand. Sturdy plastic, with action levers to move figures back and forth. Figures easily removable for individual play.

Send your name, address zip code; and proof-of-purchase seal (shown at right) from 2 STAR WARS Action Figure packages along with *$2.00* to:

STAR WARS Action Collector's Stand
P.O. Box 1313
ONE Industrial Drive
Maple Plain, Minn. 55348

Collector's Action Stand **FREE** with proofs-of-purchase from 12 STAR WARS Action Figures.

Allow 8-10 weeks for delivery. Offer expires May 1, 1979. Void where prohibited, taxed, or otherwise regulated.

General Mills FUN GROUP STAR WARS™ ACTION FIGURES

MADE IN HONG KONG.

© GENERAL MILLS FUN GROUP, INC. 1977   Characters: © 1977 TWENTIETH CENTURY FOX FILM CORP.   KENNER PRODUCTS, Cincinnati, Ohio 45202

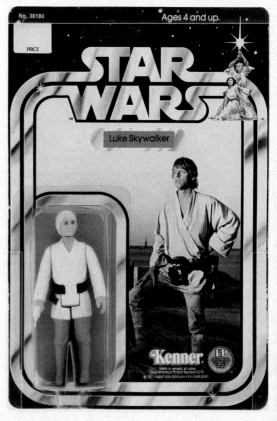

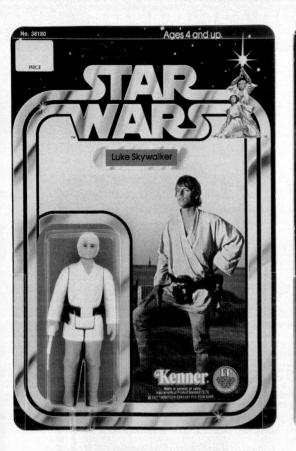

	PR/GD	VG/EX	NM/MT
Boba Fett	$700	$3,800	$6,900
Death Star Droid	$275	$1,175	$2,150
Greedo	$310	$855	$1,535

	PR/GD	VG/EX	NM/MT
Hammerhead	$245	$950	$1,575
Luke Skywalker (X-Wing Pilot)	$330	$750	$1,200
Power Droid	$290	$710	$1,125
R5-D4	$310	$1,480	$2,620
Snaggletooth	$190	$605	$1,030
Walrus Man	$220	$675	$1,130

STAR WARS
THE EMPIRE STRIKES BACK
31/32-BACKS

	PR/GD	VG/EX	NM/MT
Bespin Security Guard (white)	$185	$265	$345
Bossk	$225	$1,225	$2,225
FX-7	$215	$555	$1,090

	PR/GD	VG/EX	NM/MT
Han Solo (Hoth Outfit)	$125	$495	$865
IG-88	$215	$375	$535
Imperial Stormtrooper (Hoth Battle Gear)	$255	$520	$785
Lando Calrissian	$125	$480	$840
Luke Skywalker (Bespin Fatigues)	$405	$990	$1,575
Princess Leia Organa (Bespin Gown)	$175	$595	$1,015
Rebel Soldier (Hoth Battle Gear)	$120	$260	$405
Yoda	$110	$360	$610

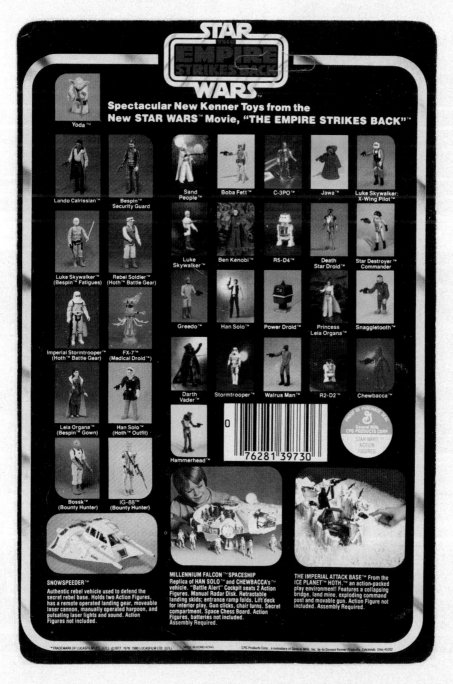

	PR/GD	VG/EX	NM/MT
2-1B	$120	$510	$900
4-LOM	$175	$890	$1,600
AT-AT Commander	$80	$205	$330
AT-AT Driver	$170	$445	$720
Bespin Security Guard (black)	$170	$360	$550
C-3PO (Removable Limbs)	$330	$550	$910

	PR/GD	VG/EX	NM/MT
Cloud Car Pilot	$145	$190	$260
Dengar	$155	$475	$740
Han Solo (Bespin Outfit)	$330	$900	$1,500
Imperial Commander	$200	$550	$1,000
Imperial TIE Fighter Pilot	$190	$280	$375
Lobot	$130	$400	$630
Luke Skywalker (Hoth Battle Gear)	$330	$520	$715
Princess Leia Organa (Hoth Outfit)	$360	$615	$850
R2-D2 (with Sensorscope)	$150	$380	$615
Rebel Commander	$145	$400	$660
Ugnaught	$200	$305	$450
Zuckuss	$145	$405	$660

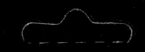

STAR WARS™ ACTION FIGURES
Collect all 45!

1. (Twin Pod) Cloud Car Pilot™
2. Bespin Security Guard™
3. AT-AT Commander™
4. Luke Skywalker™ (Hoth Battle Gear)
5. C-3PO™ (Removable Limbs)
6. R2-D2™ (With Sensorscope™)
7. Rebel Commander™
8. Lobot™
9. Han Solo™ (Bespin Outfit)
10. 2-1B™
11. Yoda™
12. Imperial Commander™
13. AT-AT Driver™
14. Dengar™
15. Leia Organa™ (Hoth Outfit)
16. Lando Calrissian™
17. Ugnaught™
18. FX-7™ (Medical Droid)
19. Han Solo™ (Hoth Outfit)
20. Bossk™ (Bounty Hunter)
21. Rebel Soldier™ (Hoth Battle Gear)
22. IG-88™ (Bounty Hunter)
23. Bespin Security Guard™
24. Imperial Stormtrooper™ (Hoth Battle Gear)
25. Luke Skywalker™ (Bespin Fatigues)
26. Leia Organa™ (Bespin Gown)
27. Jawa™
28. Princess Leia Organa™
29. Luke Skywalker™
30. Han Solo™
31. Boba Fett™
32. Sandpeople™
33. Power Droid™
34. Star Destroyer Commander™
35. Darth Vader™
36. Hammerhead™
37. Snaggletooth™
38. Greedo™
39. Chewbacca™
40. Walrus Man™
41. R5-D4™
42. Ben Kenobi™
43. Luke Skywalker™ (X-Wing Pilot)
44. Death Star Droid™
45. Stormtrooper™

SPECIAL OFFER
Star Wars™ Action Figure
DISPLAY ARENA

The Display Arena includes four 7½″ long, "L"-shaped display stands—each holds 14 STAR WARS Action Figures—plus four backdrops with different photographs from STAR WARS and THE EMPIRE STRIKES BACK on each side. You can connect the display stands in many different ways to set up your own unique Display Arena.

ACTION
FIGURES
SOLD
SEPARATELY

YOU CAN INTERCONNECT STANDS MANY WAYS

YOU CAN GET THE DISPLAY ARENA BY:
• Purchasing any 10 STAR WARS Action Figures.
• Remove Proof-of-Purchase Seals.
• Send 10 Seals plus $2.00 with your name and address to:
STAR WARS ACTION FIGURE DISPLAY ARENA
P.O. BOX 4153
MONTICELLO, MINNESOTA 55365

• Allow 10-12 weeks for delivery. • Offer expires May 31, 1982.

IN THE INTEREST OF BETTER QUALITY AND VALUE, WE ARE CONSTANTLY IMPROVING AND UPDATING OUR PRODUCTS. CONSEQUENTLY, PICTURES ON THIS PACKAGE MAY SOMETIMES DIFFER FROM THE MODEL ENCLOSED.

0

76281 69570

PROOF OF PURCHASE SEAL
General Mills
CPG PRODUCTS CORP.
STAR WARS
ACTION
FIGURES

S

STAR WARS™
ACTION FIGURES Collect all 48!

1. Imperial TIE Fighter™ Pilot
2. Zuckuss™
3. 4-LOM™
4. Cloud Car™ Pilot
5. Two-Onebee (2-1B)™
6. AT-AT™ Commander
7. Artoo-Detoo (R2-D2)™ (with Sensorscope™)
8. See-Threepio (C-3PO)™ (with removable limbs)
9. Luke Skywalker® (Hoth™ Battle Gear)
10. Bespin™ Security Guard
11. Rebel Commander™
12. Han Solo™ (Hoth™ Battle Gear)
13. Princess Leia Organa® (Hoth™ Outfit)
14. Han Solo™ (Bespin™ Outfit)
15. Star Destroyer Commander™
16. AT-AT™ Driver
17. Ugnaught™
18. Dengar™
19. Yoda™
20. Imperial Stormtrooper™ (Hoth™ Battle Gear)
21. Imperial Commander™
22. IG-88™
23. Power Droid™
24. Han Solo™
25. Bespin™ Security Guard
26. Luke Skywalker® (Bespin™ Fatigues)
27. FX-7™
28. Lando Calrissian™
29. Rebel Soldier™
30. Boba Fett™
31. Stormtrooper™
32. Princess Leia Organa® (Bespin™ Gown)
33. Tusken Raider™ (Sand People®)
34. R5-D4™
35. Lobot™
36. Death Star Droid™
37. Bossk™
38. Luke Skywalker® (X-Wing Fighter® Pilot)
39. Walrus Man™
40. Chewbacca™
41. Luke Skywalker®
42. Princess Leia Organa®
43. Ben (Obi-Wan) Kenobi®
44. Greedo®
45. Hammerhead®
46. Snaggletooth®
47. Jawa®
48. Darth Vader®

SPECIAL OFFER!
FREE ADMIRAL ACKBAR™
FIGURE FROM STAR WARS:
REVENGE OF THE JEDI™
WITH SIX PROOFS-OF-PURCHASE

Now, get a special free action figure from the next chapter of the STAR WARS™ saga, REVENGE OF THE JEDI™, premiering in May 1983! Just purchase six Star Wars™ Action Figures, send in the six proof-of-purchase seals with your name and address to the address below:

"REVENGE OF THE JEDI" FIGURE OFFER
P.O. BOX 909
YOUNG AMERICA, MINNESOTA 55399

• Offer expires January 31, 1983.
• Allow 10 to 12 weeks for processing.
• Offer void where prohibited, taxed or otherwise regulated.
• Offer good in U.S.A. only.

PROOF OF PURCHASE SEAL
General Mills
CPG PRODUCTS CORP. S
STAR WARS™
ACTION FIGURES

© LUCASFILM LTD. (LFL) 1982. TM. ® TRADEMARKS OWNED BY LFL AND USED BY KENNER UNDER AUTHORIZATION CPG Products Corp., a subsidiary of General Mills, Inc. by its Division Kenner Products. Cincinnati, Ohio 45202.

MADE IN HONG KONG

0   7 6281 69570

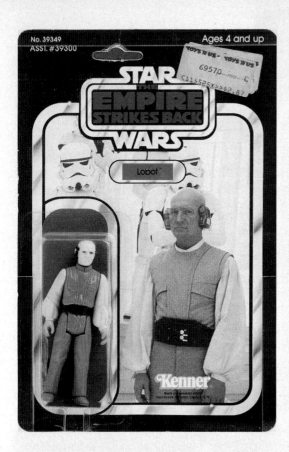

STAR WARS RETURN OF THE JEDI 65-BACKS

	PR/GD	VG/EX	NM/MT
Admiral Ackbar	$65	$235	$405
Bib Fortuna	$55	$315	$565
Biker Scout	$160	$250	$340
Chief Chirpa	$125	$170	$225
Emperor's Royal Guard	$100	$200	$305

	PR/GD	VG/EX	NM/MT
Gamorrean Guard	$95	$205	$415
General Madine	$55	$70	$100
Klaatu	$80	$165	$255
Lando Calrissian (Skiff Guard Disguise)	$100	$275	$440
Logray (Ewok Medicine Man)	$65	$95	$125
Luke Skywalker (Jedi Knight Outfit)	$205	$380	$560
Nien Nunb	$90	$160	$230
Princess Leia Organa (Boushh Disguise)	$125	$320	$535
Rebel Commando	$50	$215	$375
Ree-Yees	$50	$150	$250
Squid Head	$55	$220	$390
Weequay	$105	$260	$415

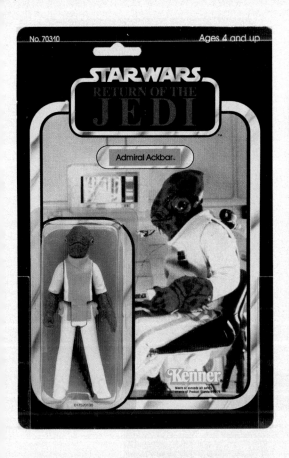

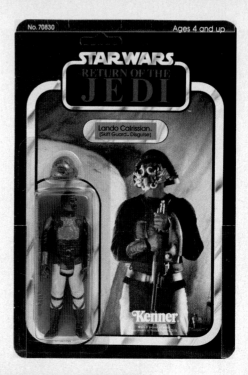

STAR WARS RETURN OF THE JEDI 77/79-BACKS

	PR/GD	VG/EX	NM/MT
8D8	$40	$140	$230
AT-ST Driver	$80	$240	$460
B-Wing Pilot	$100	$170	$255
The Emperor	$200	$520	$865

STAR WARS. ACTION FIGURES
Collect all 77!

1. Prune Face™
2. Klaatu™ (In Skiff Guard™ Outfit)
3. 8D8™
4. Nikto™
5. Wicket W. Warrick™
6. Rancor Keeper™
7. The Emperor™
8. Han Solo™ (Trench Coat)
9. Teebo™
10. AT-ST Driver™
11. Princess Leia Organa™ (In Combat Poncho)
12. B-Wing Pilot™
13. Squid Head™
14. Ree-Yees™
15. Luke Skywalker® (Jedi Knight® Outfit)
16. Biker Scout™
17. Boushh™
18. Emperor's Royal Guard™
19. Rebel Commando™
20. Logray™ (Ewok™ Medicine Man)
21. Bib Fortuna™
22. Klaatu™
23. General Madine™
24. Lando Calrissian™ (Skiff Guard™ Disguise)
25. Gamorrean Guard™
26. Chief Chirpa™
27. Weequay™
28. Nien Nunb™
29. Admiral Ackbar™
30. Imperial TIE Fighter® Pilot
31. 4-LOM™
32. Zuckuss®
33. Cloud Car™ Pilot
34. Darth Vader™
35. Yoda, The Jedi Master™
36. Boba Fett®
37. Jawa™
38. Artoo-Detoo (R2-D2)® with Sensorscope™
39. See-Threepio (C-3PO)® (with removable limbs)
40. Luke Skywalker® (Hoth™ Battle Gear)
41. Bespin™ Security Guard
42. Rebel Commander®
43. Imperial Commander®
44. Two-Onebee (2-1B)®
45. Imperial Stormtrooper® (Hoth™ Battle Gear)
46. Bespin™ Security Guard
47. Tusken Raider® (Sand People)®
48. Luke Skywalker® (Bespin™ Fatigues)
49. Princess Leia Organa® (Bespin™ Gown)
50. Lando Calrissian™
51. Han Solo® (Bespin™ Outfit)
52. Luke Skywalker® (Bespin™ Outfit)
53. Han Solo® (Hoth™ Battle Gear)
54. AT-AT™ Driver
55. Lobot®
56. AT-AT™ Commander
57. Princess Leia Organa® (Hoth™ Outfit)
58. Ugnaught®
59. Chewbacca®
60. Luke Skywalker® (X-Wing Fighter® Pilot)
61. Rebel Soldier®
62. IG-88®
63. Star Destroyer® Commander
64. Ben (Obi-Wan) Kenobi®
65. Power Droid™
66. Stormtrooper®
67. Snaggletooth®
68. Han Solo®
69. Princess Leia Organa®
70. FX-7®
71. Hammerhead®
72. Greedo®
73. Walrus Man®
74. Dengar®
75. Death Star® Droid
76. Artive-Defour (R5-D4)®
77. Bossk® (Bounty Hunter)

Look for these new toys from STAR WARS : RETURN OF THE JEDI™ collection in your favorite stores. (U.S.A. only)

Action Figures sold separately

Action Figures sold separately

SY SNOOTLES AND THE REBO BAND™

EWOK™ COMBAT GLIDER

EWOK™ ASSAULT CATAPULT

RANCOR MONSTER™

ACTION FIGURES SOLD SEPARATELY

Figures made in Hong Kong

® TM & © Lucasfilm Ltd. (LFL) 1983. All rights reserved.
Kenner Products, a Div. of CPG Products Corp., Authorized User.
Kenner is a trademark of CPG Products Corp., by its Div. Kenner
Products, Cincinnati, Ohio 45202.

0

76281 69570

PROOF OF PURCHASE SEAL
General Mills
CPG PRODUCTS CORP.
STAR WARS™
ACTION
FIGURES

	PR/GD	VG/EX	NM/MT
Han Solo (in Trench Coat)	$125	$215	$310
Klaatu (in Skiff Guard Outfit)	$75	$110	$150
Lumat	$70	$105	$150
Nikto	$50	$325	$620
Paploo	$90	$140	$180
Princess Leia Organa (in Combat Poncho)	$70	$230	$400
Prune Face	$100	$200	$300
Rancor Keeper	$90	$140	$180
Teebo	$60	$135	$200
Wicket W. Warrick	$55	$215	$375

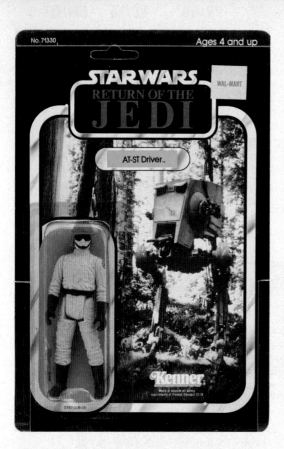

STAR WARS POWER OF THE FORCE 92-BACKS

	PR/GD	VG/EX	NM/MT
Amanaman	$280	$425	$590
Anakin Skywalker	$825	$5,480	$10,135
A-Wing Pilot	$150	$305	$565
Barada	$100	$210	$320

STAR WARS® ACTION FIGURES.   Collect all 92!

1. EV-9D9™
2. Artoo-Detoo (R2-D2)® with pop-up Lightsaber™
3. Han Solo™ (In Carbonite Chamber)
4. Warok™
5. Imperial Dignitary™
6. Romba™
7. Barada™
8. Lando Calrissian® (General Pilot)
9. Anakin Skywalker™
10. Luke Skywalker™ (Imperial Stormtrooper Outfit)
11. Imperial Gunner™
12. Luke Skywalker™ (In Battle Poncho)
13. A-Wing Pilot™
14. Paploo™
15. Amanaman™
16. Lumat™
17. 8D8™
18. Han Solo™ (In Trench Coat)
19. Prune Face™
20. Princess Leia Organa™ (In Combat Poncho)
21. Klaatu™ (In Skiff Guard™ Outfit)
22. Wicket W. Warrick™
23. Bib Fortuna™
24. Rancor Keeper™
25. Luke Skywalker™ (Jedi Knight™ Outfit)
26. AT-ST Driver™
27. The Emperor™
28. Emperor's Royal Guard™
29. Klaatu™
30. Princess Leia Organa™ (Boushh™ Disguise)
31. Nikto™
32. B-Wing Pilot™
33. Teebo™
34. Squid Head™
35. Princess Leia Organa™ (In Combat Poncho Outfit)
36. Luke Skywalker™ (Hoth™ Battle Gear)
37. Bespin™ Security Guard
38. 4-LOM™
39. Darth Vader™
40. Cloud Car™ Pilot
41. Zuckuss™
42. Imperial TIE Fighter™ Pilot
43. Admiral Ackbar™
44. Lando Calrissian™ (Skiff Guard™ Disguise)
45. Chief Chirpa™
46. Weequay™
47. Logray™ (Ewok™ Medicine Man)
48. Ree-Yees™
49. Rebel Commando™
50. Nien Nunb™
51. General Madine™
52. Gamorrean Guard™
53. Biker Scout™
54. Luke Skywalker™
55. AT-AT™ Driver
56. Han Solo™ (Bespin™ Outfit)
57. Lando Calrissian™
58. See-Threepio (C-3PO)® with removable limbs
59. Greedo®
60. Princess Leia Organa® (Bespin™ Gown)
61. Rebel Commander™
62. Lobot™
63. Han Solo™ (Hoth™ Battle Gear)
64. AT-AT™ Commander
65. Boba Fett®
66. Chewbacca®
67. Bespin™ Security Guard
68. Two-Onebee (2-1B)®
69. Snaggletooth®
70. Dengar®
71. Imperial Commander™
72. Luke Skywalker® (Bespin™ Fatigues)
73. Imperial Stormtrooper™ (Hoth™ Battle Gear)
74. Imperial Stormtrooper™
75. Princess Leia Organa®
76. Rebel Soldier™
77. Ben (Obi-Wan) Kenobi®
78. Han Solo™
79. Star Destroyer™ Commander
80. FX-7®
81. Hammerhead®
82. Walrus Man®
83. Tusken Raider® (Sand People)®
84. IG-88®
85. Artive-Defour (R5-D4)®
86. Ugnaught®
87. Jawa®
88. Power Droid™
89. Yoda, The Jedi Master®
90. Luke Skywalker® (X-Wing Fighter™ Pilot)
91. Death Star® Droid
92. Bossk® (Bounty Hunter)

SPECIAL STAR WARS™ COINS
COLLECT ALL 62!

Now you can get a Special STAR WARS™ Collectors Coin with each Action Figure you buy. The front shows a STAR WARS® character. The back side tells you about his role in the STAR WARS® movies. Collect them or trade them. There's never been anything like it.

FRONT   BACK

WAROK
EWOK

An EWOK warrior who helps the EWEKS overcome the deadly SCOUT WALKERS

Meets or exceeds all safety requirements of Product Standard 72-76.

7628169570

®, TM & © LucasFilm Ltd. (LFL) 1984. All rights reserved. Kenner Products, a Div. of CPG Products Corp., Authorized User. ® Kenner is a trademark of CPG Products Corp., by its Div. Kenner Products, Cincinnati, Ohio 45202. Made in Hong Kong

General Mills, CPG PRODUCTS CORP.
STAR WARS® ACTION FIGURES
HT

	PR/GD	VG/EX	NM/MT
EV-9D9	$250	$395	$565
Han Solo (in Carbonite Chamber)	$280	$350	$425
Imperial Dignitary	$100	$215	$340
Imperial Gunner	$210	$350	$490
Lando Calrissian (General Pilot)	$135	$805	$1,490
Luke Skywalker (in Battle Poncho)	$120	$315	$500
Luke Skywalker (Stormtrooper Outfit)	$475	$1,230	$2,000
R2-D2 (with pop-up Lightsaber)	$425	$720	$1,300
Romba	$75	$190	$295
Warok	$120	$160	$205

	PR/GD	VG/EX	NM/MT
C-3PO	$580	$910	$1,200
Jann Tosh	$100	$170	$215
Jord Dusat	$80	$115	$140
Kea Moll	$50	$110	$150
Kez-Iban	$100	$160	$225
R2-D2	$515	$1,380	$2,360
Sise Fromm	$560	$765	$975
Thall Joben	$100	$155	$250
Tig Fromm	$280	$550	$710
Uncle Gundy	$120	$205	$470

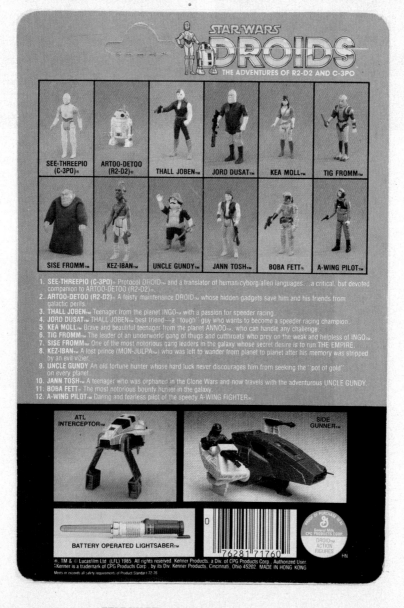

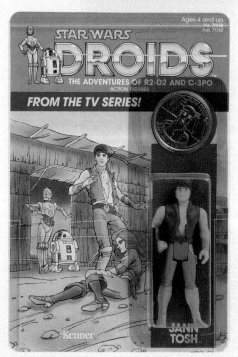

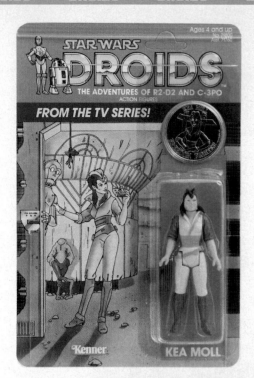

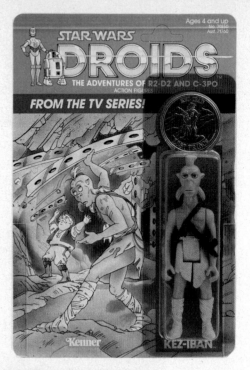

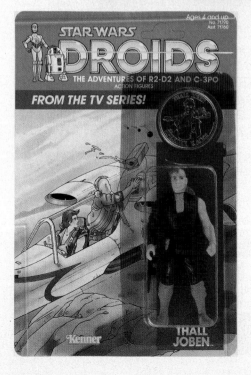

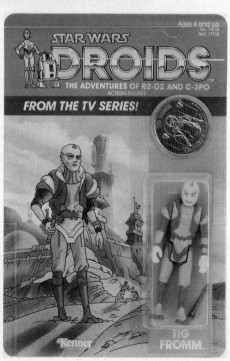

	PR/GD	VG/EX	NM/MT
Dulok Scout	$50	$95	130
Dulok Shaman	$70	$110	$175
King Gorneesh	$65	$120	$180
Logray	$95	$160	$220
Urgah Lady Gorneesh	$60	$120	$200
Wicket W. Warrick	$190	$280	$375

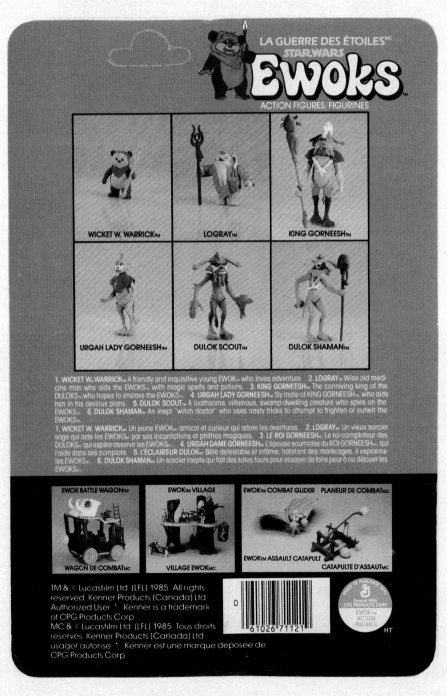

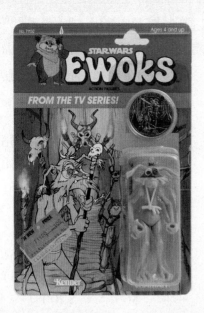

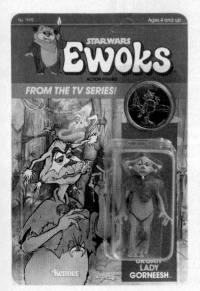

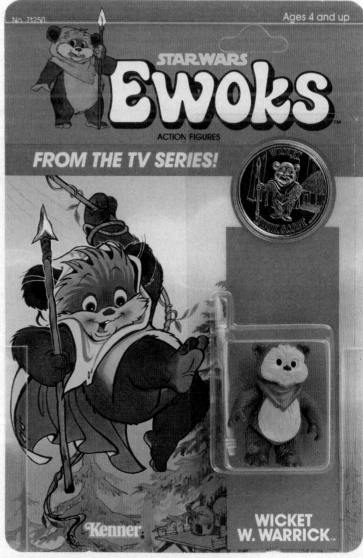

	PR/GD	VG/EX	NM/MT
Dulok Scout	$50	$95	$130
Ben Kenobi	$80	$170	$350
Boba Fett (Star Wars)	$150	$1,890	$3,630
Boba Fett (Empire Strikes Back)	$575	$4,650	$8,850
C-3PO	$300	$750	$1,205
Chewbacca	$125	$335	$550
Darth Vader	$450	$2,970	$5,500
Han Solo	$465	$3,450	$6,435
IG-88	$220	$655	$1,160
Jawa	$65	$200	$340
Luke Skywalker	$225	$395	$740
Princess Leia Organa	$1,500	$2,850	$5,495
R2-D2	$150	$260	$450
Stormtrooper	$220	$2,450	$9,670

Boba Fett

SEE THREEPIO (C-3PO)

No. 38630   Ages 4 and up

STAR WARS

• "chromed" head "clicks" • button opens secret
compartment • removable Death Star Plans
• simulated "electronic circuit" card.

ACTION FIGURE…
NOT A RADIO CONTROL TOY.

Contents: 7½" Poseable Droid Figure

Kenner

ARTOO-DETOO (R2-D2)

LARGE SIZE ACTION FIGURE
NOT A RADIO CONTROL TOY.

No. 39180   Ages 4 and up

STORMTROOPER

LARGE SIZE ACTION FIGURE

STAR WARS

Contents: 12" Poseable Action Figure with movable arms,
legs, and wrists; distinctive white and black armor; "Laser"
rifle can be held in hand or hung on belt.

Kenner

STORMTROOPER

PLAYSET AND VEHICLE PRICES

Similar to action figures, *Star Wars* playsets and vehicles sell in a wide range based on condition, rarity, and desirability. The following price list comprises the values of playsets and vehicles based on prices of carded or boxed graded toys that were sold in auctions in recent years. The list is organized by film release, then alphabetically. The values listed are based on toys in conditions of Poor/Good, Very Good/Excellent, and Near Mint/Mint.

STAR WARS PLAYSETS

	PR/GD	VG/EX	NM/MT
Cantina Adventure Set	$575	$2,000	$8,100
Creature Cantina Action Playset	$125	$310	$785
Death Star Space Station	$450	$2,500	$8,435
Droid Factory	$230	$950	$1,325
Land of the Jawas Action Playset	$90	$220	$415

No. 39120   Ages 4 and up

STAR WARS
CREATURE CANTINA
ACTION PLAYSET

Contents: Plastic Cantina base with 2 battle action levers, opening front door, circular bar and chipboard backdrop with pictures of STAR WARS Cantina band.   ASSEMBLY REQUIRED   ACTION FIGURES NOT INCLUDED

Kenner

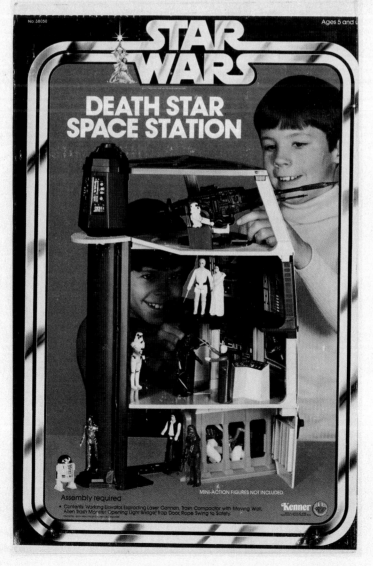

No. 38050   Ages 5 and up

STAR WARS
DEATH STAR
SPACE STATION

MINI-ACTION FIGURES NOT INCLUDED

Assembly required
• Contents: Working Elevator Exploding Laser Cannon, Trash Compactor with Moving Wall, Alien Trash Monster, Opening Light Bridge, Trap Door, Rope Swing to Safety.

Kenner

No. 39150   Ages 5 and up

STAR WARS
DROID FACTORY

- Robot parts and pieces interchangeable.
- Build up to 5 different robots at the same time.
- Make hundreds of different combinations.
- Robot building instruction blueprint booklet included.
- Build your own R2-D2 .

ACTION FIGURES NOT INCLUDED

Contents: Factory base with swivel crane, 38 robot parts.

Kenner

No. 39130   Ages 4 and up

STAR WARS
LAND OF THE JAWAS
ACTION PLAYSET

REFUNDS UP TO $3.00

Contents: Tatooine Desert Base with boulders, cave, battle action lever, escape pod rocket with opening hatch and corrugated Jawa Sandcrawler, with manual elevator.

ASSEMBLY REQUIRED   ACTION FIGURES NOT INCLUDED

Kenner

THE EMPIRE STRIKES BACK PLAYSETS

	PR/GD	VG/EX	NM/MT
Cloud City Playset	$400	$1,200	$4,600
Dagobah Action Playset	$80	$475	$900
Darth Vader's Star Destroyer Action Playset	$205	$730	$2,140
Hoth Ice Planet Adventure Set	$40	$120	$175
Imperial Attack Base	$85	$170	$225
Rebel Command Center Adventure Set	$295	$915	$1,555
Turret/Probot Playset	$1,295	$3,090	$4,890

RETURN OF THE JEDI PLAYSETS

	PR/GD	VG/EX	NM/MT
Ewok Village	$300	$1,200	$2,785
Jabba the Hutt Action Playset	$100	$325	$700
Jabba the Hutt Dungeon Action Playset (with EV-9D9, Amanaman, Barada)	$80	$155	$325
Jabba the Hutt Dungeon Action Playset (with Klaatu, Nikto, 8D8)	$75	$120	$200

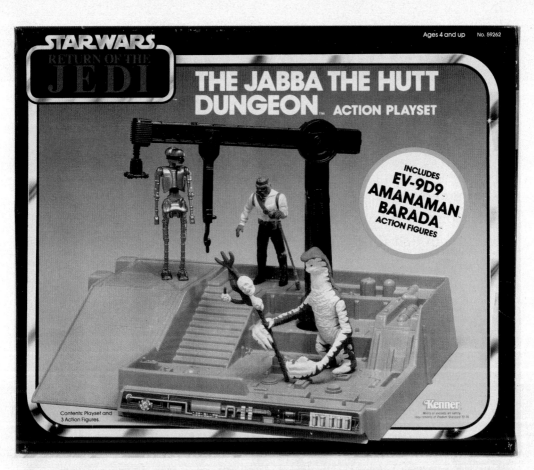

STAR WARS VEHICLES

	PR/GD	VG/EX	NM/MT
Darth Vader TIE Fighter	$405	$1,200	$2,000
Imperial Troop Transporter	$85	$190	$300
Land Speeder	$145	$785	$1,355
Millennium Falcon	$465	$1,750	$3,000
Radio Controlled Jawa Sandcrawler	$225	$900	$1,600
Sonic Controlled Land Speeder	$505	$2,995	$13,885
TIE Fighter	$250	$550	$7,135
X-Wing Fighter	$175	$1,495	$4,720

NO. 38020

Ages 5 and up

STAR WARS

LAND SPEEDER

MINI-ACTION FIGURES NOT INCLUDED.

Kenner

Contents: 1 Land Speeder™ Space Vehicle With Floating Suspension
Scaled For STAR WARS™ Mini-Action Figure.

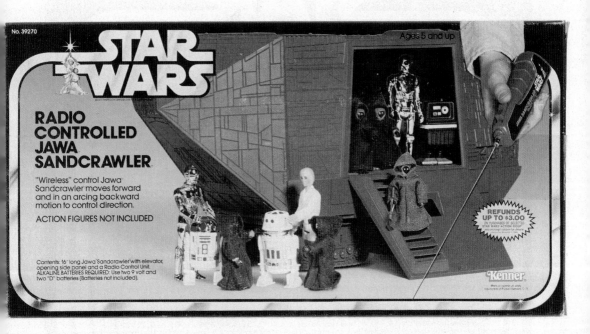

No. 39270

Ages 5 and up

STAR WARS

RADIO CONTROLLED JAWA SANDCRAWLER

"Wireless" control Jawa
Sandcrawler moves forward
and in an arcing backward
motion to control direction.

ACTION FIGURES NOT INCLUDED

REFUNDS
UP TO $3.00

Contents: 16" long Jawa Sandcrawler with elevator,
opening side panel and a Radio Control Unit.
ALKALINE BATTERIES REQUIRED: Use two 9 volt and
two "D" batteries (Batteries not included).

Kenner

THE EMPIRE STRIKES BACK
VEHICLES

	PR/GD	VG/EX	NM/MT
AT-AT	$500	$2,000	$3,495
Battle Damaged X-Wing Fighter	$170	$510	$2,855
Imperial Cruiser	$350	$650	$2,500
Rebel Armored Snowspeeder	$120	$695	$2,725
Rebel Transport	$120	$450	$1,200
Scout Walker	$175	$650	$1,500
Slave I	$305	$720	$2,360
Twin-Pod Cloud Car	$50	$105	$190

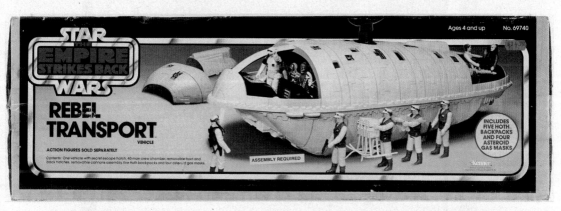

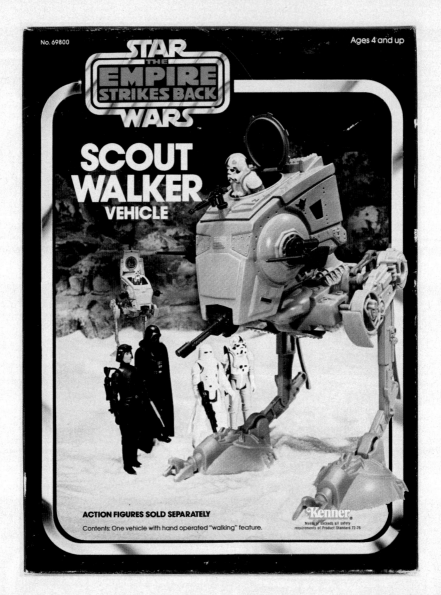

RETURN OF THE JEDI
VEHICLES

	PR/GD	VG/EX	NM/MT
Battle Damaged Imperial TIE Fighter	$270	$1,385	$2,500
B-Wing Fighter	$170	$400	$990
Imperial Shuttle	$310	$630	$2,595
Speeder Bike	$70	$200	$430
TIE Interceptor	$205	$550	$1,640
Y-Wing Fighter	$160	$225	$350

POWER OF THE FORCE
VEHICLES

	PR/GD	VG/EX	NM/MT
Ewok Battle Wagon	$220	$295	$370
Tatooine Skiff	$365	$650	$1200

DROIDS VEHICLES

	PR/GD	VG/EX	NM/MT
A-Wing Fighter	$140	$295	$450
ATL Interceptor	$260	$920	$3,890
Side Gunner	$130	$375	$530

	PR/GD	VG/EX	NM/MT
Darth Vader TIE Fighter	$60	$260	$595
Imperial Cruiser	$105	$500	$1,295
Land Speeder	$135	$200	$355
Millennium Falcon	$100	$325	$785
TIE Fighter	$110	$220	$410
X-Wing Fighter	$95	$225	$635
Y-Wing Fighter	$90	$300	$825

THE EMPIRE STRIKES BACK
DIECAST

	PR/GD	VG/EX	NM/MT
Slave I	$305	$700	$1,005
Snowspeeder	$145	$320	$650
TIE Bomber	$625	$1,140	$2,400
Twin-Pod Cloud Car	$80	$200	$590

THE EMPIRE STRIKES BACK
MINI-RIGS

	PR/GD	VG/EX	NM/MT
CAP-2	$60	$120	$300
INT-4	$40	$120	$215
MLC-3	$60	$105	$175
MTV-7	$120	$380	$885
PDT-8	$45	$120	$360
Radar Laser Cannon	$30	$95	$245
Tri-Pod Laser Cannon	$45	$80	$165
Vehicle Maintenance Energizer	$20	$45	$60

RETURN OF THE JEDI MINI-RIGS

	PR/GD	VG/EX	NM/MT
AST-5	$30	$60	$130
Desert Sail Skiff	$60	$135	$325
Endor Forest Ranger	$40	$95	$175
ISP-6	$65	$120	$1,535

POWER OF THE FORCE
MINI-RIGS

	PR/GD	VG/EX	NM/MT
Imperial Sniper	$60	$200	$270
Sand Skimmer	$70	$135	$230
Security Scout	$90	$165	$250

THE EMPIRE STRIKES BACK MICRO COLLECTION

	PR/GD	VG/EX	NM/MT
Bespin Control Room Action Playset	$30	$90	$165
Bespin Freeze Chamber Action Playset	$70	$125	$200
Bespin GantryAction Playset	$45	$100	$165
Bespin World Action Playset	$140	$400	$2,185
Death Star Compactor Action Playset	$45	$110	$225
Death Star Escape Action Playset	$35	$80	$140
Death Star World Action Playset	$75	$130	$565
Hoth Generator Attack Action Playset	$50	$120	$175
Hoth Ion Cannon Action Playset	$50	$225	$1,555
Hoth Turret Defense Action Playset	$40	$60	$100
Hoth Wampa Cave Action Playset	$30	$60	$85
Hoth World Action Playset	$165	$235	$1,000
Imperial TIE Fighter	$50	$130	$300
Millennium Falcon	$130	$300	$475
Snowspeeder	$75	$160	$250
X-Wing Fighter	$60	$130	$200

STAR WARS CREATURES

	PR/GD	VG/EX	NM/MT
Patrol Dewback	$130	$300	$2,075

THE EMPIRE STRIKES BACK CREATURES

	PR/GD	VG/EX	NM/MT
Tauntaun	$120	$440	$700
Wampa	$95	$190	$850

RETURN OF THE JEDI CREATURES

	PR/GD	VG/EX	NM/MT
Rancor Monster	$80	$160	$285
Sy Snootles and the Rebo Band	$80	$175	$350

THE CHALLENGE OF PRICING MULTIPACKS

Pricing collectibles takes a tremendous amount of research. For some items, there are significant established pieces of data, prices realized through auctions, dealers, and private sales, shared on message boards, and printed in publications. This evidence can be used to cement and guide to their values in respective conditions.

But for some collectibles, a lack of sufficient sale prices makes it difficult to anticipate an item's value.

Star Wars action figures – on card or loose, third party graded or not – are bountifully available on the secondary market. The multipack sets, however, are a different story. Sales of the three-packs on card or six-packs in-box have been minimal in recent years.

Which prompts the question of: why?

Have they been underwhelming because the figures are already available by themselves and multipacks didn't offer any new figures? Is it because figures like Luke, Han,

even Ugnaught, are repeated within the multipack series? Or do people anticipate that first releases of characters sold as single figures will be more valuable than what could be considered reissues as multipacks, similar to how comic book fans hunt for first appearances and title debuts?

More than likely, it boils down to rarity. Single figures were much cheaper to produce, package, and sell, than the multipacks. The multipacks had a considerably lower distribution rate, which meant that they were far less available when they originally came out. Additionally, the packages took up more space on store shelves, resulting in fewer overall sales opportunities for the store, which likely translated to smaller orders made to distributors.

During the run of Kenner's *Star Wars* action figures, only 16 varieties of three-packs were made and just two six-packs. The three-packs all have *Star Wars* or *The Empire Strikes Back* packaging, suggesting that sales weren't strong enough to warrant a new wave in *Return of the Jedi* packaging.

Now, on the secondary market, it's a different situation. There's a completist mentality to procure all 16 of the three-packs. This is certainly a goal among the 92-backs as well, but many of those figures were reissued later. So, if collectors want a Princess Leia Organa figure but can't find a 12-back, they can get a 20-back or even the later issued version on *ESB* and *ROTJ* cards.

Finding the three-packs, especially ones that are still on card and in mid to high grade condition is much more challenging.

"These are a packaging format which makes them difficult to find in a 100% sealed state, where they won't be refused or receive a qualified grade by AFA," CPPA Accredited Appraiser Joe Fiore said. "In cases such as the Hero or Rebel set, they are sold so infrequently that I don't believe grade would be as much a factor, although factors of completeness and a sealed state would draw in higher paying buyers."

Collectors have likely held on to these, knowing their rarity, which creates its own difficulty for auction houses and dealers to accurately price for sales.

"Our estimates are always an educated guess, but more times than not, it has to do with our past auction results or other known and vetted sales," Hake's Auctions President Alex Winter said. "However, in the case of the very rare, like the multipacks, there are very little results to go by. That is when we then go by more of a gut feeling than anything else."

Auction results are evidentiary support to gauge interest in an item and anticipate future prices. For dealers and private sales, setting prices can result in significant differences. A quick search comparison of the Android set results in an AFA 80 listed for under $5,000 by one dealer versus an AFA 75 listed for $8,500 by another.

"As three-packs are rare, the prices can fluctuate a great deal," Toy & Comic Heaven owner and operator, James Gallo said. "If someone is trying to put a set together it

A Bespin Set in similar grade sold for $4,897 and $1,200 in recent years.

An Imperial Set sold for $9,086 in a 2018 auction and one in similar condition cleared only $1,300 in a 2014 auction.

A Droid Set estimated at $2,000-$5,000 cleared for $6,490 in 2018 and one estimated at $300-$500 reached $2,000 in 2017.

may force prices higher for a period of time. At times dealers will list items at over-inflated prices because they don't really want to sell them or because they paid higher than normal just to get a rare item in inventory."

Collectibles have their own economic system, with completed sales creating a baseline for other examples in similar conditions. But when something very rare hits the market, it can spike significantly. Across most of the *Star Wars* toys, prices are currently on the rise, and as a group, multi-packs seem to be jumping in value more than single issue figures.

Because they don't come up that often, it can create bidding wars. In their July 2018 auction, Hake's Auctions offered a six-pack action figure set AFA 90 that carried an estimate of $2,000 to $5,000, but ended up selling for $28,556. Similar auction results from 2017 and 2018 have shown several other three-pack special action figure sets far exceeding their estimates.

When asked for his attribution to the high result of the six-pack, Winter noted factors surrounding the toy.

"We keep our preauction estimates on the conservative side," Winter said. "For much of the items from the Russell Branton collection, our estimates were eclipsed. The six-pack was one of the biggest prices realized over our estimate. A lot has to do with the excitement the Branton collection has generated. And since most of his material was high grade, or highest known, the sold prices are reflective of this. Such was the case of the six-pack. It is a coveted item all the way around and in the auction environment, it really flourished."

These and other sales in recent years have made the news – mainstream and in the collecting communities – which means that more could hit the market as owners of the toys seek to capitalize on the potential rising value by selling now. High dollar sales certainly instigate more examples to be offered for sale, but if more come fresh to the market, then the prices could start leveling off. In the meantime, accurately predicting what they'll sell for to a hungry market is quite challenging. As Fiore put it, they have "become darlings of the vintage *Star Wars* collecting hobby, emerging as the cream of the crop when collectors realized they were much scarcer than the single/individual character MOCs."

This six-pack action figure set graded AFA 90 was estimated at $2,000-$5,000 and sold for $28,556 at Hake's Auctions.

To demonstrate the challenges in pricing multipacks for the current market, a few experts from the collecting field were asked to offer their estimates for a sample of multipacks. Those experts are:

- Joe Fiore, CPPA Accredited Appraiser and *Overstreet Comic Book Price Guide* Advisor
- James Gallo, Owner and Operator of Toy & Comic Heaven
- Jesse Cedar Soberman, Experienced Star Wars Collector
- Alex Winter, President of Hake's Auctions

Each was given the same list of figure sets that have not been sold in high profile settings over the last few years, based on the expectation that the sets in question were graded AFA 80.

ANDROID SET
C-3PO
R2-D2
Chewbacca

Fiore: $7,000
Gallo: $6,000-$10,000
Soberman: $7,000
Winter: $5,000-$7,000

Bespin Set

C-3PO
Ugnaught
Cloud Car Pilot

Fiore: $15,000
Gallo: $8,000-$12,000
Soberman: $13,000-$14,000
Winter: $7,000-$10,000

Hero Set

Luke (X-Wing Pilot)
Ben Kenobi
Han Solo

Fiore: $8,000
Gallo: $8,000-$10,000
Soberman: $8,500
Winter: $15,000-$20,000

IMPERIAL SET
Imperial Commander
Dengar
AT-AT Driver

Fiore: $10,000
Gallo: $10,000-$12,000
Soberman: $6,500
Winter: $7,000-$10,000

REBEL SET
2-1B
Princess Leia (Hoth Outfit)
Rebel Commander

Fiore: $17,500
Gallo: $10,000-$12,000
Soberman: $12,000-$13,000
Winter: $7,000-$10,000

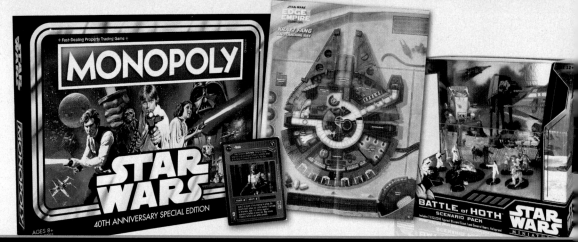

ROLL TO USE THE FORCE
STAR WARS AND TABLETOP GAMES

By Carrie Wood

Star Wars is about as pervasive as a media franchise can possibly get, and accordingly the series has seen numerous tabletop gaming adaptations. Much like how the series has managed to touch nearly every possible genre of video games, it's also managed to see its universe portrayed in nearly every type of tabletop game – from in-depth role-playing adventures to simple childhood board games, and everything in between.

While the amount of tabletop options from the *Star Wars* universe is indeed vast, they can essentially be broken into a handful of categories: role-playing games, card games, wargames, and board games.

ROLE-PLAYING GAMES

Fans of stories from a galaxy far, far away have enjoyed a pretty significant variety when it comes to *Star Wars* RPGs, with systems having been published by West End Games in 1987 (*Star Wars: The Roleplaying Game*), Wizards of the Coast in 2000 (*Star Wars Roleplaying Game*), and Fantasy Flight in 2013 (*Star Wars: Edge of the Empire; Star Wars: Age of Rebellion;* and *Star Wars: Force and Destiny*).

West End Games' *Star Wars: The Roleplaying Game* arrived with the *1st Edition* in 1987; this was followed up with the *2nd Edition* in 1992, and the *2nd Edition Revised and Expanded* in 1996. The game took a lot of its mechanics from West End's earlier RPG based on *Ghostbusters*, making use of the same d6 (6-sided die) System. Each edition had a core rulebook, with numerous smaller supplements released to help guide players through stories and create their own adventures. *Star Wars: The Roleplaying Game*

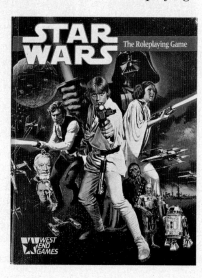

proved to be wildly popular thanks not just to its source material, but to the fact that the RPG system was easy to learn for newcomers while still being interesting to veterans.

The West End game was discontinued after the company declared bankruptcy in the late 1990s, at which point Wizards of the Coast picked up the license. In 2000, Wizards published their own *Star Wars Roleplaying Game* with the first edition of the rulebook. A *Revised Edition* was released in 2002, and in 2007 the company released the *Saga Edition*, which made far more significant changes in order to help streamline the rules. This game made use of the d20 system published by Wizards, which was also in use for *Dungeons & Dragons*; that both *Star Wars* and *D&D* ran on the same system made it easy for fans of one to pick up the other. *Star Wars* offered numerous different species and classes for players to build a character with – player characters could be anything from a human, to an Ewok, to a Twi'lek, or even a Droid. Classes included Scoundrels, Soldiers, and various kinds of Jedi, with the option to pick a "Prestige Class" for further specialization. In early 2010, Wizards announced that they wouldn't be renewing the license, and the final book published for their *Star Wars Roleplaying Game* released that April.

Fantasy Flight Games picked up the license at that point, and went on to publish their own *Star Wars Roleplaying Game* beginning in 2012 (with the *Beta* edition). Their game actually has three different smaller standalone games within it, all focused on different kinds of characters: *Edge of the Empire* (for playing bounty hunters and mercenary types), *Age of Rebellion* (for playing Rebellion soldiers) and *Force and Destiny* (for playing Jedi). All three games are set within the Original Trilogy, and numerous supplementary materials have been released in the years since they launched.

When it comes to collecting these games, books and minis from the West End Games production tend to have higher prices than pieces from the newer games, simply due to their vintage. Fantasy Flight Games has actually reprinted the original West End books in a deluxe format, making them available for a whole new generation of fans and collectors (though in a way this has only increased demand for the original printing). However, materials from all three publishers are generally easy to find for usually no more than $30-$50.

CARD GAMES

The 1990s saw a massive boom in collectible card games thanks to the arrival of *Magic: The Gathering*, and multiple *Star Wars* CCGs have since been produced. The first was the *Star Wars: Customizable Card Game*, which was produced from 1995 to 2001 by Decipher, Inc.

A unique aspect of this game was that one player *must* play with a Light Side deck, while the other plays with a Dark Side deck. In casual play, participants would often specialize in one or the other, but when it came to official tournaments, players needed to have both Light and Dark decks prepared. Similar to how Mana worked in *MTG*, the *SW: CCG*'s main resource to draw from was Force, which would be built up and drawn upon in order to unleash attacks on the opponent.

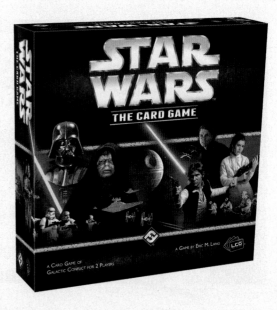

The "Premiere" set for this game debuted in 1995, and was followed by numerous expansions, including *Hoth, Dagobah, Cloud City, Jabba's Palace, Tatooine, Coruscant,* and more. A handful of expansions in the early 2000s were planned, but ultimately canceled.

Lucasfilm ultimately chose to end Decipher's license at the end of 2001, and the game officially was discontinued at that point. However, the game still has a fairly active community even today, with a strong core base of fans that continues to hold tournaments and even release (obviously unofficial) "virtual expansions" online for players to add to their decks.

The *Customizable Card Game* was succeeded in 2002 by *Star Wars: The Trading Card Game*, published by Wizards of the Coast and designed by Richard Garfield of *Magic: The Gathering* fame. Designed for two players, the *Star Wars Trading Card Game*'s goal is to take control of the in-game arenas. Players control various units to battle for the arenas, and units can only be placed in certain arenas based on what type of card they are (Character, Ground or Space). From 2002 to 2005, Wizards produced various sets and expansions for the game: *Attack of the Clones, Sith Rising, A New Hope, Battle of Yavin, Jedi Guardians, The Empire Strikes Back, Rogues and Scoundrels, The Phantom Menace, Return of the Jedi,* and *Revenge of the Sith.*

In 2005, Wizards of the Coast put the game on an indefinite hiatus, and they have not produced any further sets since. But, much like the game that preceded it, a group of fans, the "*Star Wars Trading Card Game* Independent Development Committee," has developed new sets of cards in the years since, and has made them available to fans for free online.

Both of these discontinued games can still be found online fairly cheaply (or, in the case of the fan-made expansions, for free). The more expensive products tend to be booster boxes or deck releases, and those can run anywhere from $100 to $300 or more depending on if they're still factory sealed and on the exact set expansion involved.

In 2012, Fantasy Flight Games debuted *Star Wars: The Card Game*, which instead of a typical CCG is what's called a "living card game." Living card games are a twist on the random nature of building up a deck in a traditional CCG; rather than buying blind packs, players purchase core sets and expansions that have predetermined cards in them. LCGs also go through various "cycles" that advance an over-arching story told through the outcomes of the game matches.

The first cycle for *Star Wars: The Card Game* was *Hoth*, followed by *Echoes of the Force, Rogue Squadron, Endor, Opposition,* and *Alliances*. The *Alliances* cycle was confirmed to be the final content addition by the publisher in early 2018.

Fantasy Flight also produces *Star Wars: Destiny* as of late 2016. This game also incorporates heavy use of dice, and is more focused on character-based decks that help players experience various "what-if" style battles between some of the icons of the franchise.

WARGAMES

With the amount of space warfare that takes place within the *Star Wars* universe, it seems to be a pretty obvious choice that some tabletop wargames would eventually be produced based on the series.

West End Games – having already published the RPG for the series in the mid-1980s – entered this area of gaming in 1989 with *Star Wars Miniatures Battles*. The game saw a second edition in 1990, and won the Origins Award for Best New Miniatures Rules in 1991. *Miniatures Battles* used various metal and plastic minis produced by West End, and the stats for the characters could actually be easily converted for use with the company's *Star*

Wars RPG, enabling some crossover action. When West End lost the license to publish *Star Wars* games, *Miniatures Battles* was accordingly discontinued. However, the game was popular enough during its lifespan that it saw some fairly significant print runs, and the minis for the game are fairly easy to find still in-box in various online auctions. The most that a collector would be paying would be for one of the larger sets, such as the *Mos Eisley Cantina* set, which can sometimes run for $50 or more. But even smaller packs of minis can be found for only a few bucks, making it an easy addition to a collection (especially for those not looking to actually play the game).

Much like how Wizards of the Coast would follow up on West End's RPG with a system of their own in the aughts, they did the same thing with a miniatures game, simply called *Star Wars Miniatures*. The game, which was published from 2004 to 2010, focused on point-based squads where players would build up an army from one of several different factions (such as Rebel, Imperial, New Republic, Sith, and so on). Each faction had their own separate line of minis to build up an army with; only the neutral "Fringe" action could use minis from any faction in order to build a squad. Minis in the Wizards game had a heavier collectability value; each mini released had a different level of rarity. Boosters would contain seven figures, with four common minis, two uncommon minis, and one rare or "very rare" mini in a set. Most of the popular characters from the films would either be rare or very rare, making them inherently more difficult to get. *Star Wars Miniatures* would be discontinued in 2010, though the minis can still be found fairly cheaply – usually for $25 or less even for entire lots of figures.

At Gen Con 2012, Fantasy Flight debuted *Star Wars: X-Wing*, which features dog-fighting mechanics between some of the more iconic space fighters in the franchise. The game was designed with newcomers to wargaming in mind; unlike many other wargames, *X-Wing* matches typically take less than an hour from setup to the game being decided. The first version of the game saw more than a dozen waves of expansions. A second edition was released in September 2018, with new rules for play (though minis from the first version can still be used via a conversion kit). The Core Set for *X-Wing* usually runs about $40, with expansions running anywhere from $15 to $30 depending on the figures involved.

BOARD GAMES

There have been numerous board games released over the years with the *Star Wars* name attached, with some being just a simple rebranding of an existing game, and others being original creations entirely.

Some of the earliest games were published by Kenner in 1977, such as *Destroy Death Star*. It was pretty simple – players moved their color-coded X-wings around the board by means of a spinner, with the obvious goal of destroying the Death Star. Kenner also published *Escape from Death Star* the same year, which was a little more involved; players were to move their characters around the board, into the Control Room of the Death Star, in order to steal the blueprints. Then, they had to get to the Millennium Falcon, jump to hyperspace, and deliver the blueprints to the Rebel base. A slightly more simplistic game also published in 1977 was *Adventures of R2-D2*, which was aimed at younger chil-

dren. The game was just following along a colored path (like in *Candy Land*) and was a little more visually stimulating.

Due to high print runs, a lot of the early Kenner games are fairly easy to find. However, finding a complete-in-box vintage set that's still in good condition could likely run $50 or more in an online auction, with still-sealed copies usually hitting $100 or more.

Of the Kenner games, their 1980 release of *Yoda the Jedi Master* is one of the higher-priced examples. The game, which featured players racing to become the first to complete their training under Yoda in order to become a Jedi Knight, usually sees prices of $100 or more for a complete set, with online auctions easily seeing sealed sets go for two or three times that much.

West End Games published a few board games in addition to their RPG system. These included *Assault on Hoth* (1988),

Battle for Endor (1989), and *Escape from the Death Star* (1990). All of them leaned into RPG-style mechanics, and while *Assault on Hoth* and *Escape from the Death Star* were both designed as multiplayer adventures, *Battle for Endor* was a solitaire game.

Purchasing the West End board games will run a little more than the Kenner games, likely due to being a little harder to find; complete-in-box copies of these games can run $75, sometimes $100 or more, depending on the condition.

Parker Brothers also published a few *Star Wars* games over the years, including – for better or for worse – a handful of titles all focused on Ewoks. These included *Ewoks Save the Trees, Wicket the Ewok, Paw Pals: The Dancing Ewok Card Game,* and *Ewok Favorite Five*. Most of these were aimed at very young children and had simple mechanics, such as color-matching or counting. *Ewoks Save the Trees* was

probably the most involved of the Ewok games, with a complex board setup that involved pop-up pieces to create the creatures' home. *Wicket the Ewok* can usually be found for about $30 or so, while *Ewoks Save the Trees* can actually run up to $100 or more for a complete-in-box set.

Parker Brothers also released *Star Wars: The Interactive Board Game – Assault on the Death Star* in 1996, a game accompanied by a VHS tape. This game is of particular note because David Prowse shot new scenes on the original Death Star set and James Earl Jones recorded new lines as Vader for the first time in years for the VHS tape. The game is played by starting the VHS tape and moving pieces around the board to reach the goal (disabling the Death Star) before Vader can use the station to destroy the Rebel base. *Assault on the Death Star* used characters from other *Star Wars* material and essentially canonized them (at the time): Shira Brie from the Marvel-published *Star Wars* comics, Kyle Katarn from *Dark Forces*, and Corwin Shelvay and Erling Tredway from the West End Games RPG. It's an oddball title, and one very indicative of the time in which it was produced thanks to the VHS tape, but it's easy to find – complete copies can be found for just about $25 or so, even in good condition.

More recent games have been published by Fantasy Flight, and have included *Star Wars: Rebellion, Star Wars: Armada,* and *Star Wars: Imperial Assault.* These are all generally a little more involved and complex to play, and can often take two hours or more to complete a session – all three lean heavily into the strategy genre.

Outside of the games designed specifically with *Star Wars* in mind, there's a ton of existing board games out there that have been released as a *Star Wars* edition – multiple *Star Wars Monopoly* games, *Star Wars Sorry!, Star Wars Trouble, Star Wars Clue, Star Wars Trivial Pursuit, Star Wars Stratego, Star Wars Risk...* the list goes on seemingly forever. Most of these *Star Wars* editions can be found fairly easily (often right on the shelf at a store next to the basic edition of the same game), though due to the branding, can sometimes carry a premium price. Usually this is no more than about $10 or so more than the regular game, making these fairly easy and inexpensive to pick up and add to a collection.

The tabletop history of *Star Wars* runs deep, but it's a sect of collecting and gaming that is worth investigating even for the greenest of gamers out there.

· ROLL FOR INITIATIVE ·
A New Guide is Here!

Tabletop gaming of all kinds is bigger than ever, and Gemstone Publishing's latest "how to" book is here to provide an in-depth look at this booming hobby. *The Overstreet Guide to Collecting Tabletop Games* takes a look at tabletop games of all kinds, from pen-and-paper role-playing experiences to collectible card games, from modules to miniatures, and everything in between. This guide includes the history of tabletop adventures and other board games as well as a look at what makes them so collectible, plus interviews with veteran industry pros and seasoned collectors alike. From the publishers of *The Overstreet Comic Book Price Guide*.

Now Available!

- Classic board games
- Tabletop RPGs
- Card games
- Interviews with industry veterans and collectors alike
- Collecting books, miniatures, modules and more
- The rarest cards from *Magic, Pokémon* and more
- An in-depth look at the impact of crowdfunding
- The history of gaming companies
- And much more!

SOFTCOVER
$19.95

From Carrie Wood (author of *The Overstreet Guide to Collecting Video Games*) and *Game Trade Media*'s Richard Ankney.

TOY BOX TREASURES TO ADULT COLLECTIBLES:

RUSSELL BRANTON DISCUSSES HIS STAR WARS TOY COLLECTION

Most collections begin with a love of the subject matter that developed in childhood and was nurtured for years. This was the case for Russell Branton, who was mesmerized by Star Wars *the first time he saw the movie when he was a young boy. His passion for the toys was reignited many years later when one purchase of a rare piece inspired an extensive collection. Over the course of about 12 years, Branton compiled a world class collection of toys, vehicles, and related material, including many rarities and prototypes.*

Beginning in 2017, Branton started parting with the collection by selling it in auctions through Hake's Americana & Collectibles. At the time of this book's publication, three large portions of his collection have sold, garnering impressive results and records for the pieces.

In this interview, Branton reflects on his collection, how it began, the process of building it, the importance of grading, his feelings on parting with the collection and his reaction to the sales, as well as advice for other collectors.

Overstreet: What do you like about *Star Wars*?

Russell Branton (RB): Just the adventure of the story. The storyline itself. When I was a young boy I saw it for the first time with my older brother. I was star struck from the very beginning when they blew the blast door and the Stormtroopers came through and were firing – it was like magic to me. Seeing Darth Vader – I was hooked ever since. I think I've been a *Star Wars* fan as far back as I can remember. Probably, since the age of five or six years old.

Overstreet: How long have you been collecting?

RB: Well, I always had the toys, as a little boy. I was probably buying them even when I was a little bit older, like early teenager, embarrassingly enough, and that's when I realized how much I liked them beyond just playing with them as toys.

My actual collection started in 2002. It wasn't even supposed to really be a collection. My wife and I went to [Comic-Con International: San Diego] and my first piece that I bought was a rare 12-back vinyl cape Jawa. For some reason I always wanted one because when I was a little kid I didn't have one. This was sealed, graded, never been opened and I made the purchase.

Then after buying that, I of course, wanted all original 12 graded, and then the monster started. And then it turned into the 21-back [laughs] and then I just wanted all of the figures. I wanted the *Empire Strikes Back* and *Return of the Jedi*, then I wanted the

Russell Branton's collection began with the rare vinyl cape Jawa action figure.

tri-logo carded. Then basically everything I could get my hands on at that point. I wanted everything Kenner made and any kind of prototypes I could get my hands on and anything I remembered as a boy. It started with one figure, it was not supposed to be the beginning of this massive collection, but that's how it wound up. It wound up with just buying everything and building a collectible room to showcase it all. It was a life on its own. I kept getting phone calls with offers on these items to buy. For the most part, I don't think I turned anything down.

Overstreet: So, you did start with a focus on certain pieces?

RB: Yes, I started with the original 12 and that was sort of important to me. I believe even before I obtained the original 12 I opened it up to any *Star Wars* carded. After that I sort of progressed to *Empire Strikes Back* and *Return of the Jedi*. Basically everything. Anything they would sell. And if it wasn't graded, I'd actually buy it and send it in to AFA to certify and make sure it was graded. It had to be, in my mind, an 80 or better, unless it was an extremely rare piece. The higher the grade the better. At that point, I started trading figures back in to obtain a higher graded version of that particular figure. I started getting higher graded figures in my own collection. I tried to get the highest graded possible, especially in the 12-back.

Overstreet: Sending them in for grading yourself, I wondered if you estimated grades ahead of time or had a connection that estimated them.

Start your own collection of STAR WARS Action Figures and Space Vehicles!

12 authentically designed figures in realistic STAR WARS costumes. All have movable parts, scaled to fit inside STAR WARS Space Vehicles.

- **Sand People**™ (3¾") in sand fighter costume with Gaderffii Stick.™
- **See-Threepio**™ (3¾") in shining gold finish.
- **Death Squad Commander**™ (3¾") with Laser Rifle.™
- **Han Solo**™ (3¾") with Laser Pistol.™
- **Chewbacca**™ (4¼") with Laser Rifle.™
- **Princess Leia Organa**™ (3½") has a removable cape and Laser Pistol.™
- **Luke Skywalker**™ (3¾") with action Light Saber.™
- **Artoo-Detoo**™ (2¼") with movable legs and head that "clicks".
- **Darth Vader**™ (4¼") with action Light Saber™ and removable cape.
- **Stormtrooper**™ (3¾") with Laser Rifle.™
- **Ben (Obi-Wan) Kenobi**™ (3¾") with action Light Saber™ and removable cape.
- **Jawa**™ (2¼") with shining eyes and Laser Gun.™

All 12 STAR WARS Action Figures may not be available in your store at the same time.

How to work Light Saber™
When in closed position, tip of saber sticks out slightly.

Pull Saber out by tip or push Saber out using slide lever.

Tie Fighter™ with fly-off solar panels; Laser Light™ and sound.

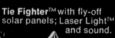

X-Wing Fighter™ with retractable wings; Laser Light™ and sound.

Land Speeder™ with "floating" motion.

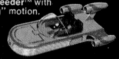

STAR WARS ACTION FIGURES NOT INCLUDED WITH COLLECTOR'S ACTION STAND.

STAR WARS
Action Collector's Stand

Display all 12 figures on this colorful STAR WARS galaxy stand. Sturdy plastic, with action levers to move figures back and forth. Figures easily removable for individual play.

Send your name, address zip code; and proof-of-purchase seal (shown at right) from 2 STAR WARS Action Figure packages along with *$2.00* to:

STAR WARS Action Collector's Stand
P.O. Box 1313
ONE Industrial Drive
Maple Plain, Minn. 55348

Collector's Action Stand **FREE** with proofs-of-purchase from 12 STAR WARS Action Figures.

Allow 8-10 weeks for delivery. Offer expires May 1, 1979. Void where prohibited, taxed, or otherwise regulated.

MADE IN HONG KONG.

© GENERAL MILLS FUN GROUP, INC. 1977   Characters: © 1977 TWENTIETH CENTURY FOX FILM CORP.   KENNER PRODUCTS, Cincinnati, Ohio 45202

The back of the packaging card showing the original
12 figures, hence the term "12-back."

His first goal was to collect all of the original 12-back figures,
including these of Princess Leia and Han Solo.

RB: Yes, I would always get a heads up where something would probably grade, which I was perfectly fine with, as long as the majority of the figures obtained an 80 or higher. But, I was always looking for an 85 or 90 and in anything, if I could get my hands on a 95, I would jump on that too.

Overstreet: What were your favorite pieces from the collection?

RB: Okay, from my collection, definitely the rare pieces. So, I had the double telescoping figures, the prototype Boba Fett. I was actually really proud that I had all three packs, so the variations of all the three packs, I had obtained those as well. I also have another prototype it's hard to get your hands on – it's a 12" *Empire Strikes Back* R2-D2. It was extremely rare. That is one of the pieces I was very proud of. Then the Vlix was one of my favorite pieces also.

Overstreet: Those are all great pieces. I really like Artoo.

RB: As a kid my favorite piece was the Gamorrean Guard. Because when I was a

kid, I looked *forever* and I couldn't find one. I had all the *Return of the Jedi* figures but for some reason that one slipped. I could not find it. I'd go in a store and they were already all gone. So for me, it was very difficult to find the figure. Eventually I was able to find a couple. I wound up with, like, 10 or 12 of them. [laughs] At the time that was one of my favorite characters.

Overstreet: Your collection is noted for having high grade material, and that was your goal when you started the collection?

RB: Yes, I wanted everything gradable. I didn't want anything open box. For the most part it had to be sealed, never opened, higher grading. The quality of the collection was important to me, more so than just obtaining all sorts of various pieces. It had to be a special circumstance for me to buy a piece that was open box or, like I said a low grade or lower grade. For me, the quality of the collection was very important and required a lot of patience. I think even having the want to buy everything, I think it still took me 12-13 years to complete the collection.

Overstreet: There are also a lot of rarities. Did you seek those out because they were rare or because they were ones you wanted?

RB: I think there's always that "holy grail" for a *Star Wars* collector. Of course, you seek them out, but again, they had to be gradable, sealed, never opened, so it was quite difficult to get all three of the double telescoping figures, the rocket-firing Boba Fett. That was an option, maybe five years into my collection, so it took some time to have something like that offered to me and I jumped at the chance. It took a lot of time, so there were certain pieces within my collection that were important for me to obtain.

But the other pieces were there and readily available 10, 12, 15 years ago. *Empire Strikes Back*, *Return of the Jedi* carded figures were okay to find, but then it obviously became harder to find if you wanted a high grade, high quality *Star Wars* carded or prototype pieces. Those are the parts that definitely took a lot longer. And vehicles. When I got into the vehicles side of it, then it became even harder because of the larger boxes. I wanted high quality boxes and graded.

Another thing that I didn't mention is that I always wanted to make sure that I got the original card for that particular figure. For instance, if they have an *Empire Strikes Back* or *Return of the Jedi* carded Darth Vader, I wasn't so much interested in those, I had to have the original 12-back Darth Vader. Same with the vehicles, I wanted an *Empire Strikes Back* boxed AT-AT Walker, as opposed to a *Return of the Jedi* AT-AT Walker because they originally came out in *The Empire Strikes Back* movie. It was very important for me to get the original package for the original figure. Unless it was rare or tri-logo Darth Vader.

Overstreet: There are tons of *Star Wars* toys. How did you learn about all the different versions of figures and the volume of items that could be collected?

RB: I think just through the years, word of mouth. I had an upper hand because I remember playing with them through the years. For me, it was important to basically obtain any piece that Kenner made.

No. 38230   Ages 4 and up.

PRICE

STAR WARS

Darth Vader

Kenner

The three action figures
with double telescoping lightsabers
are highly sought among collectors.

RB: I love everything *Star Wars*, but for the most part I think I just avoided anything that wasn't the toy line. They're all neat things, everything's cool with a *Star Wars* label on it. I specifically was toy hunting. I just looked for the toys themselves. I was offered actual pieces from the set of *Star Wars* and at the time, I wasn't too interested. Looking back on it, maybe that's what I'll start collecting next. They're obviously rare pieces. The toys were what I wanted.

Overstreet: Did you come across any controversial material? If so, how did you handle that?

RB: There was an authentic piece that really wasn't picked up on until I turned everything in to Hake's [Americana & Collectibles]. Through the years buying all these pieces, of course, you're going to have some issues. The one that stuck out to me was that it wasn't a fake piece, but it was altered. The piece, they sprayed a sheen on it, I guess to make it look more appealing or newer. Which, of course, sort of ruined the value of the product. Which was fine, because it wasn't a rare item or high-end piece. It just happened to be a piece that I need to complete the collection, so it wasn't even a big deal and I got my money back for the purchase. It was one of those items that was actually just overlooked and wasn't really an issue.

So, I wanted to get the entire Kenner line. But then, you get some more of the rare pieces that were European variations, like the European Death Star variation. That was important for me to obtain because that was different. It was a variation to the Death Star original. So that was pretty much it – Kenner line and rare pieces outside Kenner. I kind of had pretty good knowledge of the toys themselves, but then just talking to people through the years, you realize, other figures are rare and hard to obtain. Then, of course, you start looking for those figures as well.

Overstreet: Where did you buy from? Was it auctions or stores or other sources?

RB: I had a source, so I had someone that would locate what I was looking for and I would make the purchases that way. I always had someone do the groundwork for me and either say yes or no. I handled it that way. That may be another reason it took so long. [laughs]

Overstreet: Were there any specific items that you avoided getting? If so, what was the reason?

Overstreet: These collectibles sell in a pretty wide range of prices. How did you determine what was reasonable, regarding what you were willing to pay for them?

RB: I think the rarity of the item, obviously. What I would call more common items, there was a price range I would pay. Then there were the much rarer items, which I was willing to pay much more for. It had to make sense. When these pieces were locat-

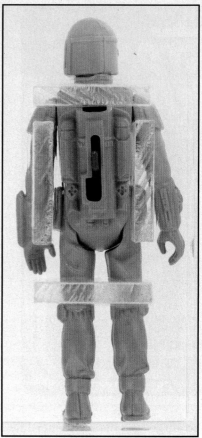

Branton also looked for prototype figures like this
rocket-firing Boba Fett figure with the "L" slot on the back.

ed for me, they knew when they brought it to my attention that it had to make sense financially. There were some items at the time that I absolutely paid top dollar for, but it was high quality, graded, no questions about the product that I bought and I felt, at the time, it was a great purchase, I guess overall, a good investment. I originally bought them all thinking I was going to give them to my kids, but unfortunately, I don't think they're going to love *Star Wars* the way that I do. So, I figured there are other things we could do with the money and take care of their college that way. [laughs]

Overstreet: Did you have any "the one that got away" experiences while you were collecting?

RB: Oh gosh, that's a great question. I have to really think hard about that. Yes. I think, I had an opportunity to buy another variation to the Boba Fett prototype. There's an

"L" and a "J" and obviously I had an "L" then I had a "J" offered to me and even at the time that would've been one heck of a purchase. It would have been a good idea, but I didn't buy it because I already had the other prototype. At the time, I was thinking that I didn't need another variation to the prototype I already had, but in hindsight, bad decision, I should've bought that one also. [laughs] So, yes, now that you have me thinking about it, I want to go beat myself up that I didn't buy that one too. [laughs]

Overstreet: Sorry about that! Earlier you touched on sending them out to AFA for grading, can you elaborate on that?

RB: Yes. I came across AFA, they had a stand at that same Comic-Con that I went to when I purchased my first vinyl cape Jawa. I had a long discussion with them about the importance of grading, why you grade, and I think that's the first year I found out about it. At that time, it was important to me that

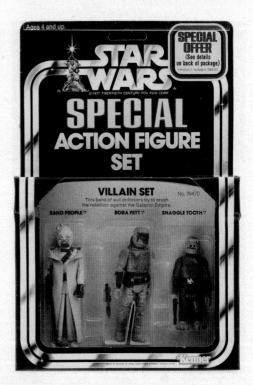

While collecting, Branton was able
to find all three packs, including
these Rebel, Villain, and Hero sets.

once I started my collection, I wanted to make sure everything was graded. Pretty much my entire toy line is graded through AFA. So, I went to AFA and they graded everything.

Overstreet: Did you have a good experience getting things graded?

RB: Absolutely. On my end, they were just terrific. I'd send stuff in, they'd take a little time, tell me the grade, and put stuff in the beautiful package casing and send it to me. I had a really good experience with AFA, I never had any issues with them at all.

Overstreet: Why did you decide to sell the collection now?

RB: I think I touched on it a little bit. I moved from Southern California to Arizona and when I moved I bought a house that had a space to display my collectibles. I kept them boxed and wrapped for, probably, a year and at that time I had a serious discussion with Hake's. Thinking long and hard about it, as I said before, I don't think my kids love it the way that I do. So, I thought it would be better to sell these items and let other people that really love *Star Wars* have an opportunity like I had to obtain these pieces. So, let them obtain these pieces that they want and I can reinvest and probably start some other type of collection down the line with my kids that they like. We'll see.

No. 38630   Ages 4 and up

STAR WARS

• "chromed" head "clicks" • button opens secret compartment • removable Death Star Plans • simulated "electronic circuit" card.

ACTION FIGURE...
NOT A RADIO CONTROL TOY.

Kenner

Contents: 7½" Poseable Droid Figure

ARTOO-DETOO (R2-D2)

LARGE SIZE ACTION FIGURE
NOT A RADIO CONTROL TOY.

Another rarity in his collection is this 12"
Empire Strikes Back R2-D2 prototype.

Overstreet: What has the experience been like seeing your collection moving into new hands?

RB: Good, and a little bit of bad. I'm happy for the person that made the purchase, because I know it makes them happy, since they bought something that they really wanted, and I know that feeling and it's a great feeling. So, you're always happy for that person. You genuinely are. You think, "Hey, that's great. They bought that piece because they love it, they probably remember it from when they were a kid, they really wanted that piece." Some are pure investors and that's fine, that's great too. They're still going to think that piece is super neat.

And then, the sad side for me would be all of the years putting that together and remembering having them displayed and seeing them all in your cases. That's not going to happen anymore, but I'll always have those memories. Completing the collection, and you have it for years, you start thinking, "What should I do with this?" Because I've had it in the room, I've looked at them long enough, I've enjoyed them. I've truly enjoyed them. I think it was important to let other people who want to enjoy them, enjoy them. A little sad, but more happy than sad, for sure.

Overstreet: Have you been happy with the sales achieved for your collectibles?

RB: Absolutely. I have to tell you – I know I've spoken with the president at Hake's and Kelly McClain at Hake's works very closely with me – and I have to tell you, the best decision that I ever made was letting Hake's handle my auctions. There's no possible way anyone else could have done this good. The way they have marketed the product, the way they have cared about the product. If anyone out there has any item that you care about and you want it taken care of and auctioned, you want it to go through Hake's. Absolutely. Hake's has been wonderful every step of the way – no issues at all of any kind. They've been phenomenal guys over there.

Overstreet: It's important that auction houses know and care about the material.

RB: Yes, absolutely and that's important. The passion that they have carries over into their job and it carries over into your collection. I think that's why they actually care about each individual piece that you're selling, not just the overall collection. They have a lot of knowledge of those pieces and I think that's really important when they put the description out there as to what they're selling, where they think it will sell at, and why. It's pretty great.

Overstreet: Have there been any sales that surprised you by going higher or lower than expected?

RB: Initially, no one knows where these items will fall. Believe it or not I was probably more concerned about your standard action figure – your *Empire Strikes Back* carded, your *Return of the Jedi* carded figure. But, they always did extremely well. I think they've done, probably, overall better than I had thought. That's pretty much it. As far as the higher end pieces that were projected to a certain number, I think they've been fairly accurate with those. Overall, I'm very pleased with where they landed.

Overstreet: Are you still collecting *Star Wars* or anything else?

RB: Nothing at the moment. [laughs] I think I'm so busy with the time that I have with the auctions themselves. When they pull pieces for the next auction I get to review the list, so it's an ongoing situation, even though there's an auction every four months, I feel like I'm getting lists of items that are pulled weekly or monthly. I'm preparing for those and then the auctions themselves go for

As a part of the Power of the Force line, this Gamorrean Guard figure came with a collectible coin.

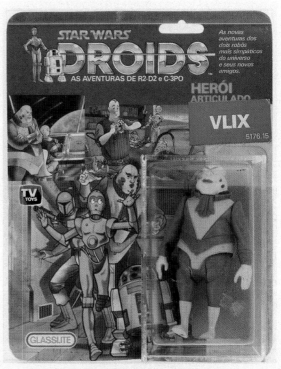

Unproduced in the United States, the Vlix figure was released in Brazil through the Glasslite company.

No. 93390   **STAR WARS**   **THE EMPIRE STRIKES BACK**   Ages 4 and up

SIX PACK

INCLUDES ALL SIX
ACTION FIGURES SHOWN

IG-88™

Yoda™

Kenner

Darth Vader™   Stormtrooper™   AT-AT Driver™   Rebel Soldier™

Along with the three packs, he owned
this six pack of figures.

22-some odd days. That takes my time. When it's all said and done, I think I'll have time to sit down and reflect and possibly start something else, for sure.

Overstreet: Do you have any advice you would give to people who are looking to start a *Star Wars* toy collection?

RB: Be patient. Be very specific about what it is you're looking for. Obviously, the most important thing you want to do when you're buying something is authenticate the product. You want to make sure you have authenticated the pieces and that's why when I said, let's go ahead and auction off the collection, I had no worries of any kind. I said, let's auction these off and there were no authenticity issues of any kind. So, if you're going to make a purchase, make sure it's graded, I would say. If you have to buy something that's not graded, I know now that they can authenticate pieces that aren't sealed boxes, and that's great too. I would say, definitely grade the item whether it's sealed or not sealed, get it graded. I think it helps with the value of the product too. And obviously, you want to buy something that you love. For sure.

No. 38240   Ages 4 and up

STAR WARS   **THE EMPIRE STRIKES BACK**

Stormtrooper™

Kenner

He also purchased many production
sample proof cards.

This Anakin Skywalker prototype figure
was used at the 1985 Toy Fair.

Branton's collection extended into vehicles like this
Sonic Controlled Land Speeder.

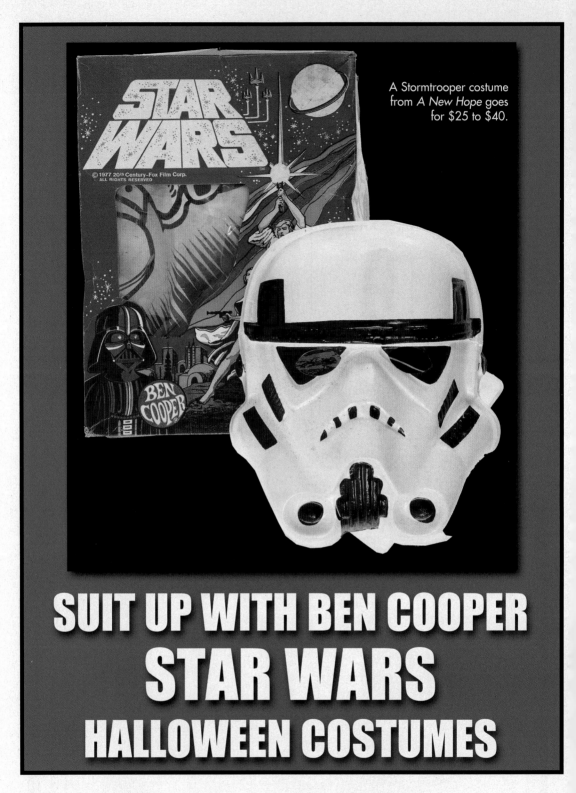

A Stormtrooper costume from *A New Hope* goes for $25 to $40.

SUIT UP WITH BEN COOPER
STAR WARS
HALLOWEEN COSTUMES

Wearing Halloween costumes is among the high points of childhood. It's the chance to be a hero, a scary monster, a funny jokester, or a fancy princess and show off the chosen persona throughout the neighborhood. After *Star Wars* was introduced to audiences young and old, Halloween costumes for the series' characters became essential for all the coolest kids on the hunt for trick or treat candy.

Though several companies have made costumes over the years, Ben Cooper is the name that is synonymous with the *Star Wars* Halloween costumes. Ben Cooper Inc. was one of the biggest costume manufacturers of the 20th century, primarily from the 1950s to mid-1980s. By taking a chance on licensed costumes from *Star Wars*, Disney, and comic book publishers, among others, they presented a new opportunity for kids to find costumes that were popular characters, yet still affordable.

Ben Cooper founded a theatrical costume business in 1927, though he was somewhat frustrated with the complications of making theatrical costumes. The piecework factor of putting them together, coupled with the more expensive garment quality for theatrical costumes caused multiple difficulties.

Ben and his brother Nat Cooper wanted to investigate other business options for mass production. As live theater saw decline due to the Great Depression and Halloween became more popular, they founded Ben Cooper, Inc., in 1937. They started creating inexpensive costumes with thin plastic masks and one or two pieces of thin cloth or vinyl-like material, and kids loved them. The Brooklyn-based company gained control of the license to sell Disney costumes using Mickey Mouse as the vehicle to entice kids and families.

Utilizing a keen sense for staying ahead of pop culture trends and their business model of gaining licenses to provide kids with more specific costumes based on characters they watched on TV and film, gave them an edge over the competition. Not only did the costumes feature popular characters, they were affordable and attractive – appealing to both consumers and retailers.

A Chewbacca costume from the first film sells in the range of $10 to $65.

That interest created the welcome problem of figuring out how to manufacture the costumes in large volumes of ready to wear pieces. Ben Cooper used vacuum forming rather than stiff cloth or other handmade operations to create the masks. They were then silk-screened with facial details rather than embroidered, saving a lot of manufacturing time. The costume pieces were created through mechanized sewing with a minimum of pieces, which also saved time. Through these processes they were able to supply more costumes to the retail base.

Mickey Mouse was joined by other early Disney costumes like Donald Duck and Snow White, as well as movie monsters like Frankenstein, superheroes like the Flash, and cartoons like Huckleberry Hound. Another of their revolutionary campaigns came in the 1950s when they created costumes with Glitter Glo, which reflected in car headlights and quelled parental concerns about kids' safety. By the '60s and

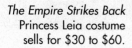

The Empire Strikes Back Princess Leia costume sells for $30 to $60.

'70s Ben Cooper had hit a solid stride as the Halloween costumer known for licensed TV and film characters.

Unfortunately, they saw financial losses in the mid-1980s following a wave of concern that candy was being tampered with, causing many parents to forgo trick or treating. Ben Cooper tried to improve the situation by encouraging different ways to celebrate Halloween, but with bankruptcy looming, some licensees pulled licenses to secure deals with other costume producers. Following several setbacks, the company closed in the early 1990s after a second bankruptcy.

During their heyday, Ben Cooper acquired the license for *Star Wars* costumes in 1977 – and quickly sold out that year. The character masks could be seen through the window box packaging, on top of costume pieces which often depicted the character rather than what they wore in the movies. But for just a few dollars, kids could sport the looks of main characters like Luke, Leia, Darth Vader, Chewbacca, C-3PO, R2-D2, and Yoda all the way to those with smaller

Klaatu, one of the rarer costumes from *Empire* reaches up to $75.

roles like Boba Fett, Wicket, Admiral Ackbar, Klaatu, and Gamorrean Guard.

In retrospect, those costumes are pretty comical looking, but nostalgia has turned them into popular, and affordable collectibles. Collectors prefer the full costume in box, but will buy out of box at a lower

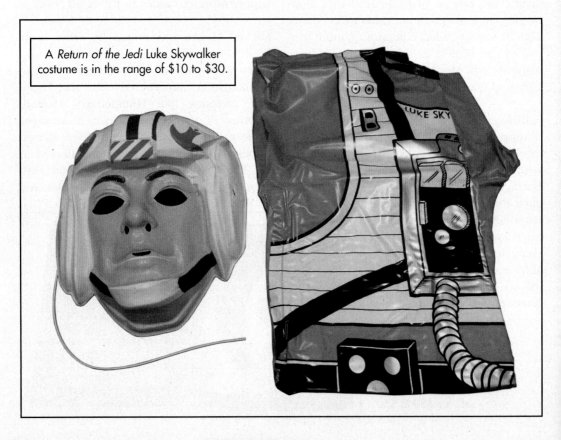

A *Return of the Jedi* Luke Skywalker costume is in the range of $10 to $30.

The Wicket costume from *Return of the Jedi* averages $45.

The rare Gamorrean Guard costume from *Return of the Jedi* hits $80.

rate. Occasionally just the mask or the cloth pieces will be sold, for significantly less, however the mask by itself will sell for more than the costume pieces.

Because the costumes and boxes are not especially sturdy material, they are hard to find in better conditions. Ones that are in above average to near mint condition can raise the price with the rarer costumes taking more drastic jumps.

Though characters like Luke, Leia, and Darth Vader are primary characters in the series, their costumes were more readily available and average lower prices in the secondary market than some character costumes that weren't made at the same volume. Because details on the sequels were kept vague, some mistakes were made on costumes for *The Empire Strikes Back* and *Return of the Jedi*, resulting in color variations like the blue Yoda mask or silver Boba Fett mask. Another interesting feature of some *Empire* costumes is that they display the early *Revenge of the Jedi* title before the movie was retitled, making for intriguing collectibles.

A New Hope costumes for Luke Skywalker and Princess Leia average $40-$65, while Chewbacca and Darth Vader sell in the range of $10-$65. A C-3PO costume can be found for just $10-$30, while the rarer R2-D2 goes for $80, and a Stormtrooper goes for $25-$40.

The Empire Strikes Back Luke and Boba Fett costumes are very affordable, typically in the $10-$45 range. Princess Leia, Yoda, and Darth Vader sell for a bit more at $30-$60. The higher value costumes from *Empire* include Chewbacca at $65, Klaatu and Wicket at $50-$75, and Admiral Ackbar at $75.

Costumes from *Return of the Jedi* are typically the most affordable among the series. Leia, Luke, Darth Vader, and Boba Fett sell for $10-$30. A Wicket costume averages $45, Klaatu goes for $50-$75, and the Gamorrean Guard is one of the rarer ones, selling for $80.

THAT'S A WRAP!
Collecting Screen-Used Items and Production Material

From beginning to end, movie-making is a complicated process. There are logistical and technical details with script revisions and storyboards, makeup and costume tests, prop and mask creation, set designing, location scouting, lighting needs, securing permits, and legal documents. Then comes the actual filmmaking with the director, actors, and hundreds of on-site crew members handling myriad tasks. After that, there's special effects, the editing process, scoring, and other work before a film is finally completed. The process is truly monumental.

It's also the basis for a slew of collecting opportunities, and in the case of *Star Wars*, they appeal to both series fans and general film buffs. Screen-used items and production material includes everything from costumes and props seen on film to models and call sheets. They are as small as film strips and as large as set pieces. Though collectors may anticipate that screen-used and production material is expensive, the prices achieved in auctions are from $20 to $200,000.

SCREEN-USED MEMORABILIA

Buying things that were used onscreen gives collectors the chance to own a physical part of the movie. With *Star Wars*, the level of creativity involved in the movies amplifies the amount of collecting options with costumes, helmets, masks, a bevy of props, puppets, models, and maquettes.

Values are impacted by which film the item is from, with pieces from earlier or more popular films achieving higher prices. Other contributing factors to the price include the

Helmets, like this Stormtrooper, sell in a wide range from $3,000 to $225,000 depending on detail and rarity.

Models of ships in the series reach $40,000 to $95,000 at auction.

Pieces of the Death Star miniature go for $650 to $1,600, depending on size.

significance of the character, amount of screen time, and popularity. For instance, an Ewok costume mask from *Return of the Jedi* has sold for $22,700, while a Rodian mask from *The Phantom Menace* reached $30,000. Now, *Return* is universally considered better than *Phantom*, but there's long been polarizing opinions regarding the Ewoks within the fandom; meanwhile, the Rodian is the species of the popular bounty hunter Greedo, which could account for its outselling the Ewok mask.

For characters with multiple versions (Stormtroopers, Rebels, background creatures) the rarer or more stylish helmets, props, or costumes sell for more. A Stormtrooper helmet used in *Return* has sold for $80,000 while a rarer Snowtrooper helmet from *The Empire Strikes Back* cleared $225,000. On the opposite end of the spectrum, a basic Rebel helmet from *Empire* that is undecorated and was used for longer shots sold for only $3,000.

The original trilogy used a lot of practical effects, including models and miniatures for ships and scenes in space.

Models of the ships achieve high dollar sales: Y-Wing and X-Wing Fighter miniatures from *A New Hope* sell for $40,000 to $95,000, and Luke Skywalker's X-Wing Fighter miniature from *Empire* reached $180,000 at auction. But some of these mementos can be found for hundreds and lower thousands. The Imperial Shuttle Tydirium motion control 1" model from *Return* has sold for $5,000 and a small surface piece of the original Death Star miniature used in *A New Hope* goes for $650 to $1,600, depending on the size.

Star Wars lightsabers, blasters, and other weaponry are consistently popular with collectors and drive value. A Stormtrooper blaster from *A New Hope* can clear $35,000 while a Stormtrooper blaster rifle from that

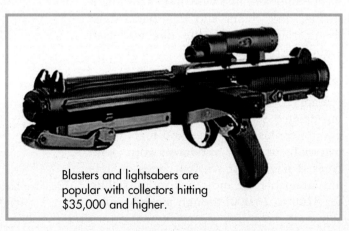

Blasters and lightsabers are popular with collectors hitting $35,000 and higher.

movie goes up to $85,000. One rarity, a Stepper motor-driven turbolaser tower from *Return* netted $75,000. When it comes to lightsabers, Luke Skywalker is king, as his saber from *A New Hope* and *Empire* sold for an incredible $240,000.

Though most major props from *Star Wars* reach impressive heights in value, there are many nestled outside of these five and six-figure prices. A Darth Vader stunt lightsaber from *Return* has sold for $5,200 and an incomplete Rebel blaster rifle (with pieces missing due to recycling for other props) from *Empire* sold for $3,000. A Tauntaun head casting or animatronic head sells for $3,000 to $8,000. Collectors can pick up a Sarlacc tentacle for $1,000, a lock of Chewbacca fur for under $500, or a *Rogue One* Rebel Communications bag with goggles, radio, wrench, and gloves for $1,000.

PRODUCTION MATERIAL

Off camera, there are logistical collectibles, such as production binders with unit breakdowns, shooting schedules, call sheets, and contact lists. This category also has pitch folders for special effects, makeup, and costuming that were presented to directors and producers for approval. Collectors can buy actual storyboards that mapped out the movies or blueprints and concept designs used to create set pieces and customized vehicles. Even filming location displays, expense reports, as well as parking passes and dashboard cards used during filming can be purchased. There's also clapperboards, on-set photos and reference images, technical equipment like viewfinders and light testers, and chairs and chairback signs designating seats for the director, cast, and other crew members.

Production-used scripts are leaders in this category. There are early drafts featuring deleted scenes or unused characters, editing copies with notes and highlighted material, or final versions worn with creased pages and scuffed edges. Scripts are attainable for most collectors, selling for $100 to $3,000, though signed copies or those used by directors, writers, and principal cast will sell for significantly more.

Similar to the scripts, most production material falls between a hundred and a few thousand at auctions. Production slides average $1,000 to $2,500, storyboard art sells in the range of $200 to $3,000, and a production wardrobe planning and continuity bible can reach $3,000. Things like production notes, set photos, call sheets, concept art, technical crew booklets, film strips, and transparencies are often lumped together in group lots at auctions. Individually, these items can sell for as little as $30 and in groups, they go for up to $6,500.

Tauntaun head castings and animatronic heads can realize $3,000 to $8,000.

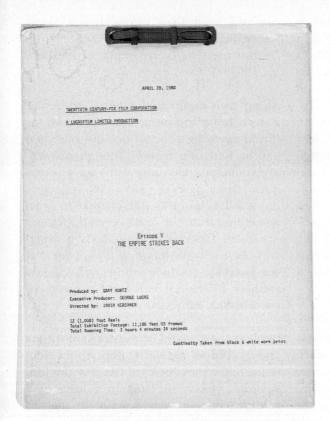

Scripts are popular collectibles within production material, realizing $100 to $3,000, depending on condition, film, and if they are signed.

From concept to completion film crews consist of hundreds of people working on lighting and sound, drivers, caterers, stand-ins, second unit groups, restroom services, medical technicians, practical effects, special effects, wardrobe, editing, accounting – the list goes on. Many folks who work as part of a film crew are often given shirts, jackets, and hats that designate them as such. These are modestly priced collectibles, typically selling for $50 to $200 from throughout the series. What's additionally interesting about this type of collectible is that the shirts and hats can depict working titles and logos. *Return of the Jedi* crew sweatshirts with original *Revenge of the Jedi* title and crew hats from *The Last Jedi* with the logo for the working title, *Space Bear*, have popped up in auctions.

CHALLENGES OF BUYING SCREEN-USED AND PRODUCTION MATERIAL

These types of collectibles instantly become highly coveted entries into any film fan's collection. However, there are some challenges inherent in buying this type of material, chiefly among them authenticity and accuracy.

The most important factor in buying screen-used and production items is to buy from reputable auction houses and dealers with established credibility. Places like Profiles in History, Premiere Props, and Screenbid specialize in this type of material. Auction houses like Hake's Americana & Collectibles and Heritage Auctions deal in a wide range of memorabilia, including film collectibles. Several others can be found through research on websites like Live Auctioneers.

Better auction houses, like the ones listed above, will research the provenance of items to confirm their authenticity, ensuring that their customers can buy with confidence. They'll include a certificate of authenticity (COA) or letter of authenticity (LOA), often included in item descriptions. These authentications come from sources like Lucasfilm, Twentieth Century Fox, Industrial Light and Magic, and Pinewood Studios, though other sources for this documentation can be from the prop master, mask creator, costumer, actor, or a reputable prop house. Not only do COAs and LOAs protect collecting investments, the verifiable provenance can quell any controversy or disputes when it comes time to sell to a new collector.

When purchasing screen-used material, be sure to read the description. It cannot be overstated how important this is when determining how much to spend. Because *Star Wars* is so significant to pop culture there are many authorized replicas for use in advertising, official appearances, film crew mementos, and those sold to the public. Lucasfilm provided examples of helmets, costumes, and armor to other companies for the purpose of making replicas to be used on tours. These items may not have been used on-screen but they can still fetch high prices, like a Darth Vader helmet and shoulder armor from *Empire* used to create replicas that sold for $90,000.

Along with authorized replicas, there are also costume and props that were used for the filmmaking process but not onscreen and/or with the actors. Though discerning collectors may only want screen-used items, these types of pieces give collectors on smaller budgets the chance to own something from the movie even if it wasn't onscreen. One such example is a Jango Fett blaster from *Attack of the Clones* that was used for costume fittings and recently sold for $750 – far below what a screen-used blaster achieves.

Replicas and stand-in versions of props and costumes regularly pop up in auctions. Since they look exactly like the film versions, reputable auction houses will acknowledge in their description that an item is a replica, its point of origin, and previous purpose or use.

It cannot be overstated that doing research will produce the best collecting experience. If a person or auction house offers screen-used memorabilia at a curiously low price, there's a strong possibility that it isn't authentic. Having a working knowledge of what things typically sell for helps in estimating the expected price and guides collectors to identify the real deal collectibles versus fakes or copies.

Collecting memorabilia that was used in the filmmaking process is a gratifying hobby, connecting cinephiles to the movies they love. It transports collectors' emotions to the sets where they can imagine walking by Luke Skywalker, see George Lucas concentrating in his director chair, hear Princess Leia's biting wit, and peek behind the curtain at models of Star Destroyers.

Crew jackets, shirts, and hats are affordable to most collectors, ranging from $50 to $200.

LAWRENCE KASDAN
Writing the Wars

SHOOTING
SCRIPT
FOURTH DRAFT

Is the pen mightier than the lightsaber? It is when it's wielded by a talented writer like Lawrence Kasdan. A behind the scenes triple threat – screenwriter, director, and producer – Kasdan is a three-time screenplay Oscar nominee and has written scripts for four of the *Star Wars* films.

Raised in Morgantown, West Virginia, Kasdan studied at the University of Michigan where he earned a degree in education, with a plan to be an English teacher. Unable to find a teaching job, he became an advertising copywriter in Detroit and then in Los Angeles.

He broke into the film business when Warner Bros. bought his script for *The Bodyguard* in the mid-1970s. For several years, the script languished before finally being made in 1992 with Whitney Houston and Kevin Costner.

As that script circled development, Kasdan continued writing, catching the attention of George Lucas who hired him to write the screenplay for *Raiders of the Lost Ark*. Impressed with that script, Lucas brought Kasdan into *The Empire Strikes Back* to complete the screenplay after the passing of Leigh Brackett, who had written the first draft. Lucas had written a few drafts and revisions, which included the major plot twist that Darth Vader was Luke Skywalker's father. Kasdan came in to write the final drafts, making it a more serious film with a darker storyline and higher stakes. It has been included on several "greatest movies" lists and was selected for preservation in the U.S. National Film Registry by the Library of Congress.

Following that movie's success, Lucas hired Kasdan to write the screenplay for *Return of the Jedi*. The script was still going through the revision process when the movie was already in preproduction. When it came time for the shooting script, Lucas, Kasdan, and director Richard Marquand spent a few weeks discussing ideas, which Kasdan used to finish and polish the script. One area of disagreement came with how to handle Han Solo's story. Both Kasdan and Harrison Ford believed that Han should die by sacrificing himself to save the others, which would instill the "no one is safe" mentality. Lucas was against the concept in favor of a more optimistic ending with all three leads alive and happy.

Through the '80s and '90s, Kasdan wrote, directed, and produced *The Big Chill*, *Silverado*, *The Accidental Tourist*, *Grand Canyon*, *Wyatt Earp*, and *Mumford*, among others. He returned to *Star Wars* in 1996 to write the *Star Wars: Shadows of the Empire* video game script in which a mercenary named Dash Rendar goes through missions to help save Luke Skywalker and Princess Leia.

With the announcement of 2015's *The Force Awakens*, came the news that Kasdan was returning to write the script. The first draft had been written by Michael Arndt, but he was struggling with the timetable. Arndt left the project and Kasdan took over writing duties, along with J.J. Abrams, who would direct the movie. They planned the story together and their first draft was done in a few weeks. Their goal was to return to the roots of *Star Wars* with an emotional story rather than lengthy exposition.

Kasdan co-wrote 2018's *Solo: A Star Wars Story*, the second standalone movie in the series. He had actually been writing the movie before he got the job for *The Force Awakens*. When he needed to take a break to write *The Force Awakens*, Kasdan brought his son Jonathan in to continue work on *Solo*. The goal for the movie was to plot the backstory of how Han Solo became the smuggler and pilot who made the Kessel Run in 12 parsecs. The Kasdan duo were able to create a believable history for Han, including some nice nods to what would happen in his future.

After George Lucas, Kasdan is credited with more writing contributions to *Star Wars* films than any other writer. He has helped to define beloved characters, create emotional dialogue, and make large scale stories feel personal and tangible.

Scoring the Galaxy:
Star Wars Soundtracks

By Jon Steffens

ORIGINAL SOUNDTRACK COMPOSED AND CONDUCTED BY JOHN WILLIAMS
PERFORMED BY THE LONDON SYMPHONY ORCHESTRA

The original *Star Wars* soundtrack sells for $10 to $45.

Both the magnificent, instantly recognizable "Main Title" theme and Lord Vader's militaristic "The Imperial March" have long been ingrained into the collective pop culture psyche. The music of the *Star Wars* films, primarily written and conducted by renowned composer John Williams, is as iconic to the franchise as the Death Star or the Millennium Falcon.

Whether to immerse themselves in the music and let their imaginations drift to a galaxy far, far away or simply to collect and display, *Star Wars* collectors have been buying the soundtracks to the beloved series of space operas for decades.

Though brilliant work in every field of moviemaking has been poured into these beloved films, they simply wouldn't have the impact they do if it wasn't for Williams' music. Majestic, epic, and filled with emotion, the soundtracks to the *Star Wars* films enchant viewers, carrying a weight to them that make one feel that the stakes in the storylines are very real and meaningful to their lives.

The 2016 double picture disc reissue for *A New Hope* reaches up to $90.

The first *Star Wars* soundtrack is not only special because it's the first of its kind, but because it also features the grandiose, orchestral "Main Title" theme used in nearly every following film to prime the viewer for the epic action about to unfold on screen. It's a piece that triggers excitement and nostalgia in equal measures – especially for those that grew up with the original trilogy. The "Main Title" was released as a single alongside the full soundtrack album in 1977, peaking at the number 10 spot on the *Billboard* Hot 100. A disco version of the theme was also released that year, and in October became a No. 1 hit. The soundtrack went on to win a multitude of awards, including a Grammy, an Oscar, and a Golden Globe in the categories of Best Film Score and Soundtrack Album, and would go on to sell over one million copies in the United States. The original two-disc vinyl release included a poster of a painting of the film's final battle by artist John Berkey.

Originally released on May 16, 1980, the soundtrack album from *The Empire Strikes Back* contains a piece that likely ties the "Main Title" in recognition: "The Imperial March (Darth Vader's Theme)." As cold and brutal as it is majestic, "The Imperial March" is a leitmotif that captures Vader's strength, his calculating demeanor – his very essence – perfectly. Composed like its predecessor by Williams and performed by the London Symphony Orchestra (the LSO would go on to perform the score for *Return of the Jedi* and the prequel trilogy as well), the soundtrack also includes "Yoda's Theme," a light, whimsical piece reflecting the aloof nature of the diminutive Jedi master.

Unlike the first two, the soundtrack album for *Return of the Jedi* was released as a single-disc edition, though it is the lengthiest score of any of the original trilogy. The score's final piece is titled "Ewok Celebration and Finale." Commonly referred to as "Yub Nub," the uplifting jungle-themed piece was written by Williams with Ewok-language lyrics by Ben Burtt of ILM.

Riding on the fans' love of the Ewoks, two made for television movies focused on the fuzzy little warriors, were released in '84 and '85. Titled *Caravan of Courage: An Ewok Adventure* and *Ewoks: The Battle for Endor*, both films were scored by Peter Bernstein, who also reworked brief parts of Williams'

The Empire Strikes Back 2016 reissue
averages $29 to $62.

An original copy of Return of the Jedi sells
in the range of $10 to $100.

Ewok theme from *Return of the Jedi* into both scores. A soundtrack LP incorporating music from each of the Ewok outings, titled *Ewoks – Original Soundtracks*, saw release from Varèse Sarabande in 1986.

The music from the prequel trilogy is remembered more fondly than the films themselves. Again, composed by the inimitable Williams and performed by the LSO, the prequel soundtracks are filled with the magnificent, epic moments *Star Wars* fans love, especially "Duel of the Fates" from *The Phantom Menace*. Sweeping, grand, and filled with excitement, the choral-orchestral piece is a masterwork of film music.

Featuring music by noted television composer Kevin Kiner, popular animated spinoff series *Star Wars: The Clone Wars* and *Star Wars: Rebels* received their own vinyl soundtrack releases in 2014 and 2015, respectively. Both issued on Walt Disney Records, *Star Wars: The Clone Wars – Seasons One Through Six* hit the shelves in a single-disc edition in 2014, while on April 18, 2015, the theme from *Rebels* was released on a 7" picture disc in a limited edition of 3,500 copies.

Williams again returned to the *Star Wars* universe to compose the scores for *The Force Awakens* and *The Last Jedi*. While the

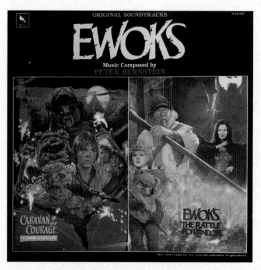

The *Ewoks – Original Soundtrack*
realizes $25 to $55.

The double vinyl reissue for *The Phantom Menace*
goes for $17 to $40.

music is a traditional mix of familiar cues and new themes, they are each a departure in that they were performed by freelance orchestras, instead of the previously used London Symphony Orchestra. Both soundtracks charted on the Billboard Top 20, with *The Force Awakens* debuting in the No. 5 spot.

Much like the film itself, the soundtrack to *Rogue One: A Star Wars Story* is a more radical departure in that it was composed not by Williams, but by Michael Giacchino, though Giacchino did incorporate several of Williams' classic themes from the series. Composed in a mere four and a half weeks, the film's score is filled with the drama, emotion, and excitement we've come to expect in a *Star Wars* film.

The *Rebels* soundtrack averages $10 to $20.

Released only digitally and on compact disc on May 25, 2018, the score from *Solo: A Star Wars Story* features John Powell (*How to Train Your Dragon*, *Ferdinand*) as the film's main composer, with Williams guesting on the soundtrack. Not only were previous Williams themes and motifs used throughout, the beloved composer wrote and conducted "The Adventures of Han" theme. Both composers' styles blend quite well, resulting in an effort that's as exciting as it is nostalgic.

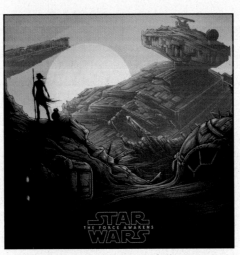

The 2017 "Rey" edition of *The Force Awakens* goes for up to $150.

There are many ways to collect the soundtracks to these beloved movies, from digital files for those only concerned with the music, to physical media – vinyl records, cassette tapes, and CDs. For those of us who are truly collection-oriented, only physical media will do. Compact discs and cassettes may hit the spot for those looking to recapture a prize from their youth, but vinyl records are where it's at as far as most value and rarity is concerned. As with most collectibles, condition greatly affects the value of each piece, so those looking to build a collection with the most value should steer clear of copies with tattered covers, heavy ring-wear, label wear, and deep scratches to the vinyl. Original pressings often carry the greatest value, but high-end reissues – especially picture discs – can fetch very good sums as well.

All soundtrack prices are for original vinyl pressings unless otherwise noted.

Star Wars
1977; 20th Century Records
Composed by John Williams; performed by the London Symphony Orchestra
$10 to $45

Star Wars: Episode IV – A New Hope
2016; Sony Classical, 20th Century Records
Double Picture Disc Reissue
Composed by John Williams; performed by the London Symphony Orchestra
$27 to $90

The Story of Star Wars
1977; Buena Vista Records
$10 to $35

*Star Wars: Episode V – The Empire
Strikes Back*
1980; RSO
Composed by John Williams; performed by
the London Symphony Orchestra
$15 to $50

*Star Wars: Episode V – The Empire
Strikes Back*
2016; RSO, Sony Classical
Double Picture Disc Reissue
Composed by John Williams; performed by
the London Symphony Orchestra
$29 to $62

*Star Wars: Episode VI – Return of
the Jedi*
1983; RSO
Composed by John Williams; performed by
the London Symphony Orchestra
$10 to $100

*Star Wars: Episode VI – Return of
the Jedi*
1997; RCA Victor
2-CD Remastered Box Set
Composed by John Williams; performed by
the London Symphony Orchestra
$12 to $40

*Star Wars: Episode VI – Return of
the Jedi*
2016; RSO, Sony Classical
Barnes & Noble Exclusive Release on
Gold Vinyl
Composed by John Williams; performed by
the London Symphony Orchestra
$27 to $50

*Star Wars: Episode I – The Phantom
Menace*
2015; I Am Shark
Double Vinyl Reissue/Black with White Splatter
Composed by John Williams; performed by
the London Symphony Orchestra
$17 to $40

Ewoks – Original Soundtracks
1986; Varèse Sarabande
Composed by Peter Bernstein
$25 to $55

*Star Wars: The Clone Wars –
Seasons One Through Six*
2014; Walt Disney Records
LP Vinyl Edition
Composed by Kevin Kiner
$10 to $20

Star Wars: Rebels
2015; Walt Disney Records
7" Vinyl Picture Disc
Composed by Kevin Kiner
$10 to $20

Star Wars: The Force Awakens
2016; Walt Disney Records, Lucasfilm Ltd.
Double LP Vinyl Edition
Composed by John Williams
$25 to $45

Star Wars: The Force Awakens
2017; I Am Shark
Double LP "Rey" Edition on Yellow/
Orange/Brown Marbled Vinyl
Composed by John Williams
$68 to $150

Rogue One: A Star Wars Story
2017; Walt Disney Records
Double LP Vinyl Edition
Composed by Michael Giacchino
$15 to $45

Star Wars: The Last Jedi
2018; Walt Disney Records
Double LP Vinyl Edition
Composed by John Williams
$20 to $30

Solo: A Star Wars Story
2018; Walt Disney Records
Compact Disc/Digital
Composed by John Powell and
John Williams
$10 to $20

The Story Of... Records

One interesting group of collectibles related to the *Star Wars* film soundtracks are the "Story of..." LPs released by Buena Vista Records in conjunction with the release of each movie. Unlike the full score soundtracks, these records consist of movie dialog, narration, pieces of music and sound effects from each movie to present an abbreviated version of the film. In a time before home video, or before the medium was affordable to nearly everyone, these albums were the only way most devoted fans could own their favorite *Star Wars* movies.

The first, released in 1977, is *The Story of Star Wars*. Produced by George Lucas and Alan Livingston and narrated by Roscoe Lee Brown (Emmy Award-winning stage and screen actor of *Barney Miller, The Cosby Show*, and *Two Trains Running* fame), the original pressing included a 16-page full-color booklet filled with stills from *A New Hope*. Fans scooped them up from stores in droves, propelling the album onto the charts, where it went gold. *The Story of Star Wars* was released in several other formats, including 8-track tape, 4-track reel-to-reel, and cassette tape.

The Story of The Empire Strikes Back and *The Story of Return of the Jedi* followed in 1980 and 1983, respectively. *Empire* was narrated by Malachi Throne (*Star Trek, Lost in Space*), while Chuck Riley (noted movie trailer voiceover artist) voiced *Return*. Each of these also originally included 16-page souvenir booklets, making them quite an immersive media experience for the time. Not incredibly rare while still highly sought, these can be found at relatively affordable prices. That said, international versions – from Canada, Australia, France, etc. – tend to command slightly higher prices. If you happen upon any of them in good condition – especially with the original souvenir booklets – don't pass them up!

The Story of Star Wars record averages $35.

FROM THE ORIGINAL SOUNDTRACK

THE STORY OF STAR WARS™

John Williams:

The Man Behind the Music

By Jon Steffens

Born in Floral Park, New York on February 8, 1932, John Williams is an American film composer whose name is synonymous with the work of Steven Spielberg. Aside from the scores of every single *Star Wars* film excluding *Rogue One*, Williams' music can be heard in *Jaws, Close Encounters of the Third Kind, Raiders of the Lost Ark, E.T. the Extra-Terrestrial, Indiana Jones and the Temple of Doom, Jurassic Park, Schindler's List*, and other generation-defining Spielberg blockbusters.

Music has always been in Williams' life. His father was a musician and Williams started taking piano lessons when he was a kid. After the family moved to Los Angeles in 1948, he studied at the University of California at Los Angles for a brief period then was drafted into the U.S. Air Force in 1951. Following three years in the military, Williams moved back to New York City where he attended Juilliard School. It was at the prestigious school when he was inspired to become a composer.

He returned to Los Angeles and worked as a movie studio musician, including in films like *Some Like It Hot* and *To Kill a Mockingbird*. He also played piano for a few TV programs and began composing music for shows like *Gilligan's Island* and *Lost in Space*.

Along with his popular work in *Star Wars* and Spielberg films, the prolific composer's scores can also be heard in three *Harry Potter* films, the first two *Home Alone* movies, Richard Donner's *Superman, Catch Me If You Can*, Oliver Stone's conspiracy drama *JFK*, and multitudes of other huge films.

With a neoromantic style influenced by Richard Wagner and Pyotr Tchaikovsky, his scores utilize large-scale orchestration to evoke a wide range of emotion from the drama and action unfolding onscreen, and by extension, the audience. His work has been nominated for more than 50 Academy Awards, with the scores from *Jaws, Star Wars: Episode IV, E.T., Schindler's List*, and a 1971 production of *Fiddler on the Roof* taking home the Oscar.

With over 100 film scores – and countless other recordings – to his name, John Williams is set to retire from composing *Star Wars* movies after scoring the J.J. Abrams-helmed *Star Wars: Episode IX*, set for release on December 20, 2019. Needless to say, a long time ago, in a galaxy far, far away would surely sound – and feel – much different without his masterful touch.

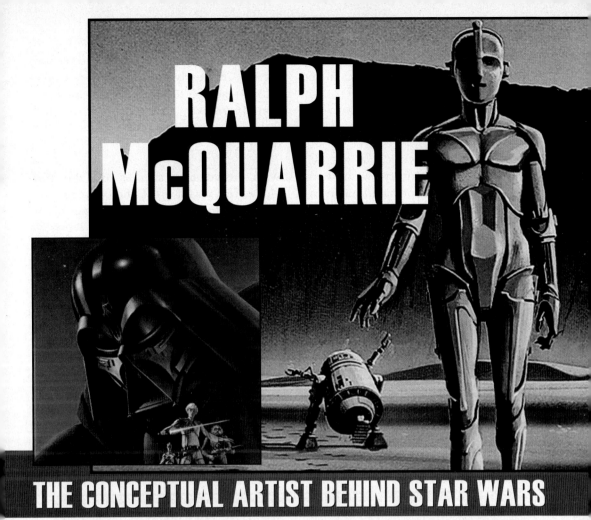

RALPH McQUARRIE

THE CONCEPTUAL ARTIST BEHIND STAR WARS

The filmmaking process is a complicated endeavor that involves hundreds of people performing myriad tasks. While the director and writer may have a vision for the project, it takes talented designers, artists, prop masters, set builders, and costumers to realize those images. When it comes to *Star Wars*, one of the most pivotal members of that creative team was Ralph McQuarrie.

As a conceptual designer and illustrator, McQuarrie has worked on *Battlestar Galactica*, *E.T. the Extra-Terrestrial*, and *Cocoon*, but he is lauded most for *Star Wars*. He created the series' "used futuristic" look. Prior to *Star Wars*, science fiction relied on a sterile, clean look for futuristic and otherworldly creatures, props, and designs. McQuarrie made futuristic technology and vehicles look used, even dirty and in need of repair, which gave a realistic appearance to the advanced galaxy.

McQuarrie was born on June 13, 1929 in Gary, Indiana, then grew up on a farm near Billings, Montana. After serving in the army during the Korean War he moved to California to study at the Art Center School in Los Angeles. His early artist jobs involved drawing teeth and equipment for a dentistry firm, then he drew diagrams of jets as an artist and preliminary design illustrator for Boeing Company. Next, he designed film posters and animation for CBS News' coverage of the Apollo space program. His next job defined the trajectory of his career.

Hal Barwood and Matthew Robbins hired McQuarrie to create some illustrations for a science fiction film they were working on. Though that project was not made, George Lucas saw the designs and was impressed with McQuarrie's work. The pair met to discuss the idea for *Star Wars*, and in 1975, Lucas commissioned

McQuarrie to illustrate scenes for the film. McQuarrie ended up designing some of the most notable characters, including Darth Vader, C-3PO, R2-D2, and Chewbacca, as well as drawing many concepts for the sets.

McQuarrie's concept work was a crucial part of getting 20th Century Fox on board for the film. His concept paintings included scenes on Tatooine, inside the Mos Eisley cantina, inside the Death Star, and the moon of Yavin. Lucas made sure that scenes in the movie matched McQuarrie's paintings.

When it came to the film's main villain, Lucas wanted his costume to resemble the look of samurai armor. Since Darth Vader needed to travel between ships, McQuarrie was the first to suggest that Darth Vader should have a breathing device and be in a space suit. Lucas agreed with the suggestion, so McQuarrie blended the two concepts, giving him a breathing mask with a samurai helmet.

His painting of R2-D2 and C-3PO in the desert of Tatooine was the first to be completed. That early interpretation of C-3PO, which resembled the robot in Fritz Lang's film *Metropolis*, inspired actor Anthony Daniels to take the part of the protocol droid.

With his design success on the film, McQuarrie was a great choice to produce cover art for the *Star Wars* novelization. The first edition, *Star Wars: From the Adventures of Luke Skywalker*, was published in 1976 depicting his version of Darth Vader's helmet on the cover. He was commissioned to create art for nearly two dozen titles for Del Rey Books (a branch of Ballantine books) over the next decade.

Once Lucas started working on *The Empire Strikes Back*, McQuarrie was hired for conceptual artwork. His art established the iconic looks of Yoda and the AT-AT Walkers, and his design for the Cloud City was adapted from one of his early

The cover of *The Star Wars Portfolio* by Ralph McQuarrie features his Darth Vader design that combines a samurai with a space suit.

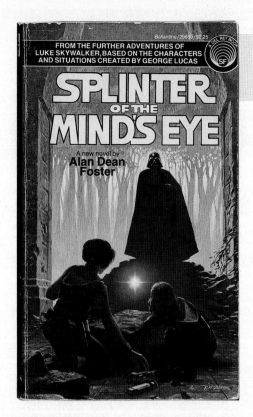

sketches of Alderaan made in 1975 for an early draft of *Star Wars*.

He added actor to his résumé in *ESB* with an uncredited cameo during the opening sequence, appearing on the Rebel base as a character named General Pharl McQuarrie. He was added to the action figure line as General McQuarrie in 2007 for the 30th anniversary. Other figures were made based on his conceptual versions of Vader, Han Solo, Chewbacca, Artoo, Threepio, Boba Fett, Yoda, Obi-Wan Kenobi, and the Imperial Stormtrooper.

By the time of *Return of the Jedi*, he was dealing with some creativity challenges since he felt that his best designs were already in the series. Consequently, fewer of his design ideas were used in the final version of *ROTJ*.

He was offered the position of designer for the prequel trilogy but turned it down. Though he was retired from creating new work for the series, McQuarrie's concept paintings were displayed in art exhibitions and books on the series.

McQuarrie died on March 3, 2012 when he was 82 years old. He was survived by his wife Joan, who he married in '83.

The current films and related media are still utilizing McQuarrie's concepts from 40 years ago. Some of his unused designs made it into the animated series, *Star Wars: The Clone Wars* and *Star Wars Rebels*. The planet Orto Plutonia was based on his original design of Hoth, Zeb Orrelios was based on Chewbacca, and Chopper was based on R2-D2.

McQuarrie's realization of Lucas' visions established the look of the *Star Wars* universe. His contributions brought imagination to life with creativity, functionality, fanciful realism, and even some dirt.

His cameo from *The Empire Strikes Back* was turned into a General McQuarrie action figure in 2007.

STAR WARS TRADING CARDS

THE POCKET-SIZED COLLECTIBLES

An unopened box of *Star Wars* Series 1 cards can reach $750 or more in auctions.

Over the past century, trading cards have been easily accessible, steadily popular collectibles. Depicting athletes, cowboys, teen heartthrobs, and game characters, they can appeal to any kid and are often the first steps in budding collections. For *Star Wars* fans, the collecting opportunities number into the thousands in (mostly) affordable ranges.

Trading cards, also called non-sport cards, are themed around a series or title. Typically produced to promote the movies, they depict still images from the films as well as original art. Most new cards that are issued are available through major retailers, but some specialty cards are issued exclusively through specific sources.

In 1977, The Topps Company became the first to produce and release *Star Wars* trading cards to coincide with the first film. Since then, they have remained the official producer in the U.S., though cards are manufactured by various other companies domestically and around the world.

Topps has utilized many different design styles and configurations for the cards, which are released in contained series. In addition to the regular cards, they can also include stickers, autograph cards, costume cards, specialty promos, and mail-away cards. As new sets are released, they feature new characters and scenes while also offering the potential for cards connected to older films.

Star Wars Series 1-5 and the Wonder Bread set were released in 1977, and the Topps Sugar Free Gum Wrappers were out in '77-'78. Each of Series 1-5 includes 66 cards and 11 stickers, which are sequentially numbered to follow the previous set. Series

1 comprises cards 1-66 (blue border) and stickers 1-11, Series 2 adds cards 67-132 (red border) and stickers 12-22, Series 3 includes cards 133-198 (yellow border) and stickers 23-33, Series 4 features cards 199-264 (green border) and stickers 34-44, and Series 5 adds cards 265-330 (orange border) and stickers 45-55. The Wonder Bread set contains 16 cards and the Topps Sugar Free Gum Wrappers have 56 wrappers.

In 1980 five series were added for *The Empire Strikes Back*. Series 1 has 132 cards (red border) and 33 stickers, Series 2 adds 132 cards (blue border) and 33 stickers, Series 3 has 88 cards (yellow border) and 22 stickers, The Giant Photo Cards contains 30 cards at 5" x 7" size, and the Star Wars Burger King set features 36 cards.

Return of the Jedi added Series 1 with 132 cards (red border) and 33 stickers and Series 2 added 88 cards (blue border) and 22 stickers – both in 1983.

From '93 to '99, several more sets were added before the prequel era. The first three new sets were titled *Star Wars* Galaxy, featuring another 365 base cards, plus silver stamped bases, and some with refractor foil, holographic, Lucas art, etched foil, and clear-zone cards. Five Widevision sets for the first three films were released with base cards and a variety of steel cards, chromium, and poster cards – totaling over 450. Other sets included the Topps *Star Wars* Caps, Master Visions, *Shadows of the Empire*, Vehicles, and Trilogy sets. Along with the base sets, specialty cards include slammer caps, galaxy cards, matrix, embossed, foil, motion, cut-away, 3D, laser, hologram, chrome, and clear cards. Most of these sets contained 60 to 90 each.

Luke Skywalker is depicted on the first card in *Star Wars* Series 1.

From '99 to 2005, new trading card sets were focused on the prequel trilogy era. *The Phantom Menace* had two Widevision Series, each with 80 base cards, plus expansion, chrome, foil, embossed, and stickers. There was also a 3D set with 46 base cards and a few multi-motion cards. *Attack of the Clones* had a regular set and Widevision set with over 200 cards in base sets, silver foil, panoramic, promos, and autograph cards. *Revenge of the Sith* also had a regular set and Widevision set containing etched foil, morphing, holograms, tattoo, embossed foil, stickers, chrome, autographs, and others. This period also saw release of a *Clone Wars* set that included battle motion and artist sketch cards.

A *Star Wars* Series 2 uncut card sheet like this can sell for up to $300.

A 30th anniversary set was released in 2007, featuring 120 base cards, triptych puzzle cards, autographs, sketch, foil stamped box loaders, animation cels, magnet cards, bonuses, and promos. From 2008 to 2010, *Clone Wars* received a regular set that came with animation cels, Trading Card Stickers Set that included die-cut pop ups and tattoos, Widevision Season 1, Rise of the Bounty Hunters Season 2, and Dog Tags Trading Cards with matching dog tags. During this period, a small *Star Wars Holiday Special* set was released, as were Galaxy Series 4-7, 3D Widevision sets for *ESB* and *ROTJ*, Dog Tag Trading Cards, Jedi Legacy, an Illustrated Set, and an Evolution set.

In 2015 *Rebels* received a 100-card set, plus stickers and tattoos. A set for *The Last Jedi* came out in 2017 with portrait cards, die-cut stickers, parallel cards, and autographs. Several sets came out in 2018 including Archive Signature Series, Galactic Files, *The Last Jedi* Series 2, *Solo: A Star Wars Story*, *Rebels* Series Finale, and *A New Hope* Black & White.

Outside of Topps, cards were included in packaging and in promos for various companies and restaurants, such as General Mills, Kellogg's, Parker Brothers, Kenner/Hasbro, Doritos, Pepsi, TV Guide, Safeway, and Random House, among others.

One of the most enjoyable aspects of *Star Wars* trading cards is the affordability. Going back to the original series, cards can be bought for a few dollars. But, that doesn't mean that there aren't very valuable examples. Autograph cards, rarities, graded and encapsulated cards and stickers from the first set, and unopened boxes from the early releases can fetch prices into the thousands.

Impressive autograph card sales include a 2012 Harrison Ford *Star Wars* Galactic Files autograph card that sold for $2,275, a 2018 Leaf Metal Pop Century *Star Wars* 1/1 Daisy Ridley, Adam Driver, and Laura Dern autograph card that reached $2,500, and a 2017 *Star Wars* Masterwork 1/1 Ian McDiarmid, Hayden Christensen, and Matthew Wood

The Empire Strikes Back Series 3 unopened box can realize $150.

autograph card that hit $7,500. Notable sales of high grade, encapsulated examples include a 1977 Topps *Star Wars* Sticker #1 Luke Skywalker PSA 10 GEM Mint for $6,150, a Sticker #2 Princess Leia PSA 10 GEM Mint for $3,050, and Sticker #3 Han Solo PSA 10 GEM Mint for $3,560. Sketch cards like the 1/1 versions, and error cards like the infamous C-3PO card #207 are also valuable on the secondary market, reaching prices into the hundreds.

Whether they are swapped on the bus to school or bought through competitive auctions, *Star Wars* trading cards are part of a vivacious collecting community. There are thousands of cards, stickers, and related

Many cards, even from early sets like this *Return of the Jedi* Princess Leia card, can be bought for a few dollars.

items that represent over 40 years of franchise history. For a few bucks or a few thousand, collectors can tuck a piece of *Star Wars* into their pocket or admire it on a display shelf for years to come.

PRICING STAR WARS TRADING CARDS

Star Wars trading cards are sold on an individual basis up to unopened boxes. This list features value breakdowns for select trading card sets, focused on the ones based on each film release. The values include that of an unopened box, sales of multiple cards (10 or more) to full open sets, and single base cards.

Star Wars Series 1
1977
Unopened box: $750
Uncut card sheet: $400
Multiple cards to full set: $35 to $100
Single cards: $1 to $5
Stickers: $1 to $2

Star Wars Series 2
1977
Unopened box: $500
Uncut card sheet: $300
Multiple cards to full set: $30 to $75
Single cards: 50¢ to $3.50
Stickers: $1 to $2

Star Wars Series 3
1977
Unopened box: $300
Multiple cards to full set: $30 to $70
Single cards: 50¢ to $4
Stickers: $1 to $2

Like many sets, this "Senator Amidala Lives" card includes plot details or background information.

This "Chewbacca in Disguise" card is part of the *Shadows of the Empire* multimedia project.

Star Wars Series 4
1977
Unopened box: $300
Multiple cards to full set: $35 to $60
Single cards: 50¢ to $3
Stickers: $1 to $2

Star Wars Series 5
1977
Unopened box: $250
Multiple cards to full set: $25 to $60
Single cards: 50¢ to $2
Stickers: $1

The Empire Strikes Back Series 1
1980
Unopened box: $175
Multiple cards to full set: $20 to $70
Single cards: 50¢ to $2
Stickers: $1

The Empire Strikes Back Series 2
1980
Unopened box: $150
Multiple cards to full set: $20 to $70
Single cards: 25¢ to $2
Stickers: $1

The Empire Strikes Back Series 3
1980
Unopened box: $150
Multiple cards to full set: $25 to $50

Single cards: 25¢ to $2
Stickers: $1

Return of the Jedi Series 1
1983
Unopened box: $150
Multiple cards to full set: $20 to $50
Single cards: 25¢ to $1.50
Stickers: 50¢ to $1

Return of the Jedi Series 2
1983
Unopened box: $100
Multiple cards to full set: $15 to $30
Single cards: 25¢ to $1.50
Stickers: 50¢ to $1

Star Wars Widevision
1995
Unopened box: $60
Multiple cards to full set: $30 to $40
Single cards: 25¢ to $1

The Empire Strikes Back Widevision
1995
Unopened box: $50
Multiple cards to full set: $15 to $30
Single cards: 25¢ to $1

Return of the Jedi Widevision
1996
Unopened box: $50
Multiple cards to full set: $10 to $30
Single cards: 25¢ to $1

Shadows of the Empire
1996
Unopened box: $60
Multiple cards to full set: $10 to $25
Single cards: 25¢ to $1

The Phantom Menace Widevision Series 1-2
1999
Unopened box: $40
Multiple cards to full set: $10
Single cards: 10¢ to $1

Attack of the Clones and Widevision
2002
Unopened box: $75
Multiple cards to full set: $10 to $25
Single cards: 10¢ to $1
Clone Wars

2004
Unopened box: $60
Multiple cards to full set: $10 to $35
Single cards: 10¢ to $1

Revenge of the Sith and Widevision
2005
Unopened box: $45 to $55
Multiple cards to full set: $5 to $25
Single cards: 10¢ to $1

The Clone Wars and Widevision
2008-2009
Unopened box: $50
Multiple cards to full set: $5 to $20
Single cards: 10¢ to $1

Rebels
2015
Unopened box: $40
Multiple cards to full set: $5 to $25
Single cards: 10¢ to $1

The Last Jedi Series 1-2
2017-2018
Unopened box: $60
Multiple cards to full set: $10 to $20
Single cards: 10¢ to $1

In addition to artistic box design, most cards are sold in packs depicting creative artwork.

FROM CELLULOID TO SPINNER RACKS:
STAR WARS IN COMICS

Comic books have always been a land of enhanced imagination, housing stories of fantastical beings unconstrained by plausibility, yet made tangible through good storytelling. They provide reprieves from daily life into worlds of heroes and villains, where literally anything is possible. It's no wonder that *Star Wars* found a successful second home in comic books.

Since the first issue appeared on store shelves in 1977, *Star Wars* comics have been published by a few different companies, though predominately by Marvel Comics and Dark Horse Comics. From 1977 to 1986, Marvel published the first run of comics, which contained 107 issues and 3 annuals of film adaptations and original stories.

In 1975, the film's advertising publicity supervisor, Charles Lippincott, approached Marvel Comics' publisher, Stan Lee. Lippincott's goal was to get comics in the hands of potential viewers before the movie was in theaters as a way to promote the upcoming release. Initially, Lee did not accept the proposal, but he did agree after Roy Thomas, who wanted to work on the comics, arranged another meeting. Since movie tie-ins hadn't been successful in the past, Lee secured a deal that Lucasfilm wouldn't get royalties until sales were above 100,000.

The first installment of the six-issue movie adaptation went on

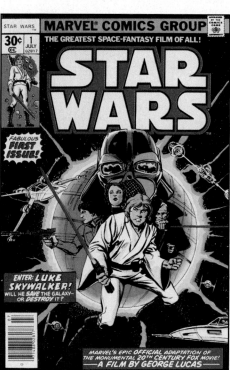

Star Wars #1 (1977) was the first installment in the six-issue movie adaptation.

sale April 12, 1977, a little over a month before *Star Wars* saw theatrical release. It became a high seller, leading to renegotiations on the royalties for Lucasfilm. The initial adaptation, written by Thomas with art by Howard Chaykin, concluded with *Star Wars* #6, the December '77 cover-dated issue. The adaptation was also collected in three oversized Marvel Treasury Edition publications. The first two reprinted three issues a piece, while the third reprinted the whole adaptation.

Before the next chapter in the movie trilogy was even a sure thing, Marvel began running original material, consisting of one-off stories and short arcs. The first original adventure, a Han Solo-Chewbacca story that introduced Jaxxon, the rabbit-like smuggler and pilot, arrived in #7 (January 1978).

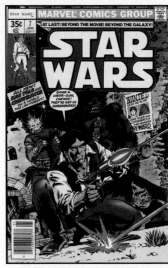
Original comic stories began in #7, with a Han Solo-Chewbacca story.

Writer Archie Goodwin and artist Carmine Infantino took over the series at #11 in May 1978. They introduced the House of Tagge, a new antagonist for the series in the guise of a scheming noble family. They own the powerful megacorporation Tagge Company, employ a private military, and support the Galactic Republic. Desiring power, family head Baron Orman Tagge even tried to usurp Vader's position at Emperor Palpatine's side.

Goodwin and Infantino also introduced the Wheel space station, a casino-filled Vegas style setting. One of Goodwin's last stories featured the Crimson Forever, a killer virus caused by gemstones.

A six-issue adaptation of *The Empire Strikes Back* by Goodwin, with art by Al Williamson and Carlos Garzon, appeared in #39-44 from September 1980 to February 1981.

Star Wars #39 began *The Empire Strikes Back* adaptation.

At #51 (September 1981), writer David Michelinie and artist Walt Simonson became the lead creative team. During this period, Lando serves as Millennium Falcon copilot, the Rebel Alliance moves to the forest planet Arbra (where Hoojibs, a race of telepathic rodent-like creatures, become spies in their employ), and Luke has a story with Shira Brie, a Force-sensitive pilot and Imperial spy.

Return of the Jedi was adapted from October 1983 to January 1984 in a separate four-issue series, handled by the team of Goodwin, Williamson, and Garzon. After the film, comics became the primary entertainment medium for continued *Star Wars* content.

Return of the Jedi was adapted in comics beginning in October 1983.

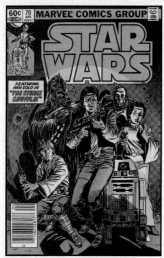

In #70, characters Rik Duel, Chihdo, and Zeltron were introduced.

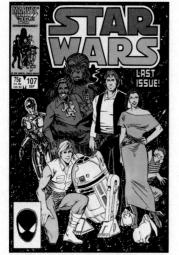

Marvel's inaugural run of *Star Wars* comics ended with #107.

Marvel U.K. began reprinting the U.S. comics in February 1978.

Mary Jo Duffy took the position of main writer at #70 and helmed the series until its conclusion. She built on the established stories, adding more depth to the characters, including features on Princess Leia. In her debut on the title, Duffy introduced Corellian smuggler Rik Duel, Greedo's cousin Chihdo, and Zeltron adventurer-thief Dani. She also reintroduced Shira Brie, who had been seemingly killed by Luke, but came back as the cyborg ninja Lumiya. Cynthia Martin became the primary artist at #93 and remained until the series ended. Together they introduced the Nagai, a species from outside the galaxy that wanted to exploit it for resources to liberate their home world from conquest.

The series came to an end with *Star Wars* #107.

From 1985 to 1987 there were also two short series based on the animated TV shows, *Star Wars: Droids* and *Star Wars: Ewoks*.

The U.S. comics were reprinted in the United Kingdom through a weekly black and white anthology by Marvel U.K. Those issues split the monthly stories from U.S. comics into smaller installments that would typically unfold over a few weeks. Along with the reprints, they also published original stories by British creators.

The series began with *Star Wars Weekly* #1, published in February 1978. The title became *The Empire Strikes Back Weekly* in May 1980 with #118 and ran that way until #139. Then it transitioned to a monthly comic with #140 in November 1980, before reverting to the original title with #159 in July 1982. As a monthly, it ran until #171 in July 1983.

Return of the Jedi Weekly, which began in June 1983 and consisted of 155 issues, became the first U.K. comic printed in color. Collectively, *Star Wars* comics at Marvel U.K. ran through 1986, featuring original content, annuals, and specials.

In more recent years, the original Marvel series was reprinted in three *Star Wars Omnibus* oversized hardcovers.

A small contingent of comics were also published outside of Marvel during the initial run. In 1978, Pendulum Press published a 31-page adaptation of *Star Wars* by Linda A. Cadrain and Charles Nicholas. It was produced with an audio tape and film strip, designed for use in classrooms, featuring vocabulary for kids. Blackthorne Publishing released a three-issue run of 3-D comics from December '87 to February '88. They were later reprinted in black and white, non-3-D by Dark Horse.

By any objective standard, Dark Horse Comics, which published *Star Wars* comics from 1991 until 2014, must be viewed as a successful steward of the franchise's comic book incarnations. With a wide variety of series and miniseries, adventures were played out across a vast tapestry of time, not just the immediate eras around the original three films. They also made the works readily available to fans with a thorough and easy-to-understand trade paperback program that kept the stories in print for many years.

It's possible that their tenure would be viewed in a different light without the surprise success of their first limited series, *Star Wars: Dark Empire*. Originally commissioned by editor Archie Goodwin when the license was still at Marvel, writer Tom Veitch and artist Cam Kennedy's follow-on was set six years after the Empire fell in *Return of the Jedi*. It depicted a galaxy still torn by fighting, and The Empire reborn with a seemingly new leader – Emperor Palpatine resurrected in cloned bodies – and a new powerful weapon.

Published from December 1991 to October 1992, it's difficult to overstate the impact its story had on *Star Wars* fandom. As difficult as that nadir might be for some to imagine, those who remember know that prior to the prequels things were getting fairly sparse. *Dark Empire* and Timothy Zahn's *Thrawn* trilogy of novels may well have reignited the spark and kept things going until the prequels were announced.

Dark Empire's story of Princess Leia and Han Solo trying to keep the New Republic together as Luke fought the pull of the Dark Side was followed by *Dark Empire II* and *Empire's End*.

Set thousands of years before the Battle of Yavin, *Star Wars: Tales of the Jedi* focused on the Great Sith War and Great Hyperspace War. The 35-issue series ran from October '93 to November '98, containing eight primary story arcs. Several people contributed to the series with Veitch and Kevin J. Anderson as the primary writers.

The *Star Wars: X-Wing Rogue Squadron* series by Michael A. Stackpole ran for 35 issues, from July 1995 to November 1998. The series featured missions of

Dark Horse Comics kicked off their *Star Wars* comics with *Star Wars: Dark Empire*.

Star Wars: Tales of the Jedi ran from October '93 to November '98.

Star Wars: X-Wing Rogue Squadron ran from July 1995 to November 1998.

the Rebel starfighters that was formed out of Red Squadron from the Battle of Yavin.

Star Wars, which began in December '98, was the first comic since the '80s to bear the franchise name with no sub-title. It provided stories from before *The Phantom Menace* until after *Revenge of the Sith*. Anakin and Obi-Wan were featured in some arcs, and the series introduced Twi'lek Jedi Aayla Secura, who would appear in the prequel trilogy films. The series was renamed *Star Wars: Republic* at #46, then became the main comic for *Clone Wars* stories. The final issue launched the title *Dark Times*, set in the early days of the Galactic Empire, it ran for 17 issues plus miniseries. Collectively, *Star Wars/Star Wars: Republic* comprised 83 issues through February 2006.

Star Wars Tales was a 24-issue series that ran from September 1999 to June 2005. An unrestricted title, it contained stories that were unrelated and from various eras, which typically ran for about 10 to 12 pages with 6 stories in each issue. There was a

16-page Free Comic Book Day issue in 2002 and six trade paperbacks.

Set around the time of the first movie, *Star Wars: Empire* featured stories about the period when the Empire was the dominate force in the galaxy. It ran for 40 issues from September 2002 to February 2006 and was continued in *Star Wars: Rebellion*.

John Jackson Miller penned *Star Wars: Knights of the Old Republic*, which was set during the same timeline as the video game. Taking place nearly 4,000 years before the films, a young Padawan who is framed for killing other Padawans goes on the run and tries to clear his name. It totaled 50 issues from January '06 to February '10.

Star Wars: Legacy, written by John Ostrander, was set over 100 years after the empire fell. The series tells stories of Cade Skywalker, one of Luke's descendants, who tries to defeat Darth Krayt to prevent the return of the Sith. It was revived for an 18-issue run about Han and Leia's descen-

Dark Horse began their *Star Wars* franchise title in December 1998.

The *Star Wars: Knights of the Old Republic* comic was set during the same time as the video game.

dant, Ania Solo. The series comprised 50 issues, running from June '06 to August '10.

Dark Horse published adaptations of the prequel trilogy, *The Thrawn Trilogy* book series, and *Splinter of the Mind's Eye* book; as well as manga adaptations of the original trilogy and *The Phantom Menace*. One of the notable miniseries was *Shadows of the Empire*, a six-issue story that was part of a multimedia project that also included a video game and novel.

Other miniseries included *Star Wars: Darth Vader* (centered around the Sith Lord), *Star Wars: Dawn of the Jedi* (featuring the origins of the Jedi and Sith), *Star Wars: Invasion* (during the early days of the Yuuzhan Vong War), *Star Wars: Jedi* (following Qui-Gon Jinn years before *The Phantom Menace*), *Star Wars: Knight Errant* (set 1,000 years before *Phantom* with a lone Jedi fighting the Sith), *Star Wars: The Old Republic* (set before the game of the same title), and *The Star Wars* (about George Lucas' original draft of the first film).

While Dark Horse had the license, the company published hundreds of *Star Wars* comics, covering thousands of years.

The Walt Disney Company acquired Marvel in 2009 and Lucasfilm in 2012, moving *Star Wars* comics back to Marvel. In 2014 it was announced that the Star Wars Expanded Universe was being rebranded as Legends, which put all of the comics published before '14 into the relabeled category. Comics that have been published since then at Marvel are considered canonical and connected to the film series. This has included prequels and further exposition on different characters.

Marvel's new wave began with three titles – *Star Wars*, *Darth Vader*, and the limited series *Princess Leia*. *Star Wars* began in March 2015 and *Darth Vader* followed a month later, both of which are currently still in production. *Star Wars* is set after the Battle of Yavin, chronicling more missions and adventures as Leia, Han, Luke, and the Rebels continue trying to thwart

Marvel's second run of *Star Wars* comics began in March 2015.

The ongoing *Darth Vader* series started in April 2015.

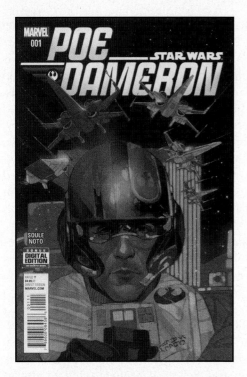

Poe Dameron and Doctor Aphra were added to Marvel's slate of ongoing series in January 2016 and June 2017, respectively.

Palpatine, Vader, and the Empire. It sticks to a mostly linear storyline, though when Luke finds Obi-Wan's journal an arc travels back to a Yoda adventure. Darth Vader's title sees the Sith Lord on his own missions for the Emperor, still hunting the remaining Jedi, and often combatting others in the Empire who seek to elevate their positions.

In addition to *Princess Leia*, there have been several limited series focused on specific characters, such as *Darth Maul*, *Mace Windu*, *Kanan*, *Lando*, *Chewbacca*, *Obi-Wan & Anakin*, *Han Solo*, and *Captain Phasma*. Other miniseries have included *Screaming Citadel*, *Shattered Empire*, a *Thrawn* book adaptation, plus the one-shots *Vader Down* and *C-3PO*.

The ongoing series *Poe Dameron*, about the X-wing pilot introduced in *The Force Awakens*, was added in January 2016; and the ongoing series *Doctor Aphra*, about the archeologist who was introduced in the *Darth Vader* comic when he recruited her, was added in June 2017.

Marvel has also published film adaptions for *The Force Awakens*, *Rogue One*, *The Last Jedi*, and *Solo*.

IDW Publishing began the *Star Wars Adventures* all-ages anthology in 2017. Unrestricted by era, the title features stories about characters from across the vast series from Rey to Mace Windu, Han to Anakin and Padmé. IDW has also released the miniseries *Forces of Destiny*, with stories about female characters in the series, and more are scheduled for the future.

Comic books have been popular storytellers for the fertile ground of *Star Wars*. Newcomers to celebrated comic industry professionals have created new worlds and characters on grand and intimate scales, much like the original material. With limitless potential for expanded content and original ideas, *Star Wars* comics could go on for a long time, much to the delight of series fans who enjoy the medium.

STAR WARS COMICS

Star Wars comics began a month before the first film premiered in theaters. Since then there have been dozens of series, miniseries, annuals, and one-shots. They include adaptations of the films and popular books, along with many original stories. Some are considered canonical while the bulk are under the Legends banner. Prices shown are from *The Overstreet Comic Book Price Guide* 48th edition (2018-2019).

Single prices listed are for Near Mint- (9.2) condition.
Three prices listed are based on conditions of Good (2.0), Fine (6.0), and Near Mint – (9.2).

MARVEL COMICS WAS THE FIRST TO PUBLISH *STAR WARS* COMICS. THE SERIES RAN FOR 107 ISSUES AND 3 ANNUALS FROM JULY 1977 TO SEPTEMBER 1986.

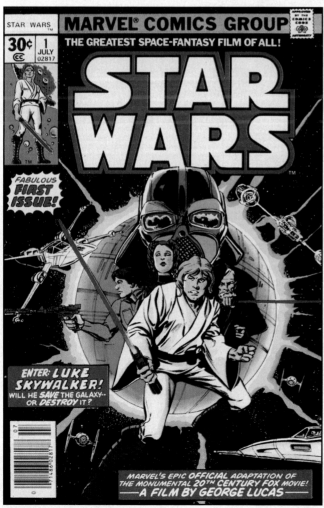

#1 35¢ COVER   JULY 1977
HOWARD CHAYKIN COVER
$367 $1101 $11,000

#1 30¢ COVER   JULY 1977
HOWARD CHAYKIN COVER
$10 $30 $215

#1 REPRINT   JULY 1977
HOWARD CHAYKIN COVER
$5 $15 $70

#2 - #9 REPRINTS
EACH **$1** **$4** **$10**

#2 35¢ COVER AUGUST 1977
RICK HOBERG COVER
$57 **$171** **$1600**

#2 30¢ COVER AUGUST 1977
RICK HOBERG COVER
$5 **$15** **$70**

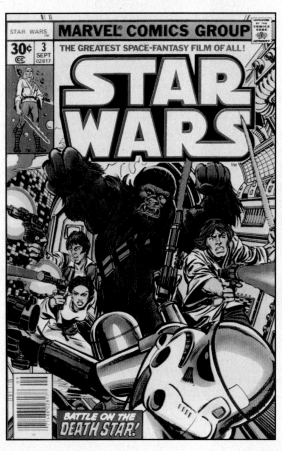

#3 35¢ COVER SEPTEMBER 19
GIL KANE COV
$57 **$171** **$16**

#3 30¢ COVER SEPTEMBER 1977
GIL KANE COVER
$5 **$15** **$70**

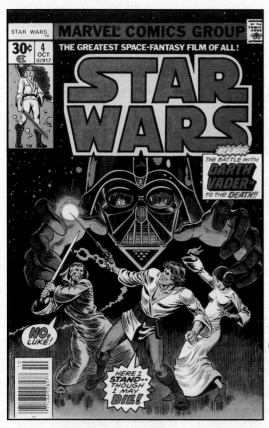

#4 35¢ COVER OCTOBER 1977
RICK HOBERG COVER
$57 $171 $1600

#4 30¢ COVER OCTOBER 1977
RICK HOBERG COVER
$5 $15 $70

#5 NOVEMBER 1977
RICK HOBERG COVER
$3 $9 $45

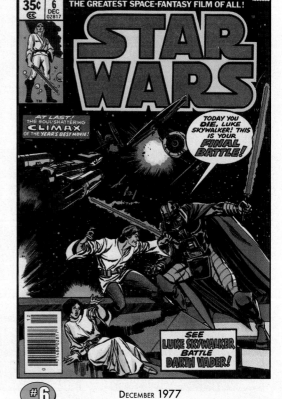

#6 DECEMBER 1977
RICK HOBERG COVER
$3 $9 $45

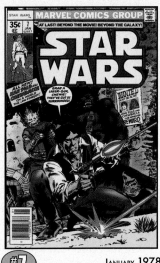

#7   JANUARY 1978
GIL KANE COVER
$2 $6 $20

#8   FEBRUARY 1978
GIL KANE COVER
$2 $6 $20

#9   MARCH 1978
GIL KANE COVER
$2 $6 $20

#10   APRIL 1978
RICK HOBERG COVER
$2 $6 $20

#11   MAY 1978
GIL KANE COVER
$2 $6 $20

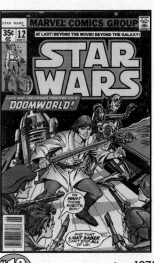

#12   JUNE 1978
CARMINE INFANTINO COVER
$2 $6 $20

#13   JULY 1978
JOHN BYRNE COVER
$2 $6 $20

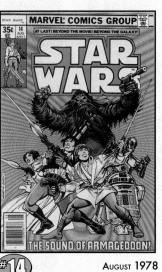

#14   AUGUST 1978
CARMINE INFANTINO COVER
$2 $6 $20

#15   SEPTEMBER 1978
CARMINE INFANTINO COVER
$2 $6 $20

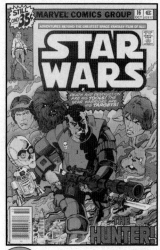

#16 OCTOBER 1978
WALT SIMONSON COVER
$2 $6 $20

#17 NOVEMBER 1978
DAVE COCKRUM COVER
$2 $6 $20

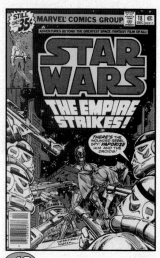

#18 DECEMBER 1978
CARMINE INFANTINO COVER
$2 $6 $20

#19 JANUARY 1979
CARMINE INFANTINO COVER
$2 $6 $20

#20 FEBRUARY 1979
CARMINE INFANTINO COVER
$2 $6 $20

#21 MARCH 1979
CARMINE INFANTINO COVER
$2 $6 $12

#22 APRIL 1979
CARMINE INFANTINO COVER
$2 $6 $12

#23 MAY 1979
CARMINE INFANTINO COVER
$2 $6 $12

#24 JUNE 1979
CARMINE INFANTINO COVER
$2 $6 $12

#25   July 1979
Carmine Infantino cover
$2 $6 $12

#26   August 1979
Carmine Infantino cover
$2 $6 $12

#27   September 1979
Carmine Infantino cover
$2 $6 $12

#28   October 1979
Carmine Infantino cover
$2 $6 $12

#29   November 1979
Carmine Infantino cover
$2 $6 $12

#30   December 1979
Carmine Infantino cover
$2 $6 $12

#31   January 1980
Carmine Infantino cover
$2 $6 $12

#32   February 1980
Carmine Infantino cover
$2 $6 $12

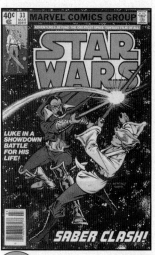

#33   March 1980
Carmine Infantino cover
$2 $6 $12

#34 APRIL 1980
CARMINE INFANTINO COVER
$2 $6 $12

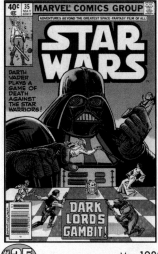

#35 MAY 1980
CARMINE INFANTINO COVER
$2 $6 $12

#36 JUNE 1980
CARMINE INFANTINO COVER
$2 $6 $12

#37 JULY 1980
CARMINE INFANTINO COVER
$2 $6 $12

#38 AUGUST 1980
MICHAEL GOLDEN COVER
$2 $6 $12

#39 SEPTEMBER 1980
AL WILLIAMSON COVER
$2 $6 $15

#40 OCTOBER 1980
AL WILLIAMSON COVER
$2 $6 $15

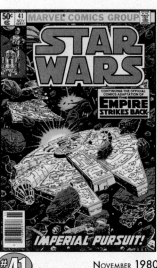

#41 NOVEMBER 1980
AL WILLIAMSON COVER
$2 $6 $15

#42 DECEMBER 1980
AL WILLIAMSON COVER
$6 $18 $110

#43   JANUARY 1981
AL WILLIAMSON COVER
$2 $6 $15

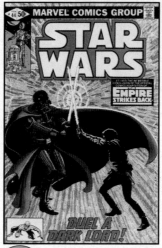

#44   FEBRUARY 1981
AL WILLIAMSON COVER
$2 $6 $15

#45   MARCH 1981
LARRY HAMA COVER
$2 $6 $12

#46   APRIL 1981
ED HANNIGAN COVER
$2 $6 $12

#47   MAY 1981
FRANK MILLER COVER
$2 $6 $12

#48   JUNE 1981
CARMINE INFANTINO COVER
$2 $6 $12

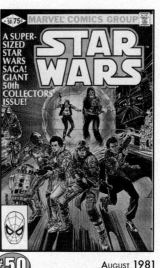

#49   JULY 1981
WALT SIMONSON COVER
$2 $6 $12

#50   AUGUST 1981
W. SIMONSON/TOM PALMER COVER
$2 $6 $12

#51   SEPTEMBER 1981
WALT SIMONSON COVER
$2 $6 $12

#52   OCTOBER 1981
WALT SIMONSON COVER
$2   **$6**   **$12**

#53   NOVEMBER 1981
WALT SIMONSON COVER
$2   **$6**   **$12**

#54   DECEMBER 1981
WALT SIMONSON COVER
$2   **$6**   **$12**

#55   JANUARY 1982
WALT SIMONSON COVER
$2   **$6**   **$12**

#56   FEBRUARY 1982
WALT SIMONSON COVER
$2   **$6**   **$12**

#57   MARCH 1982
WALT SIMONSON COVER
$2   **$6**   **$12**

#58   APRIL 1982
WALT SIMONSON COVER
$2   **$6**   **$12**

#59   MAY 1982
WALT SIMONSON COVER
$2   **$6**   **$12**

#60   JUNE 1982
WALT SIMONSON COVER
$2   **$6**   **$12**

#61   JULY 1982
WALT SIMONSON COVER
$2 $6 $12

#62   AUGUST 1982
WALT SIMONSON COVER
$2 $6 $12

#63   SEPTEMBER 1982
TOM PALMER COVER
$2 $6 $12

#64   OCTOBER 1982
JOE BROZOWSKI COVER
$2 $6 $12

#65   NOVEMBER 1982
TOM PALMER COVER
$2 $6 $12

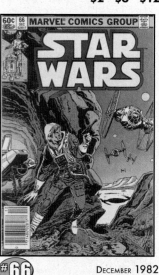

#66   DECEMBER 1982
TOM PALMER COVERR
$2 $6 $12

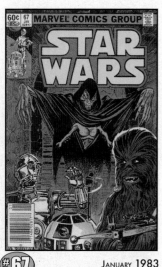

#67   JANUARY 1983
TOM PALMER COVER
$2 $6 $12

#68   FEBRUARY 1983
GENE DAY COVER
$5 $15 $70

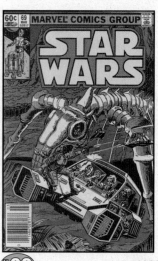

#69   MARCH 1983
TOM PALMER COVER
$2 $6 $12

#70   April 1983
Tom Palmer cover
$2 $6 $12

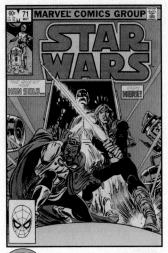

#71   May 1983
Tom Palmer cover
$2 $6 $14

#72   June 1983
Ron Frenz cover
$2 $6 $14

#73   July 1983
Ron Frenz cover
$2 $6 $14

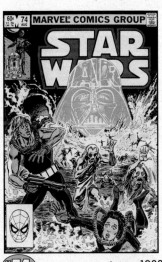

#74   August 1983
Tom Palmer cover
$2 $6 $14

#75   September 1983
Tom Palmer cover
$2 $6 $14

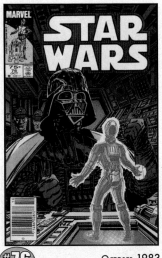

#76   October 1983
Tom Palmer cover
$2 $6 $14

#77   November 1983
Ron Frenz cover
$2 $6 $14

#78   December 1983
Bob Layton cover
$2 $6 $14

#79   JANUARY 1984
RON FRENZ COVER
$2 $6 $14

#80   FEBRUARY 1984
RON FRENZ COVER
$2 $6 $14

#81   MARCH 1984
TOM PALMER COVER
$4 $12 $50

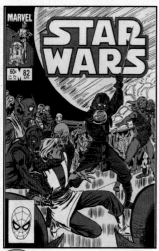

#82   APRIL 1984
RON FRENZ COVER
$2 $6 $16

#83   MAY 1984
BOB MCLEOD COVER
$2 $6 $16

#84   JUNE 1984
ROY RICHARDSON COVER
$2 $6 $16

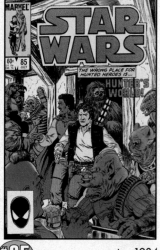

#85   JULY 1984
BOB MCLEOD COVER
$2 $6 $16

#86   AUGUST 1984
BOB MCLEOD COVER
$2 $6 $16

#87   SEPTEMBER 1984
TOM PALMER COVER
$2 $6 $16

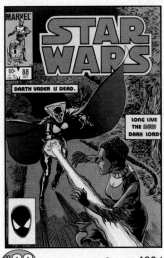

#88 OCTOBER 1984
BOB McLEOD COVER
$2 $6 $16

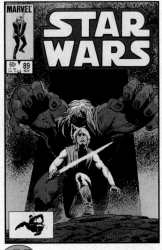

#89 NOVEMBER 1984
BRET BLEVINS COVER
$2 $6 $16

#90 DECEMBER 1984
BOB McLEOD COVER
$2 $6 $16

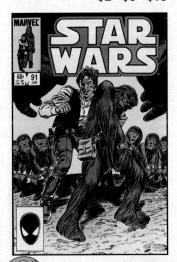

#91 JANUARY 1985
TONY SALMONS COVER
$2 $6 $20

#92 FEBRUARY 1985
CYNTHIA MARTIN COVER
$3 $9 $26

#93 MARCH 1985
CYNTHIA MARTIN COVER
$2 $6 $20

#94 APRIL 1985
CYNTHIA MARTIN COVER
$2 $6 $20

#95 MAY 1985
KENT WILLIAMS COVER
$2 $6 $20

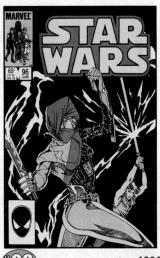

#96 JUNE 1985
CYNTHIA MARTIN COVER
$2 $6 $20

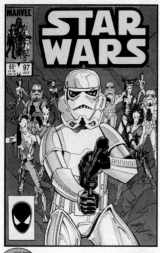

#97   July 1985
Cynthia Martin cover
$2 $6 $20

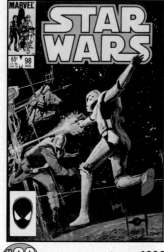

#98   August 1985
Bill Sienkiewicz cover
$2 $6 $20

#99   September 1985
Ron Frenz cover
$2 $6 $20

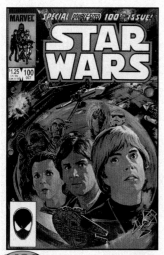

#100   October 1985
Tom Palmer cover
$3 $9 $26

#101   November 1985
Bill Sienkiewicz cover
$3 $9 $26

#102   December 1985
Kerry Gammill cover
$3 $9 $26

#103   January 1986
Cynthia Martin cover
$3 $9 $26

#104   March 1986
Cynthia Martin cover
$3 $9 $26

#105   May 1986
Cynthia Martin cover
$3 $9 $26

#106   July 1986
Cynthia Martin cover
$3 $9 $26

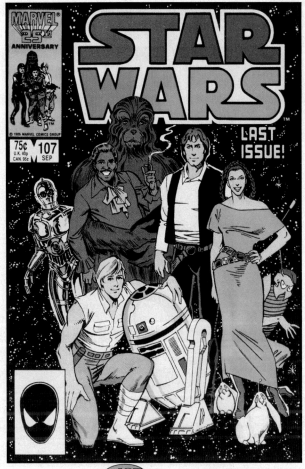

#107   September 1986
Cynthia Martin cover
$5 $15 $90

STAR WARS ANNUALS

#1   1979
Walt Simonson cover
$2 $6 $20

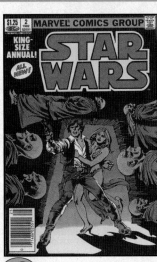

#2   1982
Carmine Infantino cover
$2 $6 $15

#3   1983
Klaus Janson cover
$2 $6 $15

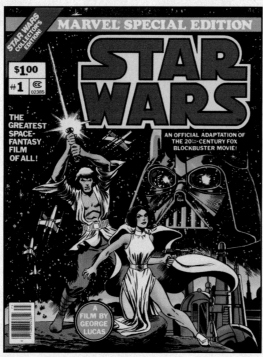

MARVEL REPRINTED THE ADAPTATION OF THE FIRST *STAR WARS* MOVIE IN THESE OVERSIZED 10" x 13" TREASURY EDITIONS

 #1

1977
RICK HOBERG COVER
$2 $6 $20
WHITMAN VARIANT $3 $9 $30

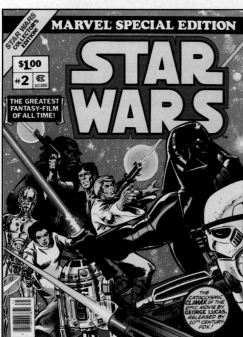

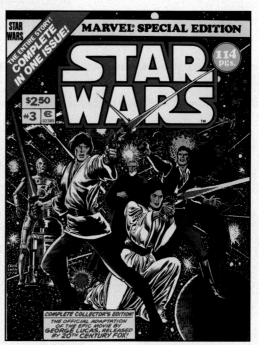

#2

1978
HOWARD CHAYKIN COVER
$2 $6 $20
WHITMAN VARIANT $3 $9 $30

#3

1978
ERNIE CHAN COVER
$3 $9 $26
WHITMAN VARIANT $3 $9 $26

MARVEL COMICS SUPER SPECIAL

MARVEL SUPER SPECIAL

#16

SPRING 1980

BOB LARKIN COVER

$4 $12 $55

#27

1983

BILL SIENKIEWICZ COVER

$2 $6 $18

MARVEL SPECIAL EDITION FEATURING ...

MARVEL ALSO REPRINTED
THE ADAPTATION OF
THE EMPIRE STRIKES BACK
IN THIS OVERSIZED
10" x 13" TREASURY EDITION
AT LATER AT COMIC-SIZE FOR
STAR WARS #39-44

VOLUME 2

SPRING 1980

BOB LARKIN COVER

$3 $9 $30

STAR WARS: RETURN OF THE JEDI

#1 OCTOBER 1983
BILL SIENKIEWICZ COVER
$2 $6 $20

#2 NOVEMBER 1983
BILL SIENKIEWICZ COVER
$2 $6 $15

#3 DECEMBER 1983
BILL SIENKIEWICZ COVER
$2 $6 $15

#4 JANUARY 1984
BILL SIENKIEWICZ COVER
$2 $6 $15

DARK HORSE COMICS

Dark Horse Comics published hundreds of issues across
dozens of series and miniseries from 1991 to 2014.

STAR WARS/STAR WARS: REPUBLIC
DARK HORSE'S FIRST STAR WARS TITLE RAN FOR 83 ISSUES FROM DECEMBER 1998 TO FEBRUARY 2006.

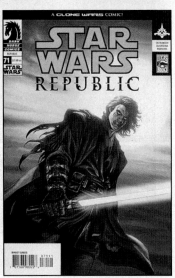

DARK HORSE'S SECOND RUN OF COMICS WITH THE FRANCHISE TITLE
RAN FROM JANUARY 2013 TO AUGUST 2014. THIS SERIES FEATURED STORIES
OF THE CLASSIC CHARACTERS AFTER THE EVENTS OF EPISODE IV.

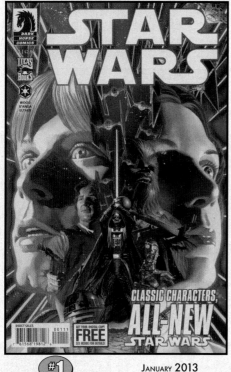

#1
JANUARY 2013
ALEX ROSS COVER
$8

#2
FEBRUARY 2013
ALEX ROSS COVER
$5

#3
MARCH 2013
ALEX ROSS COVER
$3

#4
APRIL 2013
ALEX ROSS COVER
$3

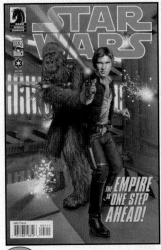

#5
MAY 2013
RODOLFO MIGLIARI COVER
$3

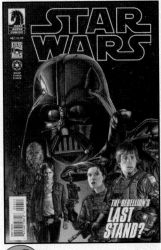

#6
JUNE 2013
RODOLFO MIGLIARI COVER
$3

#7
JULY 2013
RODOLFO MIGLIARI COVER
$3

#8
AUGUST 2013
DAVID MICHAEL BECK COVER
$3

#9
SEPTEMBER 2013
HUGH FLEMING COVER
$3

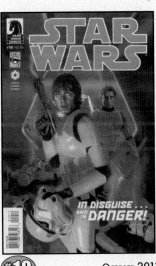

#10
OCTOBER 2013
HUGH FLEMING COVER
$3

#11
NOVEMBER 2013
SEAN COOKE COVER
$3

#12
DECEMBER 2013
HUGH FLEMING COVER
$3

#13   JANUARY 2014
HUGH FLEMING COVER
$3

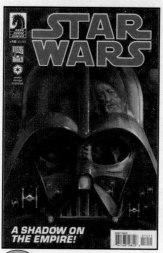

#14   FEBRUARY 2014
SEAN COOKE COVER
$3

#15   MARCH 2014
HUGH FLEMING COVER
$3

#16   APRIL 2014
SEAN COOKE COVER
$3

#17   MAY 2014
VICTOR MANUEL LEZA COVER
$3

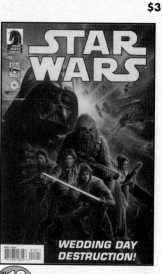

#18   JUNE 2014
VICTOR MANUEL LEZA COVER
$3

#19   JULY 2014
VICTOR MANUEL LEZA COVER
$3

#20   AUGUST 2014
HUGH FLEMING COVER
$3

MARVEL COMICS

Marvel regained the license and began publishing *Star Wars* in March 2015 and is still running.

#2 APRIL 2015
JOHN CASSADAY COVER
$4

#1 MARCH 2015
JOHN CASSADAY COVER
$5

#3 MAY 2015
JOHN CASSADAY COVER
$4

#4 JUNE 2015
JOHN CASSADAY COVER
$4

#5 JULY 2015
JOHN CASSADAY COVER
$4

#6 AUGUST 2015
JOHN CASSADAY COVER
$4

#7 SEPTEMBER 2015
JOHN CASSADAY COVER
$4

#8 OCTOBER 2015
STUART IMMONEN COVER
$4

#9 NOVEMBER 2015
STUART IMMONEN COVER
$4

#10 DECEMBER 2015
STUART IMMONEN COVER
$4

#11 JANUARY 2016
STUART IMMONEN COVER
$4

#12 JANUARY 2016
STUART IMMONEN COVER
$4

#13 FEBRUARY 2016
MARK BROOKS COVER
$4

#14 MARCH 2016
MARK BROOKS COVER
$4

#15 MARCH 2016
MIKE MAYHEW COVER
$4

#16   APRIL 2016
TERRY DODSON COVER
$4

#17   MAY 2016
TERRY DODSON COVER
$4

#18   JUNE 2016
LEINIL YU COVER
$4

#19   JULY 2016
LEINIL YU COVER
$4

#20   AUGUST 2016
MIKE MAYHEW COVER
$4

#21   SEPTEMBER 2016
DAVID AJA COVER
$4

#22   OCTOBER 2016
MIKE DEODATO COVER
$4

#23   NOVEMBER 2016
MIKE DEODATO COVER
$4

#24   DECEMBER 2016
MIKE DEODATO COVER
$4

#25   JANUARY 2017
MIKE DEODATO COVER
$5

#26   FEBRUARY 2017
STUART IMMONEN COVER
$4

#27   MARCH 2017
STUART IMMONEN COVER
$4

#28   APRIL 2017
STUART IMMONEN COVER
$4

#29   MAY 2017
STUART IMMONEN COVER
$4

#30   JUNE 2017
STUART IMMONEN COVER
$4

#31   JULY 2017
MARCO CHECCHETTO COVER
$4

#32   AUGUST 2017
MARCO CHECCHETTO COVER
$4

#33   SEPTEMBER 2017
MIKE MAYHEW COVER
$4

#34   OCTOBER 2017
MIKE MAYHEW COVER
$4

#35   OCTOBER 2017
MIKE MAYHEW COVER
$4

#36   NOVEMBER 2017
MIKE MAYHEW COVER
$4

#37   DECEMBER 2017
MIKE MAYHEW COVER
$5

#38   JANUARY 2018
DAVID MARQUEZ COVER
$4

#39   JANUARY 2018
DAVID MARQUEZ COVER
$4

#40   FEBRUARY 2018
DAVID MARQUEZ COVER
$4

#41   MARCH 2018
DAVID MARQUEZ COVER
$4

#42   MARCH 2018
DAVID MARQUEZ COVER
$4

#43 APRIL 2018
DAVID MARQUEZ COVER
$5

#44 MAY 2018
DAVID MARQUEZ COVER
$4

#45 MAY 2018
DAVID MARQUEZ COVER
$4

#46 JUNE 2018
DAVID MARQUEZ COVER
$4

#47 JULY 2018
DAVID MARQUEZ COVER
$4

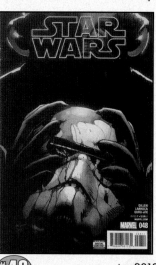

#48 JULY 2018
DAVID MARQUEZ COVER
$4

#49 AUGUST 2018
DAVID MARQUEZ COVER
$4

#50 SEPTEMBER 2018
TRAVIS CHAREST COVER
$6

#51 SEPTEMBER 2018
DAVID MARQUEZ COVER
$4

#52   October 2018
David Marquez cover
$4

#53   November 2018
David Marquez cover
$4

#54   November 2018
David Marquez cover
$4

A N N U A L S

#1   February 2016
John Cassaday cover
$5

#2   January 2017
Mike Mayhew cover
$5

#3   November 2017
Michael Walsh cover
$5

#4   July 2018
Tradd Moore cover
$5

Star Wars: Dark Empire

The *Star Wars: Dark Empire* six-part story ran from December 1991 to October 1992.

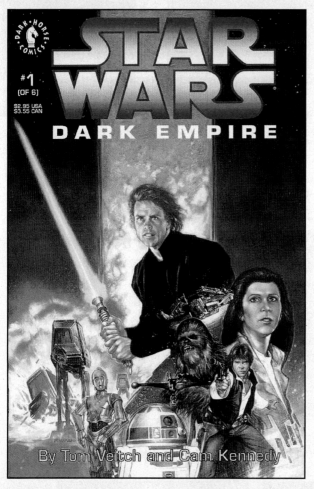

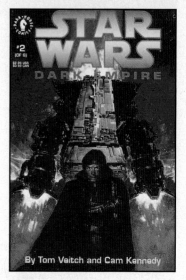

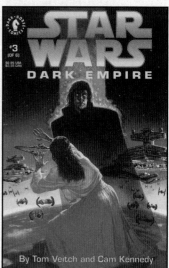

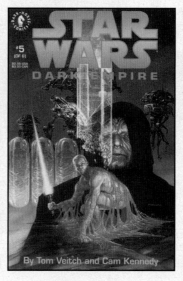

Darth Vader

Marvel has produced two *Darth Vader* series.
The first ran for 25 issues from April 2015 to December 2016.
The second series began in August 2017 and is still running.

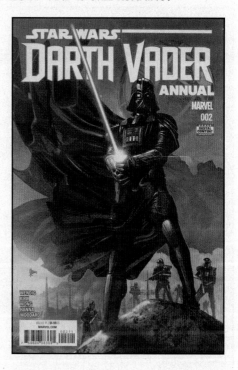

Star Wars: Doctor Aphra

Doctor Aphra became an ongoing series in June 2017.

Star Wars: Empire

Star Wars: Empire ran for 40 issues from September 2002 to February 2006.

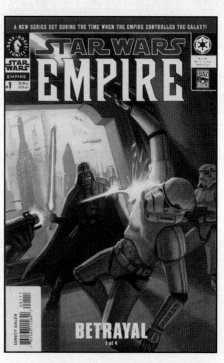

STAR WARS: KNIGHT ERRANT

The STAR WARS: KNIGHT ERRANT limited series ran from October 2010 to February 2011.

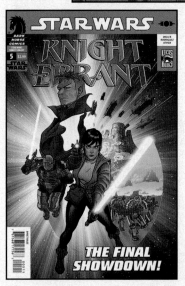

STAR WARS: KNIGHTS OF THE OLD REPUBLIC

STAR WARS: KNIGHTS OF THE OLD REPUBLIC RAN FOR 50 ISSUES FROM JANUARY 2006 TO FEBRUARY 2010.

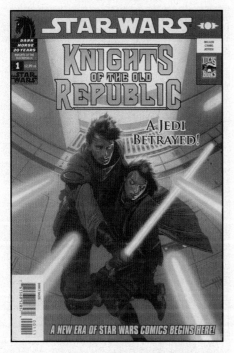

STAR WARS: LEGACY

STAR WARS: LEGACY RAN FOR 50 ISSUES FROM JUNE 2006 TO AUGUST 2010.

STAR WARS: POE DAMERON

STAR WARS: POE DAMERON BECAME AN ONGOING SERIES AT MARVEL IN JANUARY 2016.

PRINCESS LEIA

PRINCESS LEIA RAN FOR 5 ISSUES FROM MAY 2015 TO SEPTEMBER 2015.

Star Wars: Splinter of the Mind's Eye

The comic adaptation of the novel,
Splinter of the Mind's Eye,
was published from December 1995 to June 1996.

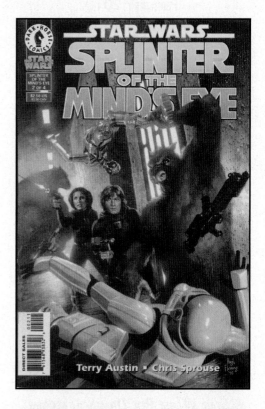

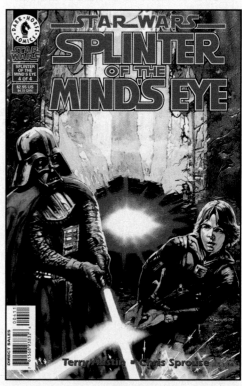

STAR WARS TALES

STAR WARS TALES RAN FOR 24 ISSUES FROM SEPTEMBER 1999 TO JUNE 2005.

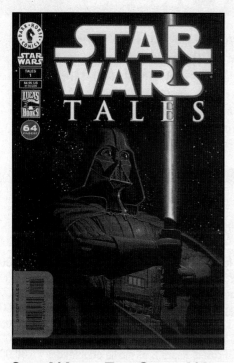

STAR WARS: TALES OF THE JEDI

STAR WARS: TALES OF THE JEDI RAN FOR 35 ISSUES FROM OCTOBER 1993 TO NOVEMBER 1998.

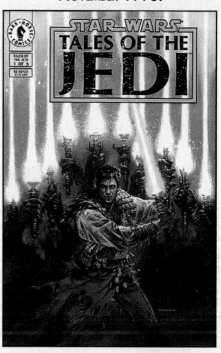

STAR WARS: THE CLONE WARS

STAR WARS: THE CLONE WARS RAN FOR 12 ISSUES FROM SEPTEMBER 2008 TO JANUARY 2010.

STAR WARS: X-WING ROGUE SQUADRON

STAR WARS: X-WING ROGUE SQUADRON RAN FOR 35 ISSUES FROM JULY 1995 TO NOVEMBER 1998.

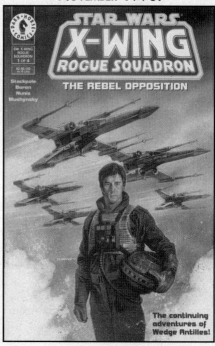

STAR WARS COMICS OVERSTREET VALUES

The Overstreet Comic Book Price Guide has been the definitive guide for collectors and dealers alike since 1970. Presented here are the listings and prices of Star Wars comics in the 48th edition (2018-2019).

Single prices listed are for Near Mint- condition (9.2).
Six prices listed are for: Good (2.0), Very Good (4.0), Fine (6.0), Very Fine (8.0), Very Fine/Near Mint (9.0) and Near Mint- (9.2).

	GD	VG	FN	VF	VF/NM	NM-
	2.0	4.0	6.0	8.0	9.0	9.2

CLASSIC STAR WARS
Dark Horse Comics: Aug, 1992 - No. 20, June, 1994 ($2.50)

1-Begin Star Wars strip-r by Williamson; Williamson redrew portions of the
   panels to fit comic book format   6.00
2-10: 8-Polybagged w/Star Wars Galaxy trading card. 8-M. Schultz-c   4.00
11-19: 13-Yeates-c. 17-M. Schultz-c. 19-Evans-c   3.00
20-($3.50, 52 pgs.)-Polybagged w/trading card   4.00
Escape To Hoth TPB ($16.95) r/#15-20   17.00
The Rebel Storm TPB - r/#8-14   17.00
Trade paperback ($29.95, slip-cased)-Reprints all movie adaptations   30.00
NOTE: *Williamson c-1-5,7,9,10,14,15,20.*

CLASSIC STAR WARS: (Title series). Dark Horse Comics
--A NEW HOPE, 6/94 - No. 2, 7/94 ($3.95)
   1,2: 1-r/Star Wars #1-3, 7-9 publ; 2-r/Star Wars #4-6, 10-12 publ. by
   Marvel Comics   4.00
--DEVILWORLDS, 8/96 - No. 2, 9/96 ($2.50)1,2: r/Alan Moore-s   3.00
--HAN SOLO AT STARS' END, 3/97 - No. 3, 5/97 ($2.95)
   1-3: r/strips by Alfredo Alcala   3.00
--RETURN OF THE JEDI, 10/94 - No.2, 11/94 ($3.50)
   1,2: 1-r/1983-84 Marvel series; polybagged with w/trading card   3.50
--THE EARLY ADVENTURES, 8/94 - No. 9, 4/95 ($2.50)1-9   3.00
--THE EMPIRE STRIKES BACK, 8/94 - No. 2, 9/94 ($3.95)
   1-r/Star Wars #39-44 published by Marvel Comics   4.00

DARTH VADER (Follows after the end of Star Wars Episode IV)
Marvel Comics: Apr, 2015 - No. 25, Dec, 2016 ($4.99/$3.99)

1-($4.99) Gillen-s/Larroca-a/Granov-c; Jabba the Hut & Boba Fett app.   5.00
2,4-12-($3.99) 6-Boba Fett app.   4.00
3-Intro. Doctor Aphra and Triple Zero   5.00
13-19,21-24: 13-15-Vader Down x-over pts. 2,4,6. 24-Flashbacks to
   Episode III   4.00
20-($4.99) The Emperor app.; back-up Triple-Zero & Beetee story   5.00
25-($5.99) Gillen-s/Larroca-a; back-up story with Fiumara-a; bonus cover
   gallery   6.00
Annual 1 (2/16, $4.99) Gillen-s/Yu-a/c   5.00
...: Doctor Aphra No. 1 Halloween Comic Fest 2016 (12/16, giveaway) r/#3
    3.00

DARTH VADER (Follows after the end of Star Wars Episode III)
Marvel Comics: Aug, 2017 - Present ($4.99/$3.99)

1-($4.99) Soule-s/Camuncoli-a/Cheung-c; back-up by Eliopoulos-s/a   5.00
2-20-($3.99) Soule-s/Camuncoli-a. 5-Vader acquires the red light saber   4.00
Annual 2 (9/18, $4.99) Wendig-s/Kirk-a/Deodato-c; Krennic app.   5.00

DOCTOR APHRA (Star Wars)(Title changes to Star Wars: Doctor Aphra with #7)
(See Darth Vader #3 for debut)
Marvel Comics: Feb, 2017 - No. 6, Jun, 2017 ($4.99/$3.99)

1-Gillen-s/Walker-a; back-up with Larroca-a; BT-1, Triple-Zero and Black
    Krrsantan app.   5.00
2-6-($3.99) Walker-a   4.00

DROIDS (Based on Saturday morning cartoon) (Also see Dark Horse Comics)
Marvel Comics (Star Comics): April, 1986 - No. 8, June, 1987

	GD	VG	FN	VF	VF/NM	NM-
1-R2D2 & C-3PO app. in all	2	4	6	13	18	22
2-8: 2,5,7,8-Williamson-a(i)	2	4	6	8	10	12

NOTE: *Romita a-3p. Sinnott a-3i.*

EWOKS (Star Wars)
Marvel Comics (Star Comics): June, 1985 - No. 14, Jul, 1987 (75¢/$1.00)

	GD	VG	FN	VF	VF/NM	NM-
1,10: 10-Williamson-a (From Star Wars)	3	6	9	17	26	35
2-9	2	4	6	8	11	14
11-14: 14-($1.00-c)	2	4	6	10	14	18

HAN SOLO (Star Wars)
Marvel Comics: Aug, 2016 - No. 5, Jan, 2017 ($3.99, limited series)

1-5-Marjorie Liu-s/Mark Brooks-a/Lee Bermejo-c; takes place between
    Episodes 4 & 5   4.00

JOURNEY TO STAR WARS: THE FORCE AWAKENS - SHATTERED EMPIRE
Marvel Comics: Nov, 2015 - No. 4, Dec, 2015 ($3.99, weekly limited series)

1-4-Rucka-s; takes place just after Episode 6 Battle of Endor; multiple covers
    on each   4.00

JOURNEY TO STAR WARS: THE LAST JEDI - CAPTAIN PHASMA
Marvel Comics: Nov, 2017 - No. 4, Dec, 2017 ($3.99, weekly limited series)

1-4-Checchetto-a/Renaud-c; takes place at the end of Episode 7 and just
    after   4.00

KANAN - THE LAST PADAWAN (Star Wars)
Marvel Comics: Jun, 2015 - No. 12, May, 2016 ($3.99)

1-12: 1-Weisman-s/Larraz-a; takes place after Episode 3; flashbacks to the
    Clone Wars. 9-11-General Grievous app.   4.00

LANDO (Star Wars)
Marvel Comics: Sept, 2015 - No. 5, Dec, 2015 ($3.99, limited series)

1-5-Soule-s/Maleev-a; Lobot & Emperor Palpatine app.   4.00

MARVEL COMICS SUPER SPECIAL, A (Marvel Super Special #5 on)
Marvel Comics: Sept, 1977 - No. 41(?), Nov, 1986 (nn 7) ($1.50, magazine)
16-Empire Strikes Back adaptation; Williamson-a

	GD	VG	FN	VF	VF/NM	NM-
	4	8	12	25	40	55
27-Return of the Jedi	2	4	6	10	14	18

MARVEL MOVIE SHOWCASE FEATURING STAR WARS
Marvel Comics Group: Nov, 1982 - No. 2, Dec, 1982 ($1.25, 68 pgs.)

	GD	VG	FN	VF	VF/NM	NM-
1-Star Wars movie adaptation; reprints Star Wars #1-3 by Chaykin; reprints-c to Star Wars #1	4	8	12	25	40	55
2-Reprints Star Wars #4-6; Stevens-r	3	6	9	16	23	30

MARVEL SPECIAL EDITION FEATURING...
Marvel Comics Group: 1975 - 1978 (84 pgs.) (Oversized)

	GD	VG	FN	VF	VF/NM	NM-
1,2-Star Wars ('77,'78) r/Star Wars #1-3 & #4-6; regular edition	2	4	6	11	16	20
1,2-Star Wars ('77,'78) Whitman variant	3	6	9	16	23	30
3-Star Wars ('78, $2.50, 116 pgs.); r/S. Wars #1-6; regular edition and Whitman variant exist	3	6	9	14	20	26
V2#2(Spring, 1980, $2.00, oversized)- "Star Wars: The Empire Strikes Back"; r/Marvel Comics Super Special #16	3	6	9	16	23	30

NOTE: *Chaykin c/a(r)-1(1977), 2, 3. Stevens a(r)-2i, 3i. Williamson a(r)-V2#2.*

OBI-WAN AND ANAKIN (Star Wars)
Marvel Comics: Mar, 2016 - No. 5, Jul, 2016 ($3.99)

1-5-Takes place a few years after Episode One; Soule-s/Checchetto-a/c	4.00

POE DAMERON (Star Wars) (Title changes to Star Wars: Poe Dameron with #13)
Marvel Comics: Jun, 2016 - No. 12, May, 2017 ($4.99/$3.99)

1-($4.99) Soule-s/Noto-a/c; prelude to The Force Awakens; back-up with Eliopoulos-a	5.00
2-6,8-12-($3.99) Black Squadron app.	4.00
7-($4.99) Anzueta-a; Leia cameo	5.00

PRINCESS LEIA (Star Wars)
Marvel Comics: May, 2015 - No. 5, Sept, 2015 ($3.99)

1-5-Mark Waid-s/Terry Dodson-a; story follows the ending of Episode IV	4.00

STAR WARS
Marvel Comics Group: July, 1977 - No. 107, Sept, 1986

	GD	VG	FN	VF	VF/NM	NM-
1-(Regular 30¢ edition)-Price in square w/UPC code; #1-6 adapt first movie; 1st issue on sale before movie debut	10	20	30	67	141	215
1-(35¢-c; limited distribution - 1500 copies?)- Price in square w/UPC code	367	734	1101	3120	7060	11,000

NOTE: *The rare 35¢ edition has the cover price in a square box, and the UPC box in the lower left hand corner has the UPC code lines running through it.*

	GD	VG	FN	VF	VF/NM	NM-
1-Reprint; has "reprint" in upper lefthand corner of cover or on inside or price and number inside a diamond with no date or UPC on cover; 30¢ and 35¢ issues published	5	10	15	30	50	70
2-9: Reprints; has "reprint" in upper lefthand corner of cover or on inside or price and number inside a diamond with no date or UPC on cover; 30¢ and 35¢ issues published	1	3	4	6	8	10
2-4-(30¢ issues). 4-Battles Darth Vader	5	10	15	30	50	70
2-4-(35¢ with UPC code; not reprints)	57	114	171	456	1028	1600
5,6: 5-Begin 35¢-c on all editions. 6-Stevens-a(i)	3	6	9	21	33	45
7-20	2	4	6	11	16	20
21-38,45-67,69,70: 50-Giant	2	4	6	8	10	12
39-41,43,44-The Empire Strikes Back-r by Al Williamson in all	2	4	6	9	12	15

	GD 2.0	VG 4.0	FN 6.0	VF 8.0	VF/NM 9.0	NM- 9.2
42-1st Boba Fett	6	12	18	41	76	110
68-Reintro Boba Fett	5	10	15	30	50	70
71-80	2	4	6	8	11	14
81-Boba Fett app.	4	8	12	23	37	50
82-90	2	4	6	9	13	16
91,93-99: 98-Williamson-a	2	4	6	11	16	20
92,100-106: 92,100-($1.00, 52 pgs.)	3	6	9	14	20	26
107 (low dist.); Portacio-a(i)	5	10	15	35	63	90
Annual 1 (12/79, 52 pgs.)-Simonson-c	2	4	6	11	16	20
Annual 2 (11/82, 52 pgs.)	2	4	6	9	12	15
Annual 3 (12/83, 52 pgs.)	2	4	6	9	12	15

... A Long Time Ago...Vol. 1 TPB (Dark Horse Comics, 6/02, $29.95)
   r/#1-14   30.00
... A Long Time Ago...Vol. 2 TPB (Dark Horse Comics, 7/02, $29.95)
   r/#15-28   30.00
... A Long Time Ago...Vol. 3 TPB (Dark Horse Comics, 11/02, $29.95)
   r/#39-53   30.00
... A Long Time Ago...Vol. 4 TPB (Dark Horse Comics, 1/03, $29.95)
   r/#54-67 & Ann. 2   30.00
... A Long Time Ago...Vol. 5 TPB (Dark Horse Comics, 3/03, $29.95)
   r/#68-81 & Ann. 3   30.00
... A Long Time Ago...Vol. 6 TPB (Dark Horse Comics, 5/03, $29.95)
   r/#82-93   30.00
... A Long Time Ago...Vol. 7 TPB (Dark Horse Comics, 6/03, $29.95)
   r/#96-107   30.00

NOTE: *Austin a-11-15i, 21i, 38; c-12-15i, 21i. Byrne c-13p. Chaykin a-1-10p; c-1. Golden c/a-38. Miller c-47p; pin-up-43. Nebres c/a-Annual 2i. Portacio a-107i. Sienkiewicz c-92i, 98. Simonson a-16p, 49p, 51-63p, 65p, 66p; c-16, 49-51, 52p, 53-62, Annual 1. Steacy painted a-105i, 106i; c-105. Williamson a-39-44p, 50p, 98; c-39, 40, 41-44p. Painted c-81, 87, 92, 95, 98, 100, 105.*

STAR WARS (Monthly series) (Becomes Star Wars Republic #46-on)
Dark Horse Comics: Dec, 1998 - No. 45, Aug, 2005 ($2.50/$2.95/$2.99)

	GD 2.0	VG 4.0	FN 6.0	VF 8.0	VF/NM 9.0	NM- 9.2
1-Prelude To Rebellion; Strnad-s	1	2	3	5	6	8

2-45: 2-6-Prelude To Rebellion; Strnad-s. 4-Brereton-c. 7-12-Outlander. 13,17-18-($2.95). 13-18-Emissaries to Malastare; Truman-s. 14-16-($2.50) Schultz-c. 19-22-Twilight; Duursema-a. 23-26-Infinity's End. 42-45-Rite of Passage   3.00
5,6 (Holochrome-c variants)   6.00
#0 Another Universe.com Ed.($10.00) r/serialized pages from Pizzazz Magazine; new Dorman painted-c   12.00
... A Valentine Story (2/03, $3.50) Leia & Han Solo on Hoth; Winick-s/ Chadwick-a/c   3.50
...: Rite of Passage (2004, $12.95) r/#42-45   13.00
...: The Stark Hyperspace War (903, $12.95) r/#36-39   13.00

STAR WARS (Monthly series)
Dark Horse Comics: Jan, 2013 - No. 20, Aug, 2014 ($2.99)

1-Takes place after Episode IV; Brian Wood-s/D'Anda-a/Alex Ross-c   8.00
2-Ross-c   5.00
3-20: 3,4-Ross-c. 5-7-Migliari-c   3.00

STAR WARS
Dark Horse Comics (Free Comic Book Day giveaways)
...: and Captain Midnight (5/13) flip book with new Captain Midnight story & Avatar   3.00

...: Clone Wars #0 (5/09) flip book with short stories of Usagi Yojimbo, Emily the Strange ... 3.00

...: Clone Wars Adventures (7/04) based on Cartoon Network series; Fillbach Bros. -a ... 3.00

...: FCBD 2005 Special (5/05) Anakin & Obi-Wan during Clone Wars ... 3.00

...: FCBD 2006 Special (5/06) Clone Wars story; flip book with Conan FCBD Special ... 3.00

...: Tales - A Jedi's Weapon (5/02, 16 pgs.) Anakin Skywalker Episode 2 photo-c ... 3.00

Free Comic Book Day and Star Wars: The Clone Wars (5/11) flip book with Avatar: The Last Airbender ... 3.00

STAR WARS (Also see Darth Vader and Star Wars: Vader Down)
Marvel Comics: Mar, 2015 - Present ($4.99/$3.99)

1-($4.99) Takes place after Episode IV; Aaron-s/Cassaday-a; multiple covers ... 5.00

2-6-($3.99) Darth Vader app.; Cassaday-a. 4-6-Boba Fett app. 6-Intro Sana Solo ... 4.00

7-24,26-36: 7-Bianchi-a; Obi-Wan flashback. 8-12-Immonen-a. 13,14-Vader Down pts. 3,5; Deodato-a. 15,20-Obi-Wan flashback; Mayhew-a. 16-19-Yu-a. 26-30-Yoda app. 31,32-Doctor Aphra app. ... 4.00

25-($4.99) Darth Vader app.; Molina-a; back-up Droids story by Eliopoulos ... 5.00

37-($4.99) SCAR Squadron app.; back-up Tusken Raiders story; Sorrentino-a ... 5.00

38-49,51,52-Larroca-a. 45-Wedge app. ... 4.00

50-(9/18, $5.99) Larroca-a; back-up with Camuncoli-a; bonus cover gallery ... 6.00

Annual 1 (2/16, $4.99) Gillen-s/Unzueta-a/Cassaday-c; Emperor Palpatine app. ... 5.00

Annual 2 (1/17, $4.99) Kelly Thompson-s/Emilio Laiso-a; intro. Pash Davane ... 5.00

Annual 3 (11/17, $4.99) Latour-s/Walsh-a ... 5.00

Annual 4 (7/18, $4.99) Bunn-s/Anindito, Boschi & Laming-a; Sana Starros app. ... 5.00

... Special: C-3PO 1 (6/16, $4.99) Robinson-s/Harris-a/c; story of C-3PO's red arm ... 5.00

STAR WARS, THE
Dark Horse Comics: Sept, 2013 - No. 8, May, 2014 ($3.99)

1-8-Adaptation of George Lucas' original rough-draft screenplay; Mayhew-a/Runge-c ... 4.00

#0-(1/14, $3.99) Design work of characters, settings, vehicles ... 4.00

STAR WARS ADVENTURES (Anthology of All-ages stories)
IDW Publishing: Sept, 2017 - Present ($3.99)

1-12: 2-Charretier-a. 3-Tudyk-s. 5-Porgs app. 6-Rose app. 10,11-Lando app. ... 4.00

Annual 2018 (4/18, $7.99) John Jackson Miller-s; Jaxxon app.; Sommariva-c ... 8.00

STAR WARS: AGENT OF THE EMPIRE - HARD TARGETS
Dark Horse Comics: Oct, 2012 - No. 5, Feb, 2013 ($2.99, limited series)

1-5: 1-Ostrander-s/Fabbri-a; Boba Fett app. ... 3.00

	GD	VG	FN	VF	VF/NM	NM-
	2.0	4.0	6.0	8.0	9.0	9.2

STAR WARS: AGENT OF THE EMPIRE - IRON ECLIPSE
Dark Horse Comics: Dec, 2011 - No. 5, Apr, 2012 ($3.50, limited series)
  1-5: 1-Ostrander-s/Roux-a; Han Solo & Chewbacca app.   3.50

STAR WARS: A NEW HOPE - THE SPECIAL EDITION
Dark Horse Comics: Jan, 1997 - No. 4, Apr, 1997 ($2.95, limited series)
  1-4-Dorman-c   4.00

STAR WARS: BLOOD TIES - BOBA FETT IS DEAD
Dark Horse Comics: Apr, 2012 - No. 4, Jul, 2012 ($3.50, limited series)
  1-4-Scalf painted-a/c   3.50

STAR WARS: BLOOD TIES: JANGO AND BOBA FETT
Dark Horse Comics: Aug, 2010 - No. 4, Nov, 2010 ($3.50, limited series)
  1-4-Scalf painted-a/c   3.50

STAR WARS: BOBA FETT
Dark Horse Comics: Dec, 1995 - No. 3, Aug, 1997 ($3.95) (Originally intended
as a one-shot)

1-Kennedy-c/a	1	2	3	5	6	8
2,3						5.00
Death, Lies, & Treachery TPB (1/98, $12.95) r/#1-3						13.00
... - Agent of Doom (11/00, $2.99) Ostrander-s/Cam Kennedy-a						3.00
... - Overkill (3/06, $2.99) Hughes-c/Andrews-s/Velasco-a						3.00
Twin Engines of Destruction (1/97, $2.95)						4.00

STAR WARS: BOBA FETT: ENEMY OF THE EMPIRE
Dark Horse Comics: Jan, 1999 - No. 4, Apr, 1999 ($2.95, limited series)
  1-4-Recalls 1st meeting of Fett and Vader   4.00

STAR WARS: CHEWBACCA
Dark Horse Comics: Jan, 2000 - No. 4, Apr, 2000 ($2.95, limited series)
  1-4-Macan-s/art by various incl. Anderson, Kordey, Gibbons; Phillips-c 3.00

STAR WARS: CLONE WARS ADVENTURES
Dark Horse Comics: 2004 - No. 10, 2007 ($6.95, digest-sized)
  1-10-Short stories inspired by Clone Wars animated series   7.00

STAR WARS: CRIMSON EMPIRE
Dark Horse Comics: Dec, 1997 - No. 6, May, 1998 ($2.95, limited series)

1-Richardson-s/Gulacy-a	1	2	3	4	5	7
2-6						5.00

STAR WARS: CRIMSON EMPIRE II: COUNCIL OF BLOOD
Dark Horse Comics: Nov, 1998 - No. 6, Apr, 1999 ($2.95, limited series)
  1-6-Richardson & Stradley-s/Gulacy-a   4.00

STAR WARS: CRIMSON EMPIRE III: EMPIRE LOST
Dark Horse Comics: Oct, 2011 - No. 6, Apr, 2012 ($3.50, limited series)
  1-6: 1-Richardson-s/Gulacy-a/Dorman-c   3.50

STAR WARS: DARK EMPIRE
Dark Horse Comics: Dec, 1991 - No. 6, Oct, 1992 ($2.95, limited series)

Preview-(99¢)						4.00
1-All have Dorman painted-c	1	3	4	6	8	10
1-3-2nd printing						4.00
2-Low print run	2	4	6	8	10	12
3						6.00
4-6						4.00
Gold Embossed Set (#1-6)-With gold embossed foil logo (price is for set)						60.00
Platinum Embossed Set (#1-6)						90.00
Trade paperback (4/93, 16.95)						17.00
Dark Empire 1 - TPB 3rd printing (2003, $16.95)						17.00
Ltd. Ed. Hardcover ($99.95) Signed & numbered						100.00

STAR WARS: DARK EMPIRE II
Dark Horse Comics: Dec, 1994 - No. 6, May, 1995 ($2.95, limited series)

1-Dave Dorman painted-c	5.00
2-6: Dorman-c in all.	4.00
Platinum Embossed Set (#1-6)	35.00
Trade paperback ($17.95)	18.00
TPB Second Edition (9/06, $19.95) r/#1-6 and Star Wars: Empire's End #1,2	20.00

STAR WARS: DARK FORCE RISING
Dark Horse Comics: May, 1997 - No. 6, Oct, 1997 ($2.95, limited series)

1-6	4.00
TPB (2/98, $17.95) r/#1-6	18.00

STAR WARS: DARK TIMES (Continued from Star Wars Republic #83)(Storyline continues in Star Wars: Rebellion #15)
Dark Horse Comics: Oct, 2006 - No. 17, Jun, 2010 ($2.99)

1-17-Nineteen years before Episode IV; Doug Wheatley-a. 11-Celeste Morne awakens. 13-17-Blue Harvest	3.00
#0-(7/09, $2.99) Prologue to Blue Harvest	3.00

STAR WARS: DARK TIMES - A SPARK REMAINS
Dark Horse Comics: Jul, 2013 - No. 5, Dec, 2013 ($3.50, limited series)

1-5-Stradley-s/Wheatley-a; Darth Vader app.	3.50

STAR WARS: DARK TIMES - FIRE CARRIER
Dark Horse Comics: Feb, 2013 - No. 5, Jun, 2013 ($2.99, limited series)

1-5-Stradley-s/Guzman-a; Darth Vader app.	3.00

STAR WARS: DARK TIMES - OUT OF THE WILDERNESS
Dark Horse Comics: Aug, 2011 - No. 5, Apr, 2012 ($2.99, limited series)

1-5-Doug Wheatley-a	3.00

STAR WARS: DARTH MAUL
Dark Horse Comics: Sept, 2000 - No. 4, Dec, 2000 ($2.95, limited series)

1-4-Photo-c and Struzan painted-c; takes place 6 months before Ep. 1	3.00

STAR WARS: DARTH MAUL (Issue #1 titled Darth Maul)
Marvel Comics: Apr, 2015 - No. 5, Sept, 2017 ($4.99, limited series)

 1-($4.99) Cullen Bunn-s/Luke Ross-a; back-up by Eliopoulos-s/a   5.00
 2-5-($3.99) Aurra Sing & Cad Bane app.   4.00
 ... Halloween Comic Fest 2017 1 (12/17, giveaway) r/#1 without Eliopoulos
     back-up   3.00

STAR WARS: DARTH MAUL - DEATH SENTENCE
Dark Horse Comics: Jul, 2012 - No. 4, Oct, 2012 ($2.99, limited series)

 1-4-Tom Taylor-s/Bruno Redondo-a/Dave Dorman-c   3.00

STAR WARS: DARTH MAUL - SON OF DATHOMIR
Dark Horse Comics: May, 2014 - No. 4, Aug, 2014 ($3.50, limited series)

 1-4-Barlow-s/Frigeri-a/Scalf-c   3.50

STAR WARS: DARTH VADER AND THE CRY OF SHADOWS
Dark Horse Comics: Dec, 2013 - No. 5, Apr, 2014 ($3.50, limited series)

 1-5-Siedell-s/Guzman-a/Massaferra-c   3.50

STAR WARS: DARTH VADER AND THE GHOST PRISON
Dark Horse Comics: May, 2012 - No. 5, Sept, 2012 ($3.50, limited series)

 1-5-Blackman-s/Alessio-a/Wilkins-c. 1-Variant-c by Sanda   3.50

STAR WARS: DARTH VADER AND THE LOST COMMAND
Dark Horse Comics: Jan, 2011 - No. 5, May, 2011 ($3.50, limited series)

 1-5-Blackman-s/Leonardi-a/Sanda-c. 1-Variant-c by Wheatley   3.50

STAR WARS: DARTH VADER AND THE NINTH ASSASSIN
Dark Horse Comics: Apr, 2013 - No. 5, Aug, 2013 ($3.50, limited series)

 1-5-Siedell-s. 1,2,4-Thompson-a. 3,5-Fernandez-a   3.50

STAR WARS: DAWN OF THE JEDI
Dark Horse Comics: No. 0, Feb, 2012 - Mar, 2014 ($3.50)

 0-Guide to the worlds, characters, sites, vehicles; Migliari-c   3.50
 ... - Force Storm (2/12 - No. 5, 6/12, $3.50) 1-5-Ostrander-s/Duursema-a/c
          3.50
 ... - Force War (11/13 - No. 5, 3/14, $3.50) 1-5-Ostrander-s/Duursema-a/c
          3.50
 ... - Prisoner of Bogan (11/12 - No. 5, 5/13, $2.99) 1-5-Ostrander-s/
     Duursema-a/c   3.00

STAR WARS: DOCTOR APHRA (See Doctor Aphra for #1-6)(See Darth Vader #3
for debut)
Marvel Comics: No. 7, Jul, 2017 - Present ($3.99)

 7-21: 7,8-Luke, Han, Leia & Sana app. 12,13-Darth Vader app. 20,21-Sana
     Starros app.   4.00
 Annual 1 (10/17, $4.99) Gillen-s/Laming & Sliney-a   5.00

STAR WARS: DROIDS (See Dark Horse Comics #17-19)
Dark Horse Comics: Apr, 1994 - #6, Sept, 1994; V2#1, Apr, 1995 - V2#8, Dec,
1995 ($2.50, limited series)

 1-($2.95)-Embossed-c   5.00
 2-6 , Special 1 (1/95, $2.50), V2#1-8   4.00

Star Wars Omnibus: Droids One TPB (6/08, $24.95) r/#1-6, Special 1, V2#1-8, Star Wars: The Protocol Offensive and "Artoo's Day Out" story from Star Wars Galaxy Magazine #1   25.00

STAR WARS: DROIDS UNPLUGGED
Marvel Comics: Aug, 2017 ($4.99, one-shot)

1-Chris Eliopoulos-s/a; short stories with R2-D2, BB-8 & a probe droid   5.00

STAR WARS: EMPIRE
Dark Horse Comics: Sept, 2002 - No. 40, Feb, 2006 ($2.99)

1-40: 1-Benjamin-a; takes place weeks before SW: A New Hope. 7,28-Boba Fett-c. 14-Vader after the destruction of the Death Star. 15-Death of Biggs; Wheatley-a   3.00
... Volume 1 (2003, $12.95, TPB) r/#1-4   13.00
... Volume 2 (2004, $17.95, TPB) r/#8-12,15   18.00
... Volume 3: The Imperial Perspective (2004, $17.95, TPB) r/#13,14,16-19
18.00
... Volume 4: The Heart of the Rebellion (2005, $17.95, TPB) r/#5,6,20-22 & Star Wars: A Valentine Story   18.00
... Volume 5 (2006, $14.95, TPB) r/#23-27   15.00
... Volume 6: In the Shadows of Their Fathers (10/06, $17.95, TPB) r/#29-34
18.00
... Volume 7: The Wrong Side of the War (1/07, $17.95, TPB) r/#34-40
18.00

STAR WARS: EMPIRE'S END
Dark Horse Comics: Oct, 1995 - No. 2, Nov, 1995 ($2.95, limited series)

1,2-Dorman-c   4.00

STAR WARS: EPISODE 1 THE PHANTOM MENACE
Dark Horse Comics: May, 1999 - No. 4 ($2.95, movie adaptation)

1-4-Regular and photo-c; Damaggio & Williamson-a   4.00
TPB ($12.95) r/#1-4   13.00
...Anakin Skywalker-Photo-c & Bradstreet-c, ...Obi-Wan Kenobi-Photo-c & Egeland-c, ...Queen Amidala-Photo-c & Bradstreet-c, ...Qui-Gon Jinn-Photo-c & Bradstreet-c   4.00
Gold foil covers; Wizard 1/2   10.00

STAR WARS: EPISODE II - ATTACK OF THE CLONES
Dark Horse Comics: Apr, 2002 - No. 4, May, 2002 ($3.99, movie adaptation)

1-4-Regular and photo-c; Duursema-a   4.00
TPB ($17.95) r/#1-4; Struzan-c   18.00

STAR WARS: EPISODE III - REVENGE OF THE SITH
Dark Horse Comics: May, 2005 - No. 4, May, 2005 ($2.99, movie adaptation)

1-4-Wheatley-a/Dorman-c   3.00
TPB ($12.95) r/#1-4; Dorman-c   13.00

STAR WARS FORCES OF DESTINY (All-ages anthology spotlighting female characters)
IDW Publishing: Jan, 2018 ($3.99, series of one-shots)

... – Ahsoka & Padme - Revis-s/Pinto-a   4.00
... – Hera - Grayson-s/Widermann-a   4.00
... – Leia - Charretier-a; Leia on planet Hoth before the events of Empire 4.00

... – Rey - Houser-s/Florean-a; Rey meets BB-8 on Jakku   4.00
... – Rose & Paige - Dawson-s/Baldari-a; the sisters before the events of
     The Last Jedi   4.00

STAR WARS: GENERAL GRIEVOUS
Dark Horse Comics: Mar, 2005 - No. 4, June, 2005 ($2.99, limited series)

  1-4-Leonardi-a/Dixon-s   3.00
TPB (2005, $12.95) r/#1-4   13.00

STAR WARS HANDBOOK
Dark Horse Comics: July, 1998 - Mar, 2000 ($2.95, one-shots)

...X-Wing Rogue Squadron (7/98)-Guide to characters and spacecraft   4.00
...Crimson Empire (7/99) Dorman-c   4.00
...Dark Empire (3/00) Dorman-c   4.00

STAR WARS: HEIR TO THE EMPIRE
Dark Horse Comics: Oct, 1995 - No.6, Apr, 1996 ($2.95, limited series)

  1-6: Adaptation of Zahn novel   4.00

STAR WARS: INFINITIES - A NEW HOPE
Dark Horse Comics: May, 2001 - No. 4, Oct, 2001 ($2.99, limited series)

  1-4: "What If..." the Death Star wasn't destroyed in Episode 4   3.00
TPB (2002, $12.95) r/ #1-4   13.00

STAR WARS: INFINITIES - THE EMPIRE STRIKES BACK
Dark Horse Comics: July, 2002 - No. 4, Oct, 2002 ($2.99, limited series)

  1-4: "What If..." Luke died on the ice planet Hoth; Bachalo-c   3.00
TPB (2/03, $12.95) r/ #1-4   13.00

STAR WARS: INFINITIES - RETURN OF THE JEDI
Dark Horse Comics: Nov, 2003 - No. 4, Mar, 2004 ($2.99, limited series)

  1-4:"What If..." ; Benjamin-a   3.00

STAR WARS: INVASION
Dark Horse Comics: July, 2009 - No. 5, Nov, 2009 ($2.99)

  1-5-Jo Chen-c   3.00
#0-(10/09, $3.50) Dorman-c; Han Solo and Chewbacca app.   3.50
... - Rescues 1-6 (5/10 - No. 6, 12/10) Chen-c   3.00
... - Revelations 1-5 (7/11 - No. 5, 11/11, $3.50) Luke Skywalker app.;
     Scalf-c   3.50

STAR WARS: JABBA THE HUTT
Dark Horse Comics: Apr, 1995 ($2.50, one-shots)

nn, ...The Betrayal, ...The Dynasty Trap, ...The Hunger of Princess Nampi   4.00

STAR WARS: JANGO FETT - OPEN SEASONS
Dark Horse Comics: Apr, 2002 - No. 4, July, 2002 ($2.99, limited series)

  1-4: 1-Bachs & Fernandez-a   3.00

STAR WARS: JEDI
Dark Horse Comics: Feb, 2003 - Jun, 2004 ($4.99, one-shots)

... - Aayla Secura (8/03) Ostrander-s/Duursema-a   5.00
... - Count Dooku (11/03) Duursema-a   5.00

... - Mace Windu (2/03) Duursema-a   5.00
... - Shaak Ti (5/03) Ostrander-s/Duursema-a   5.00
... - Yoda (6/04) Barlow-s/Hoon-a   5.00

STAR WARS: JEDI ACADEMY - LEVIATHAN
Dark Horse Comics: Oct, 1998 - No. 4, Jan, 1999 ($2.95, limited series)
  1-4: 1-Lago-c. 2-4-Chadwick-c   4.00

STAR WARS: JEDI COUNCIL: ACTS OF WAR
Dark Horse Comics: Jun, 2000 - No. 4, Sept, 2000 ($2.95, limited series)
  1-4-Stradley-s; set one year before Episode 1   3.00

STAR WARS: JEDI QUEST
Dark Horse Comics: Sept, 2001 - No. 4, Dec, 2001 ($2.99, limited series)
  1-4-Anakin's Jedi training; Windham-s/Mhan-a   3.00

STAR WARS: JEDI - THE DARK SIDE
Dark Horse Comics: May, 2011 - No. 5, Sept, 2011 ($2.99, limited series)
  1-5: 1-Qui-Gon Jinn 21 years befor Episode 1; Asrar-a   3.00

STAR WARS: JEDI VS. SITH
Dark Horse Comics: Apr, 2001 - No. 6, Sept, 2001 ($2.99, limited series)
  1-6: Macan-s/Bachs-a/Robinson-c   3.00

STAR WARS: KNIGHT ERRANT
Dark Horse Comics: Oct, 2010 - No. 5, Feb, 2011 ($2.99)
  1-5: 1-John Jackson Miller-s/Federico Dallocchio-a   3.00
... - Deluge 1-5 (8/11 - No. 5 12/11, $3.50) 1-Miller-s/Rodriguez-a/
    Quinones-c   3.50
... - Escape 1-5 (6/12 - No. 5 10/12, $3.50) 1-Miller-s/Castiello-a/Carré-c
    3.50

STAR WARS: KNIGHTS OF THE OLD REPUBLIC
Dark Horse Comics: Jan, 2006 - No. 50, Feb, 2010 ($2.99)
  1-50-Takes place 3,964 years before Episode IV. 1-6-Brian Ching-a/
    Travis Charest-c   3.00
... Handbook (11/07, $2.99) profiles of characters, ships, locales   3.00
.../Rebellion #0 (3/06, 25¢) flip book preview of both series   3.00
... - War 1-5 (1/12 - No. 5, 5/12, $3.50) J.J. Miller-s/Mutti-a   3.50
... Vol. 1 Commencement TPB (11/06, $18.95) r/#0-6   19.00
... Vol. 2 Flashpoint TPB (5/07, $18.95) r/#17-12   19.00
... Vol. 3 Days of Fear, Nights of Anger TPB (1/08, $18.95) r/#13-18   19.00

STAR WARS: LANDO - DOUBLE OR NOTHING
Marvel Comics: Jul, 2018 - No. 5, Nov, 2018 ($3.99, limited series)
  1-5: 1-Barnes-s/Villanelli-a; young Lando & L3-37 before Solo movie   4.00

STAR WARS: LEGACY
Dark Horse Comics: No. 0, June, 2006 - No. 50, Aug, 2010 ($2.99)
Volume 2, Mar, 2013 - No. 18, Aug, 2014 ($2.99)
  0-(25¢) Dossier of characters, settings, ships and weapons; Duursema-c 3.00
  0 1/2-(1/08, $2.99) Updated dossier of characters, settings, ships, and
    history   3.00

1-50: 1-Takes place 130 years after Episode IV; Hughes-c/Duursema-a.
    4-Duursema-c. 7,39-Luke Skywalker on-c. 16-Obi-Wan Kenobi app.
    50-Wraparound-c   3.00
...: Broken Vol. 1 TPB (4/07, $17.95) r/#1-3,5,6   18.00
...: One for One (9/10, $1.00) reprints #1 with red cover frame   3.00
... Volume Two 1 (3/13 - No. 18, 8/14, $2.99) 1-18: 1-Bechko-s/Hardman-a/
    Wilkins-c   3.00
... War 1-6 (12/10 - No. 6, 5/11, $3.50) 1-Ostrander-s/Duursema-a;
    Darth Krayt app.   3.50

STAR WARS: LOST TRIBE OF THE SITH - SPIRAL
Dark Horse Comics: Aug, 2012 - No. 5, Dec, 2012 ($2.99, limited series)
  1-5-J.J. Miller-s/Mutti-a/Renaud-c   3.00

STAR WARS: MACE WINDU
Marvel Comics: Oct, 2017 - No. 5, Feb, 2018 ($3.99, limited series)
  1-5-Matt Owens-s/Denys Cowan-a; follows after the Battle of Geonosis 4.00

STAR WARS: MARA JADE
Dark Horse Comics: Aug, 1998 - No. 6, Jan, 1999 ($2.95, limited series)
  1-6-Ezquerra-a   4.00

STAR WARS: OBSESSION (Clone Wars)
Dark Horse Comics: Nov, 2004 - No. 5, Apr, 2005 ($2.99, limited series)
  1-5-Blackman-s/Ching-a/c; Anakin & Obi-Wan 5 months before Episode III
                                              3.00
...: Clone Wars Vol. 7 (2005, $17.95) r/#1-5 and 2005 Free Comic Book Day
    edition   18.00

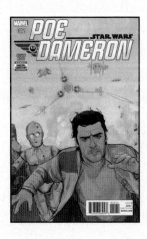

STAR WARS: POE DAMERON (Titled Poe Dameron for #1-12)
Marvel Comics: No. 13, Jun, 2017 - No. 31 ($3.99)
  13-28: 13-Soule-s/Noto-a. 14-22-Unzueta-a. 20-25-Lor San Tekka app.
    26-28-Recounts events from Episode VII & VIII   4.00
  Annual 1 (8/17, $4.99) Thompson-s/Virella-a; General Organa app.   5.00

STAR WARS: PURGE
Dark Horse Comics: Dec, 2005 ($2.99, one-shot)
nn-Vader vs. remaining Jedi one month after Episode III; Hughes-c/Wheatley-a
                                            5.00
... - Seconds To Die (11/09, $3.50) Vader app.; Charest-c/Ostrander-s 3.50
... - The Hidden Blade (4/10, $3.50) Vader app.; Scalf-c/a; Blackman-s 3.50
... - The Tyrant's Fist 1,2 (12/12 - No, 2, 1/13, $3.50) Vader app.; Freed-s/
    Dan Scott-c   3.50

STAR WARS: QUI-GON & OBI-WAN - LAST STAND ON ORD MANTELL
Dark Horse Comics: Dec, 2000 - No. 3, Mar, 2001 ($2.99, limited series)
  1-3: 1-Three covers (photo, Tony Daniel, Bachs) Windham-s   3.00

STAR WARS: QUI-GON & OBI-WAN - THE AURORIENT EXPRESS
Dark Horse Comics: Feb, 2002 - No. 2, Mar, 2002 ($2.99, limited series)
  1,2-Six years prior to Phantom Menace; Marangon-a   3.00

STAR WARS: REBEL HEIST
Dark Horse Comics: Apr, 2014 - No. 4, Jul, 2014 ($3.50)
  1-4-Kindt-s/Castiello-a; two covers by Kindt and Adam Hughes on each 3.50

STAR WARS: REBELLION (Also see Star Wars: Knights of the Old Republic
flip book)
Dark Horse Comics: Apr, 2006 - No. 16, Aug, 2008 ($2.99)
  1-16-Takes place 9 months after Episode IV; Luke Skywalker app.
    1-Badeaux-a/c   3.00
Vol. 1 TPB (2/07, $14.95) r/#0 (flip book) & #1-5   15.00

STAR WARS: REPUBLIC (Formerly Star Wars monthly series)
Dark Horse Comics: No. 46, Sept, 2002 - No. 83, Feb, 2006 ($2.99)
  46-83-Events of the Clone Wars   3.00
...: Clone Wars Vol. 1 (2003, $14.95) r/#46-50   15.00
...: Clone Wars Vol. 2 (2003, $14.95) r/#51-53 & Star Wars: Jedi - Shaak Ti
                                                                   15.00
...: Clone Wars Vol. 3 (2004, $14.95) r/#55-59   15.00
...: Clone Wars Vol. 4 (2004, $16.95) r/#54, 63 & Star Wars: Jedi - Aayla
    Secura & Dooku   17.00
...: Clone Wars Vol. 5 (2004, $17.95) r/#60-62, 64 & Star Wars: Jedi - Yoda
                                                                   18.00
...: Clone Wars Vol. 6 (2005, $17.95) r/#65-71   18.00
(Clone Wars Vol. 7 - see Star Wars: Obsession)
...: Clone Wars Vol. 8 (2006, $17.95) r/#72-78   18.00
...: Clone Wars Vol. 9 (2006, $17.95) r/#79-83 & Star Wars: Purge   18.00
...: Honor and Duty TPB (5/06, $12.95) r/#46-48,78   13.00

STAR WARS: RETURN OF THE JEDI (Movie)
Marvel Comics Group: Oct, 1983 - No. 4, Jan, 1984 (limited series)
  1-Williamson-p in all; r/Marvel Super Special #27
                                 | 2 | 4 | 6 | 11 | 16 | 20 |
  2-4-Continues r/Marvel Super Special #27
                                 | 2 | 4 | 6 | 9 | 12 | 15 |
  Oversized issue (1983, $2.95, 10-3/4x8-1/4", 68 pgs., cardboard-c)-r/#1-4
                                 | 2 | 4 | 6 | 10 | 13 | 16 |

STAR WARS: RIVER OF CHAOS
Dark Horse Comics: June, 1995 - No. 4, Sept, 1995 ($2.95, limited series)
  1-4: Louise Simonson scripts   4.00

STAR WARS: ROGUE ONE ADAPTATION
Marvel Comics: Jun, 2017 - No. 6, Nov, 2017 ($4.99/$3.99, limited series)
  1-($4.99) Houser-s/Laiso & Bazaldua-a; Noto-c; afterword by director
    Gareth Edwards   5.00
  2-6-($3.99) 3-Villanelli-a. 4-6-Laiso-a   4.00
Star Wars: Rogue One - Cassian & K2-SO Special 1 (10/17, $4.99)
    Swierczynski-s   5.00

STAR WARS: SHADOWS OF THE EMPIRE
Dark Horse Comics: May, 1996 - No. 6, Oct, 1996 ($2.95, limited series)
  1-6: Story details events between The Empire Strikes Back & Return of the Jedi;
    Russell-a(i)   4.00

STAR WARS: SHADOWS OF THE EMPIRE - EVOLUTION
Dark Horse Comics: Feb, 1998 - No. 5, June, 1998 ($2.95, limited series)
1-5: Perry-s/Fegredo-c.   4.00

STAR WARS: SHADOW STALKER
Dark Horse Comics: Sept, 1997 ($2.95, one-shot)
nn-Windham-a.   4.00

STAR WARS: SPLINTER OF THE MIND'S EYE
Dark Horse Comics: Dec, 1995 - No. 4, June, 1996 ($2.50, limited series)
1-4: Adaption of Alan Dean Foster novel   4.00

STAR WARS: STARFIGHTER
Dark Horse Comics: Jan, 2002 - No. 3, March, 2002 ($2.99, limited series)
1-3-Williams & Gray-c   3.00

STAR WARS: TAG & BINK ARE DEAD
Dark Horse Comics: Oct, 2001 - No. 2, Nov, 2001($2.99, limited series)
1,2-Rubio-s   3.00
Star Wars: Tag & Bink Were Here TPB (11/06, $14.95) r/both SW: Tag &
    Bink series   15.00
Star Wars: Tag & Bink Were Here (Marvel, 7/18, $7.99) r/both SW: Tag &
    Bink series   8.00

STAR WARS: TAG & BINK II
Dark Horse Comics: Mar, 2006 - No. 2, Apr, 2006($2.99, limited series)
1-Tag & Bink invade Return of the Jedi; Rubio-s. 2-Tag & Bink as Jedi
    younglings during Ep II   3.00

STAR WARS TALES
Dark Horse Comics: Sept, 1999 - No. 24, Jun, 2005 ($4.95/$5.95/$5.99,
anthology)
1-4-Short stories by various   6.00
5-24 ($5.95/$5.99-c) Art and photo-c on each   6.00

STAR WARS: TALES FROM MOS EISLEY
Dark Horse Comics: Mar, 1996 ($2.95, one-shot)
nn-Bret Blevins-a.   4.00

STAR WARS: TALES OF THE JEDI (See Dark Horse Comics #7)
Dark Horse Comics: Oct, 1993 - No. 5, Feb, 1994 ($2.50, limited series)
1-5: All have Dave Dorman painted-c. 3-r/Dark Horse Comics #7-9 w/new
    coloring & some panels redrawn   5.00
1-5-Gold foil embossed logo; limited # printed-7500 (set)   50.00
Star Wars Omnibus: Tales of the Jedi Volume One TPB (11/07, $24.95) r/#1-5,
    ... - The Golden Age of the Sith #0-5 and ... - The Fall of the Sith Empire
    #1-5   25.00

STAR WARS: TALES OF THE JEDI-DARK LORDS OF THE SITH
Dark Horse Comics: Oct, 1994 - No. 6, Mar, 1995 ($2.50, limited series)
1-6: 1-Polybagged w/trading card   4.00

STAR WARS: TALES OF THE JEDI-REDEMPTION
Dark Horse Comics: July, 1998 - No. 5, Nov, 1998 ($2.95, limited series)
  1-5: 1-Kevin J. Anderson-s/Kordey-c   4.00

STAR WARS: TALES OF THE JEDI-THE FALL OF THE SITH EMPIRE
Dark Horse Comics: June, 1997 - No. 5, Oct, 1997 ($2.95, limited series)
  1-5   4.00

STAR WARS: TALES OF THE JEDI-THE FREEDON NADD UPRISING
Dark Horse Comics: Aug, 1994 - No. 2, Nov, 1994 ($2.50, limited series)
  1,2   4.00

STAR WARS: TALES OF THE JEDI-THE GOLDEN AGE OF THE SITH
Dark Horse Comics: July, 1996 - No. 5, Feb, 1997 (99¢/$2.95, limited series)
  0-(99¢)-Anderson-s   3.00
  1-5-Anderson-s   4.00

STAR WARS: TALES OF THE JEDI-THE SITH WAR
Dark Horse Comics: Aug, 1995 - No. 6, Jan, 1996 ($2.50, limited series)
  1-6: Anderson scripts   4.00

STAR WARS: THE BOUNTY HUNTERS
Dark Horse Comics: July, 1999 - Oct, 1999 ($2.95, one-shots)
  ...Aurra Sing (7/99)   4.00
  ...Kenix Kil (10/99)   4.00
  ...Scoundrel's Wages (8/99) Lando Calrissian app.   4.00

STAR WARS: THE CLONE WARS (Based on the Cartoon Network series)
Dark Horse Comics: Sept, 2008 - No. 12, Jan, 2010 ($2.99)
  1-12: 1-6-Gilroy-s/Hepburn-a/Filoni-c   3.00

STAR WARS: THE FORCE AWAKENS ADAPTATION (Episode VII movie)
Marvel Comics: Aug, 2016 - No. 6, Jan, 2017 ($4.99, limited series)
  1-6: 1-Chuck Wendig-s/Luke Ross-a/Esad Ribic-c. 3-Marc Laming-a   5.00

STAR WARS: THE FORCE UNLEASHED (Based on the LucasArts video game)
Dark Horse Comics: Aug, 2008 ($15.95, one-shot graphic novel)
GN-Intro. Starkiller, Vader's apprentice; takes place 2 years before
    Battle of Yavin   16.00

STAR WARS: THE JABBA TAPE
Dark Horse Comics: Dec, 1998 ($2.95, one-shot)
  nn-Wagner-s/Plunkett-a   4.00

STAR WARS: THE LAST COMMAND
Dark Horse Comics: Nov, 1997 - No. 6, July, 1998 ($2.95, limited series)
  1-6: Based on the Timothy Zaun novel   4.00

STAR WARS: THE LAST JEDI ADAPTATION
Marvel Comics: Jul, 2018 - No. 6, Nov, 2018 ($4.99/$3.99, limited series)
  1-($4.99) Whitta-s/Walsh-a/Del Mundo-c   5.00
  2-5-($3.99) 2-Shirahama-c. 3-Noto-c   4.00
  6-($4.99) Asrar-c   5.00

STAR WARS: THE LAST JEDI - DJ - MOST WANTED
Marvel Comics: Mar, 2018 ($4.99, one-shot)

  1-Acker & Blacker-s/Walker-a   5.00

STAR WARS: THE OLD REPUBLIC (Based on the video game)
Dark Horse Comics: July, 2010 - No. 6, Dec, 2010 ($2.99, limited series)

  1-3 (Threat of Peace)-Chestny-s/Sanchez-a. 1-Two covers   3.00
  4-6 (Blood of the Empire)-Freed-s/Dave Ross-a   3.00

STAR WARS: THE OLD REPUBLIC - THE LOST SUNS (Based on the video game)
Dark Horse Comics: Jun, 2011 - No. 5, Oct, 2011 ($3.50, limited series)

  1-5-Freed-s/Carré-c/Freeman-a   3.50

STAR WARS: THE PROTOCOL OFFENSIVE
Dark Horse Comics: Sept, 1997 ($4.95, one-shot)

nn-Anthony Daniels & Ryder Windham-s   5.00

STAR WARS: THRAWN
Marvel Comics: Apr, 2018 - No. 6 ($3.99)

  1-5-Houser-s/Luke Ross-a; Thrawn's intro to the Empire; Palpatine app. 4.00

STAR WARS: UNDERWORLD - THE YAVIN VASSILIKA
Dark Horse Comics: Dec, 2000 - No. 5, June, 2001 ($2.99, limited series)

  1-5-(Photo and Robinson covers)   3.00

STAR WARS: UNION
Dark Horse Comics: Nov, 1999 - No. 4, Feb, 2000 ($2.95, limited series)

  1-4-Wedding of Luke and Mara Jade; Teranishi-a/Stackpole-s   4.00

STAR WARS: VADER DOWN
Marvel Comics: Jan, 2016 ($4.99, one-shot)

  1-Part 1 of x-over with Star Wars (2015) #13,14 and Darth Vader #13-15;
    Deodato-a   5.00

STAR WARS: VADER'S QUEST
Dark Horse Comics: Feb, 1999 - No. 4, May, 1999 ($2.95, limited series)

  1-4-Follows destruction of 1st Death Star; Gibbons-a   4.00

STAR WARS: VISIONARIES
Dark Horse Comics: Apr, 2005 ($17.95, TPB)

nn-Short stories from the concept artists for Revenge of the Sith movie   18.00

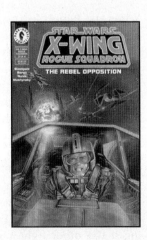

STAR WARS: X-WING ROGUE SQUADRON (Star Wars: X-Wing Rogue Squadron-The Phantom Affair #5-8 appears on cover only)
Dark Horse Comics: July, 1995 - No. 35, Nov, 1998 ($2.95)

  1/2   8.00
  1-24,26-35: 1-4-Baron scripts. 5-20-Stackpole scripts   4.00
  25-($3.95)   5.00
  The Phantom Affair TPB ($12.95) r/#5-8   13.00

STAR WARS: X-WING ROGUE SQUADRON: ROGUE LEADER
Dark Horse Comics: Sept, 2005 - No. 3, Nov, 2005 ($2.99)

  1-3-Takes place one week after the Batttle of Endor   3.00

SHIRA BRIE/LUMIYA: A STAR WARS TALE OF VENGEANCE

As seen in this panel from *Star Wars* #95 Lumiya became recognizable for her triangular headdress, cybernetics, and lightwhip.

She returned to the series in *Star Wars* #88 as Lumiya, Dark Lady of the Sith.

Star Wars reaches across several entertainment mediums to tell intriguing stories that unfold over decades. One such story – call it tragic, poetic, or just plain entertaining – was that of Shira Brie, a/k/a Lumiya. Shira's story began in *Star Wars* #56 (February 1982), she resurfaced as Lumiya in *Star Wars* #88 (October 1984), then in the 2000s she appeared in the *Legacy of the Force* book series.

Born on Imperial Center during Emperor Palpatine's reign, Shira Brie was a Force-sensitive human female who would become a Dark Lady of the Sith. Dedicating her life to the Imperial New Order doctrine, she caught Darth Vader's attention and he guided her through Imperial programs.

After she graduated from the Intelligence Academy of Carida, she was given a highly classified mission to infiltrate the Rebel Alliance and destroy Luke Skywalker, either by killing him or ruining his standing with the Rebels. She accomplished his disgrace during the Battle of the Secret Armada.

When the Rebels learned that the Imperial armada had a plan for advanced communication using Teezl (a non-sentient creature that could be a communications amplifier), they set forth a mission to attack. Luke, Shira, and two others used modified TIE Fighters to pose as returning Imperial pilots to attack the Star Destroyers and stop the Teezl. During the fight, an Imperial admiral used the Teezl to block communication, causing confusion between Imperial TIE Fighters and ones carrying Rebels. Luke finds the ship carrying the Teezl, but he sees a TIE Fighter in his line of sight. Unable to communicate because of the creature's interference, Luke uses the Force to guide him in determining if the other fighter is friend or foe. Deciding that the TIE carries an enemy, he fires at the fighter and moves on to destroy the Teezl. But upon returning to

Lumiya graced the cover of *Star Wars #96*.

the Prophets of the Dark Side cult, but suspecting his desire for power, she charged him with infiltrating the Imperial Ruling Council before he could betray her. She moved on to the planet Korriban where she could plot her next move and keep an eye on galactic events from a safe distance. Her powers grew through mastering the creation of empowered Force phantoms, which where lifelike apparitions that could be projected across the cosmos.

As she considered an invitation to join a new order of Sith on Korriban, Lumiya was almost captured by the Yuuzhan Vong as they invaded the galaxy, and the ensuing chaos solidified her belief that only a Dark Lord could create stability. She met Vergere, a Jedi turned Sith, and finally finished her training. Together they decided to pursue the creation of the next Sith Lord, targeting Jacen Solo, the grandson of Darth Vader.

Years after Vergere died, Lumiya began her plan to turn Jacen during the new conflict between the Galactic Federation of Free Alliances and Corellian systems' Five Worlds government. She orchestrated events to guide Jacen to her and then began his training. Lumiya revealed herself to the Jedi as a means of distracting them while Jacen grew to fully embrace the Dark Side and become Darth Caedus. With her mission and revenge complete, she died in combat against her lifelong nemesis Luke Skywalker.

base, Luke learns that the TIE was carrying Shira, who they know to be a Rebel. He is ostracized by fellow Rebels and put on trial.

Thought to be dead by the Rebels, Shira was found alive, but terribly disfigured. Once Vader recovered her, he rehabilitated her with cybernetic replacements akin to his. He trained her in the dark side of the Force and she took the identity of Lumiya, Dark Lady of the Sith. While Vader secretly trained her, she also worked as one of the Emperor's Hands, who were Force-trained assassins. While Lumiya was on a sojourn to the world of Ziost where she created her lightwhip, both Palpatine and Vader died in the battle of Endor. With her teachers gone, she became Mistress of the Sith, and was consumed with a need for vengeance against Luke and the Rebels.

During the Battle of Herdessa, she faced a significant loss that damaged her armor, which was replaced by the triangular headdress that, along with her lightwhip, would be her signature. While fighting alongside the Nagai during the Nagai-Tof War, she faced Luke again. Though she was defeated, Lumiya was able to escape custody, promising future revenge.

After the Nagai-Tof conflict, Lumiya retreated to the Outer Rim. Once again, she worked with Imperial Intelligence and took on former Royal Guardsman Carnor Jax as her apprentice. Together, the pair thwarted

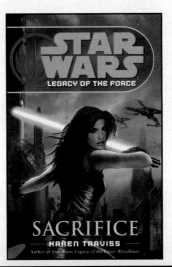

She resurfaced in the book series *Legacy of the Force* to manipulate and train Jacen Solo.

TALKING TOYS

WITH STAR WARS TOY SPECIALIST

JAMES GALLO

Like most kids, James Gallo enjoyed his toys. But, Gallo's appreciation extended into collecting, and by his mid-teens he was also a toy dealer. Now, Gallo is the owner and operator of Toy & Comic Heaven (www.thetoyheaven.com), a website specializing in toys and action figures for everything from Dungeons & Dragons *to* Thundercats.

Gallo is well versed in Star Wars *toys and the market, which he shared in this interview. He talked about his history as a collector/ dealer, discussed the current market, provided an overview of popular and rare figures, and touched on topics like grading, cleaning, and restoration.*

Toy & Comic Heaven
COMICS • VIDEO GAMES • TOYS

Overstreet: Let's start with some history. How long have you been a toy collector?

James Gallo (JG): All my life really. I was a kid of the 1980s and collected a ton of toys, I just never stopped.

Overstreet: When and how did you transition into being a toy dealer?

JG: I was setting up at shows at around 16 or so, small local comic shows with some friends and train shows with my dad.

Overstreet: Tell me about Toy & Comic Heaven.

JG: I sell comic books, toys, and collectibles from pretty much any era. I have spent some time as a baseball card dealer as well, so I do a bit of that as well. I specialize in 1980s toys, especially *Star Wars*. I have set up at just about every Star Wars Celebration worldwide except 3.

Overstreet: What's the current market like for vintage toys?

JG: It depends on the series. Some lines are very hot, like *Star Wars*, but others like *G.I. Joe* and *Transformers* are down a bit from the high levels of a few years ago. It can also vary from piece to piece. A really rare item from an otherwise soft line could go for a record price.

Overstreet: Getting into *Star Wars*, what are your favorite toys from the series?

JG: I specialize in the *Droids* and *Ewoks* animated lines from the tail-end of the original vintage run. These were all new figures from the animated shows that I just really love.

Overstreet: Do you think we'll see a market saturation point when prices dwindle or plateau?

JG: I do; not sure when that may happen but there have been some ebbs and flows on *Star Wars* 12-backs in recent years but overall, they have been pretty steady.

Overstreet: If you had to make a short list of the rarest of the rare U.S. *Star Wars* toys, what would be on it?

JG: For items issued in the U.S. the top action figures would be the double telescoping Ben, Vader, and Luke in that order. The vinyl cape Jawa is also a rarer piece that gets a lot of attention.

Overstreet: Are there particular *Star Wars* lines or types of toy collectibles that are the most popular?

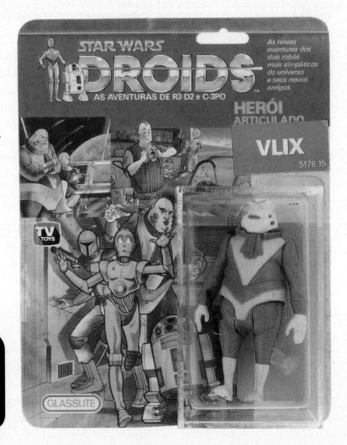

This Brazilian Vlix figure from the *Star Wars: Droids* TV series was made in 1988 by Glasslite. It was unproduced in the U.S., making it highly sought by collectors.

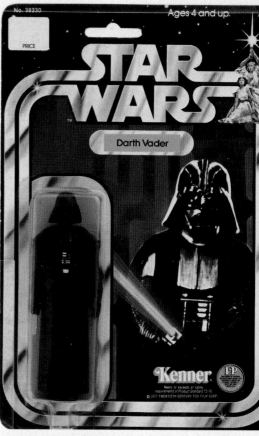

The double telescoping 12-back figures of Ben Kenobi, Darth Vader, and Luke Skywalker feature lightsabers with a second extendable piece that was not available on other toys.

JG: By far the action figures are the most popular items hands down. There are also a lot of poster collectors out there, but hands down the figures and related ships and playsets blow away anything else.

Overstreet: What sets *Star Wars* apart from other major vintage toy lines in regard to quantity, quality, and popularity?

JG: Well it has a lot of things going for it as it set a new standard in movie making and in toy production. It made the 3-3/4 scale the staple scale of action figures for 15-20 years and it has a huge following worldwide which can't be said for too many other lines. With the continuations of movies and TV shows I don't think there is anything that will compare to *Star Wars* except maybe Disney.

Overstreet: Some of the toys have different variations, Luke's hair color or light-saber size, for instance. How much do those variations effect price and can you give us insight on which ones have more notable differences in value?

JG: People really dive into the most minute differences in figures. Some figures were made over an eight-year period and in different countries, so there were a lot of both planned changes over time as well as some that were not planned. The original Han Solo figure was replaced and the "large" head was the only one available from *Empire Strikes Back* on. Luke's hair color was changed and updated on several figures over the years as was the color of his lightsaber. One of the most famous changes was the original double telescoping sabers for Luke, Ben, and Darth Vader. Their early sabers were two pieces where the inner piece extended out from the large piece. These broke with ease and were more costly to produce so they were

Ages 4 and up.

PRICE

STAR WARS

Luke Skywalker

Kenner

Meets or exceeds all safety
requirements of Product Standard 72-76
© 1977 TWENTIETH CENTURY FOX FILM CORP.

quickly changed to a one piece saber. These early sabers are some of the rarest and most expensive figures produced.

Overstreet: People are often surprised by the prices these toys achieve. Many hit the $100 mark and some are selling for over $50,000. Where do you see things going from here?

JG: It is really hard to say. There is a lot available for the more common figure so

getting into collecting doesn't have to be expensive. The five-figure sales are few and far between and are generally only for the super rare and expensive items or prototypes.

Overstreet: Most often collectibles from the early days get the highest prices. Are there any newer ones from the past 10 to 15 years that are hitting high values?

JG: There are some pieces that only had a

PRICE

Jawa

Kenner.

Meets or exceeds all safety
requirements of Product Standard 72-76
© 1977 TWENTIETH CENTURY FOX FILM CORP.

The vinyl cape Jawa is a rarity since production on the figure was pulled
shortly after release, and the cape was replaced with one made of cloth.

limited release in a certain store and over time they can increase in price. Ironically the vehicles from the last few years have done very well especially the Legacy AT-AT and Millennium Falcon which have become $300-500 pieces.

Overstreet: How big of a difference is the price between graded and ungraded toys?

JG: It really can vary from item to item and it is greatly based on the grade. An average grade might not make any difference at all but a super high grade could really boost the price a lot. A loose removable limbs C-3PO sells for about $15 ungraded and [one graded] 85 around $40, I sold a [graded] 95 for near $1,000 which is an extremely hard grade

The large head Han Solo action figure is one of the variations noted by collectors and dealers.

The removable limbs C-3PO 47-back figure comes from *The Empire Strikes Back* line.

to obtain and resulted in the super large price difference.

Overstreet: Would you say the average toy collector wants graded or ungraded toys?

JG: I think more ungraded, but it depends on why they are collecting. There are collectors of every variety so it can vary from toy line to toy line and even vary between loose and packaged.

Overstreet: In most collecting hobbies restoration produces polarizing opinions. What's the consensus among toy collectors?

JG: It hasn't been too much of an issue as there aren't a lot of items that would be worth restoring. At this point minor restoration like color touch up on a carded figure is the most common thing you would see. I think it is clearly something people do not want.

Overstreet: What tips would you give to collectors on cleaning toys?

JG: Don't go overboard – a lot can be done with warm water and dish soap. I would stay away from anything abrasive and if you're unsure, ask around. There are tons of good resources on the internet these days.

Overstreet: How about tips for storing them safely?

JG: Much like everything else: cool, dark, and dry in plastic bags or cases. Keep them away from direct light.

Overstreet: If someone is just now getting into collecting *Star Wars* toys how would you suggest they approach it?

JG: Figure out what you like and go from there. Everyone collects differently and that is great, as it makes each collection unique. Stay within your means as even though it's a ton of fun to collect toys it should not overtake your life.

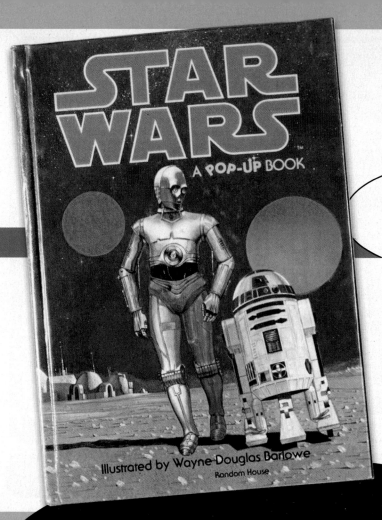

The first pop-up, *Star Wars A Pop-Up Book* sells for $5 to $100, depending on condition.

Star Wars Pop-Up Books:
Literature in Motion

The combination of imagination, adventure, foreign creatures, light spectacles, and fairy tale aspects guarantees that *Star Wars* will always find an audience with kids. Catering to those younger viewers, the series has provided additional entertainment in the form of books, comics, and TV shows. Some of the popular kid-focused additions to the series have been the pop-up books.

Pop-ups are three-dimensional books that combine story and color illustrations with movable pages that rise when opened. They are also known as movable books, tunnel books, pop-outs, transformations, and pull-downs. They can be likened to origami in the 3D aspects of the paper construction, though origami uses folding rather than the cut and glued card stock of pop-ups. In the case of *Star Wars*, children get to enjoy seeing their favorite characters, ships, and creatures physically jump out of the pages.

What's surprising is that pop-up books have been around for over 700 years and for the majority of that time, they weren't made for children. Initially, pop-up books were created by artists, book designers, and scientists to explore new ways to create litera-

A POP-UP BOOK

STAR WARS
RETURN OF THE JEDI

RANDOM HOUSE

The *Return of the Jedi A Pop-Up Book* averages $5 to $55.

ture and utilize its abilities for educational purposes. Often, they'd contain a revolving disc that could be used to teach astronomy, anatomy, even carry a secret code. Pop-up books weren't made for entertainment until the late 18th century and in the 1930s they started becoming more prominent for kids.

The *Star Wars* pop-up books started being published after the first movie, followed by a wave of them in the early 1980s, a resurgence in the mid-1990s, and an additional few in more recent years. Covering a variety of topics, the pop-up books provided film adaptations, specific stories, and subject features. Now, they can be found for as little as a few dollars, many sit comfortably in the $20 to $40 range, and some can command even higher prices – depending on condition, age, and significance.

The values below reflect the typical low to high prices achieved for the individual pop-up books. Lower values are typically due to Poor condition which can include stains, ripped or destroyed pop-up sections, even missing pages. Higher values are achieved for books in Near Mint to Mint condition with very few flaws.

Star Wars A Pop-Up Book
1978; Random House
Illustrated by Wayne Douglas Barlowe
$5 to $100

The Empire Strikes Back A Pop-Up Book
1980; Random House
Illustrated by Patricia Wynne
$5 to $50

Return of the Jedi A Pop-Up Book
1983; Random House
Illustrated by John Gampert
$5 to $55

Return of the Jedi: The Ewoks Save the Day
1983; Random House
By Kay Carroll, illustrated by James Woodend
$5 to $45

Return of the Jedi: Han Solo's Rescue
1983; Random House
By Kay Carrol, illustrated by Bryant Eastman
$10 to $25

The Mos Eisley Cantina Pop-Up Book
1995; Little Brown & Co.
By Kevin J. Anderson, Rebecca Moesta, and Lynette Ruschak, art by Ralph McQuarrie
$5 to $40

Battle of the Bounty Hunters
1996; Dark Horse Comics
By Ryder Windham, penciled by Christopher Moeller, inked by P. Craig Russell
$5 to $30

The Galactic Empire: Ships of the Fleet
1996; Little Brown & Co.
By Bill Smith, art by Barbara L. Gibson, Troy Vigil, and Ralph McQuarrie
$5 to $40

Jabba's Palace Pop-Up Book
1996; Little Brown & Co.
By Kevin J. Anderson and Rebecca Moesta, illustrated by Ralph McQuarrie
$5 to $40

The Rebel Alliance: Ships of the Fleet
1996; Little Brown & Company
By Bill Smith, art by Barbara L. Gibson and Troy Vigil
$5 to $40

The Death Star
1997; Little Brown & Co.
By John Whitman, art by Barbara Gibson
$3 to $15

Heroes in Hiding: A Super Pop-Up Book
1997; Fun Works
By Ken Steacy
$5 to $20

The Millennium Falcon
1997; Little Brown & Co.
By John Whitman, art by Barbara Gibson
$3 to $15

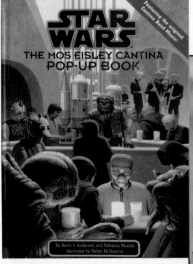

Based on the "hive of scum and villainy," *The Mos Eisley Cantina Pop-Up Book* sells for $5 to $40.

Tie Fighter: A Pocket Manual
1998; Running Press
By David West Reynolds
$2 to $20

X-Wing: A Pocket Manual
1998; Running Press
By David West Reynolds
$2 to $20

Star Wars: A Pop-Up Guide to the Galaxy
2007; Orchard Books/Scholastic Inc.
By Matthew Reinhart
$5 to $40
Limited edition: $60 to $150

The Clone Wars: Heroes – A Pop-Up Storybook
2009; Grosset & Dunlap
By Rob Valois
$3 to $20

The Clone Wars: Villains – A Pop-Up Storybook
2010; Grosset & Dunlap
by Rob Valois
$3 to $20

Star Wars: A Galactic Pop-Up Adventure
2012; Orchard Books
By Matthew Reinhart
$10 to $40

The Force Awakens Flashlight Adventure Book
2015; Phoenix International Publications, Inc.
By Erin Rose Wage
$5 to $30

Notorious gangster Jabba the Hutt is the star of *Jabba's Palace Pop-Up Book*, which also averages $5 to $40.

The limited edition version of *Star Wars: A Pop-Up Guide to the Galaxy* reaches $60 to $150.

TAKING CONTROL OF THE STORY

STAR WARS IN VIDEO GAMES

BY CARRIE WOOD

As one of the largest multimedia franchises in the world, *Star Wars* has been a popular title for video game production. With games spanning genres from shooters to role-playing games and dating back to some of the earliest years of mass-market video game availability, the history of *Star Wars* games is richer than some might expect.

THE ORIGINAL TRILOGY

Though all three films in the original trilogy would see plenty of games each, it was *Empire* that saw the first licensed video game in the form of 1982's *Star Wars: The Empire Strikes Back* for the Atari 2600. Developed and published by Parker Brothers, the game made use of the limited hardware capabilities of the time in order to render a version of the Battle of Hoth. The goal of the game was to hold off AT-AT Walkers as they advanced on the Rebel base. The difficulty of the game eventually ramps up,

FOR ATARI & SEARS' VIDEO GAME SYSTEMS

with the Walkers becoming faster in their approach; the game ends when either the player is out of lives, or the AT-AT reaches the base.

Worth noting is that, while *Star Wars: The Empire Strikes Back* was the first licensed *Star Wars* game, it wasn't the first *Star Wars* game ever produced. An unlicensed game was made and released for the Apple II computer in 1978, in which players are tasked with taking out TIE Fighters.

In 1983 the first game based on *A New Hope* released, with the arcade cabinet simply titled *Star Wars*. This game featured colorful vector graphics and, with regards to the cabinets themselves, was available in both standing and sit-down versions (though the game itself was the same). Players took control of Luke Skywalker as he piloted his X-Wing, and had to fight off Darth Vader and complete the Death Star trench run. This *Star Wars* game was ported to a number of home consoles after its release, with Parker Brothers handling many of these home versions.

Parker Brothers had another home console release with the 1983 release of *Return of the Jedi: Death Star Battle* for the Atari 2600. In accordance with the title, players took on the second Death Star, destroying its reactor and then escaping from the explosion. Notable to this particular game is how the box art was done by artist John Berkey, who had previously done some of the key artwork used in *Star Wars* movie posters. The artwork for the game shows the Millennium Falcon being pursued by a number of TIE interceptors, with the second Death Star looming in the background. Accordingly, the game with its box is valued as a collectible, with some editions of the game running for $75 or more if it's complete in box.

Due to the video game industry crash in 1983, there weren't many new *Star Wars* games released for a few years, with the one major exception being the 1985 *Star Wars: The Empire Strikes Back* arcade cabinet. Much like the first arcade title, this one featured vector graphics, though rather than taking down the Death Star, players instead fought against AT-AT Walkers and piloted the Millennium Falcon through a dangerous asteroid field. This title, too, would be ported a number of times to home consoles.

The *Return of the Jedi* arcade title, released in 1984 and developed by Atari, was the only one of the three of its era to not feature the vector graphics, instead taking a full-color, top-down approach to the presentation. Rather than a first-person view,

the game takes place in a 3/4 isometric perspective, and players control a variety of different vehicles, including speeder bikes and the Millennium Falcon.

With platformers becoming wildly popular in the late 1980s and early 1990s, *Star Wars* games too shifted into that genre, and the first such example to hit American consoles was 1991's *Star Wars*, developed by Beam Software. Following *A New Hope*, players controlled Luke Skywalker across a variety of different levels, eventually piloting the Millennium Falcon and taking on the Death Star. However, that wasn't the first *Star Wars* platformer to be released – an earlier example was 1987's *Star Wars* game for the Famicom console. Developed and published by Namco, this *Star Wars* was released exclusively in Japan and is a real weird title, memorable for its off-color graphics (Luke sported black hair) and its various deviations from the source material

(with Darth Vader having numerous shape-shifting apprentices, among other oddities). Several other platformers would be released into the early 1990s, with the most popular being the *Super Star Wars* trilogy of games for the Super Nintendo.

Overall, original trilogy titles are pretty easy to find and are generally affordable, due in large part to the fact that, thanks to the popularity of the franchise, *Star Wars* games saw massive print runs. Collectors will really only start to see prices get jacked up when they start seeking out new/shrinkwrapped copies of these games (which will see prices of more than $100) or if they want to add arcade cabinets into the mix (which will often run several thousands of dollars).

LucasArts

George Lucas had wanted to explore various other types of media and entertainment essentially from the get-go, and in 1979 the Lucasfilm Computer Division – which contained the Lucasfilm Games Group – was founded. The Games Group received funding from Atari, but was unable to develop or produce any *Star Wars* games on their own at the time, as Atari held the license rights for video games for the franchise. Instead, the company developed original titles (such as *Maniac Mansion* and *The Secret of Monkey Island*) and games based on some other popular Lucasfilm properties (like *Labyrinth* and *Indiana Jones and the Last Crusade*).

After getting the *Star Wars* license back in-house, LucasArts went to work on their first title, which was the space combat/flight simulator *X-Wing*. With a story that takes place around the same time as *A New Hope* and cutting-edge graphics, the game proved to be wildly popular. It received multiple sequels and went on to become a bestseller for the company.

LucasArts would go on to produce a plethora of video games based directly on the films throughout the '90s and well into the new millen-

nium, though many critics felt that these games began to suffer in quality fairly quickly. Most of the games based on *The Phantom Menace, Attack of the Clones* and *Revenge of the Sith* were not received well by the gaming press, and most didn't sell particularly well, either. The exception to this was *Star Wars Episode I: Racer*, which turned the podracing seen in *Episode I* into a high-octane, fast-paced racing title for both home consoles and, later, for arcades. The arcade cabinets especially proved to be popular, with players being able to sit in a replica podracer cockpit, with the ability to power and steer the machine with twin throttle controls.

While the film-to-game direct adaptations may have largely been unpopular, LucasArts succeeded in the gaming realm with their various Expanded Universe titles.

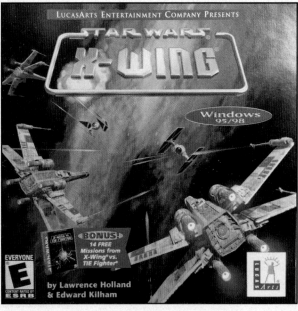

The aforementioned *X-Wing* was the first of these games, eventually seeing sequels, compilations, and upgraded ports to newer systems. *Star Wars: Rebel Assault*, released in 1993, came next; an on-rails shooter, it was notable for being one of the earliest video games to make extensive use of full-motion video. While not the biggest critical success, it was a commercial hit, and saw one sequel.

The release of *Star Wars: Dark Forces* also turned into somewhat of a benchmark for LucasArts and their *Star Wars* games. Released in 1995, the game mixed adventure gameplay with puzzles and first-person shooting and was the inaugural game in what would become the *Jedi Knight* series. It introduced the character of Kyle Katarn, who appeared in the sequel games as well as in a number of different *Star Wars* novels and in audio dramas.

Star Wars: Shadows of the Empire debuted for the Nintendo 64 in 1996, and tied into the larger multimedia project of the same name. Taking control of mercenary Dash Rendar, players fought through multiple missions in order to help save Luke and Leia. The game was mostly positively received and was a best-seller for the system. It followed roughly the same plot as outlined by the novel and comics that were created for this project, and Dash eventually saw a Kenner action figure in his likeness.

LucasArts would collaborate with a number of companies to handle development of different kinds of *Star Wars* games (with LucasArts simply acting as publisher),

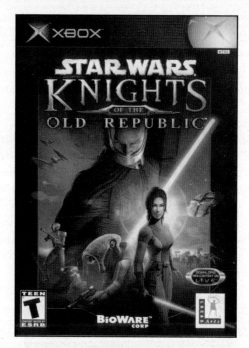

which resulted in the franchise covering a wide number of gaming genres throughout this period. One of the most significant collaborations was with BioWare, who developed the role-playing behemoth that was *Knights of the Old Republic*.

Released in 2003, *Star Wars: Knights of the Old Republic* told the story of the universe some 4,000 years before the founding of the Galactic Empire. LucasArts had actually floated the idea of doing an RPG set during the Clone Wars, but the developers instead chose to develop a game set thousands of years before any of the films in order to have the creative freedom to tell the story they wanted. The player controlled their customizable character in a bid to take down the villainous Darth Malak, a former Jedi and now a Sith Lord, who has taken a highly aggressive stance against the Republic. *KOTOR* allowed the player to go down either the Light or Dark path of the Force, with their decisions made in game ultimately impacting how the story ended. The game saw a sequel in 2005, called *The Sith Lords*, with development having been handled by Obsidian Entertainment. Both games received massive critical acclaim for their storytelling, and both picked up numerous awards. Fortunately, due to large print runs, both games are also fairly easy and inexpensive to find even today.

NEW SERIES, NEW PUBLISHERS, AND NEW CANON

While *Knights of the Old Republic* was hailed for its role-playing abilities and interesting storytelling, another sub-series of *Star Wars* games cropped up around the same time that saw just as much praise for wildly different reasons – *Star Wars: Battlefront*. Developed by Pandemic Studios, the shooter was a popular choice due to its online multiplayer as much as it was for its story mode. The game allowed players to fight for the opposing factions from both the original and prequel trilogies; it saw one direct sequel as well as multiple handheld spinoffs.

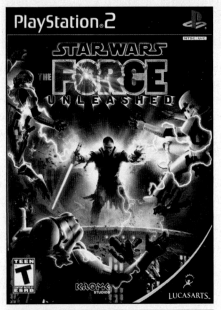

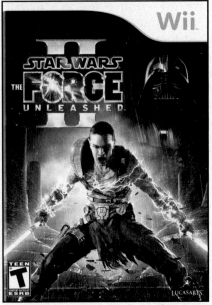

The Force Unleashed, first released in 2008, expanded upon the lore at the time with the introduction of the Starkiller character – powerful with the Force in numerous ways, he was Vader's secret apprentice. The story of Starkiller was continued with *The Force Unleashed II* in 2010. Both games were praised for their action-adventure gameplay as much as they were for their storytelling, and the original game sold more than 7 million copies worldwide.

When Lucasfilm was acquired by the Walt Disney Company in 2012, it marked some significant changes for the video games as well, particularly with what was canon and what wasn't. Basically every game that had been released previously, even if it had been canon before, was now considered non-canonical and was now a part of the *Star Wars* Legends set. In April 2013, LucasArts announced that they would cease to operate as a video game developer and publisher, and shortly thereafter, Electronic Arts was granted the license to produce *Star Wars* video games.

EA went on to reboot the *Battlefront* series, beginning with *Star Wars Battlefront* for the PlayStation 4, Xbox One and Windows PC in 2015. A sequel arrived in 2017. While both games have been somewhat praised for the actual gameplay, both have also seen heavy criticism – the first for its rushed development resulting in the lack of a single-player mode, and the second for the questionable use of microtransactions and their impact on the online multiplayer mode. EA has also announced a new title, *Star Wars Jedi: Fallen Order*, which will be developed by Respawn Entertainment and is expected to feature a story set between *Revenge of the Sith* and *A New Hope*.

A number of mobile titles for phones and other devices have also been published by EA in the years since they've had the license, including *Star Wars: Commander, Star Wars: Galaxy of Heroes, Star Wars: Uprising*, and the *Journeys* series, among others.

However, lackluster sales from the EA-published titles have led to some indus-

try rumors pointing to the potentiality of LucasArts granting video game rights to *Star Wars* to another company in the near future.

SPINOFFS AND CAMEOS

While many games in the *Star Wars* franchise would eventually be spun off and out of the main canon with the sale to Disney, some were created as spinoffs from the start. The most notable of these so far has been the *Lego Star Wars* games, which began with *Lego Star Wars: The Video Game* in 2005. Like many other *Lego* video games, these take a quirky, whimsical approach to the *Star Wars* canon by placing the stories in the brick-based world of Lego toys. All of them tell the stories of the films and allow players to control any of a wide variety of characters, most of whom have some sort of unique ability to them. They've proven to be hugely popular and commercially successful, as both Legos and *Star Wars* are popular on their own – and the games have been a family-friendly alternative to a number of the other more "hardcore" games in the *Star Wars* lineup.

Two titles were released in the *Angry Birds Star Wars* crossover, which began on mobile platforms and was eventually ported to other home and handheld consoles. The wacky crossover had the titular birds taking on the likenesses of *Star Wars* characters, complete with themed powers and abilities like lightsabers and Force movement.

The massive toys-to-life crossover of *Disney Infinity* also featured plenty of *Star Wars* characters with the third and final install-ment, *Disney Infinity 3.0*. The game featured storylines based on all three eras of films: "Twilight of the Republic" (prequel trilogy), "Rise Against the Empire" (origi-nal trilogy), and "The Force Awakens" (based on the film of the same name). As a toys-to-life game, the inclusion of *Star Wars* characters into *Disney Infinity* meant that toys were produced based on the characters. Most of these figures can still be found for $5-$10 or so, even new in box and despite the fact that they have been discontinued.

Star Wars characters have also made small-er appearances in other games. Darth Maul and Jango Fett were both unlock-able, playable characters in *Tony Hawk's Pro Skater 3* and *4*, respectively. Multiple characters were also unlockable characters in *Soulcalibur IV* in 2008: Darth Vader was exclusive for the PS3, Yoda was exclusive for the Xbox 360, and Starkiller could be unlocked in both versions. The two exclu-sive characters were later made available as purchasable downloadable content in the versions in which they did not originally appear. However, likely due to the licens-ing agreement with EA, this DLC was made unavailable as of 2016.

Thanks to the mass-market availability of video games, including *Star Wars* video games into a franchise-focused collection is a remarkably affordable way to expand that collection. Be sure to read on for a full list of pricing information and other tidbits about every *Star Wars* game worth talking about (and then some).

STAR WARS VIDEO GAME PRICES

Star Wars video games have been on the market for about as long as video games themselves have been available. The following game list contains pricing information based on an aggregated average sales price deviated from online auction results as of this book's publication, and is not meant to be a definitive buying or selling price. This list should instead serve as a starting point for your collecting purposes.

All entries on this list adhere to the following format:
Title
Year released; Game developer
System game released for
Game info: Other relevant information about this title

If a version of a game for a specific console or consoles runs significantly higher or lower than another, that version's pricing is singled out. Otherwise, pricing information should be considered to apply to any and all systems noted.

Most entries on this list contain prices for "Loose," "CIB," and "New" games. These terms are defined as follows:
<u>Loose:</u> Just the cartridge, no box.
<u>CIB:</u> Complete in box, with any additional materials that would have come in the box (such as the instruction manual or adverts).
<u>New:</u> Still has the shrink wrap or other seal present on the box; has not been taken out of the box or played.

This list covers major entries across all systems throughout the history of *Star Wars* video games. It does not include prices for games where a character only made a cameo appearance, and it does not cover browser-based or mobile titles.

Episode IV: A New Hope **Games**
Star Wars

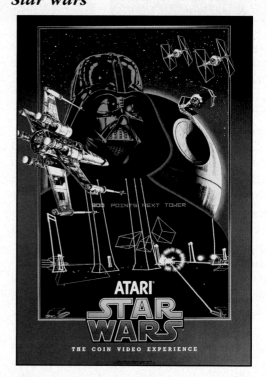

1983; Atari, Inc.
Arcade; later released for Atari 2600, Atari 5200, Atari 8-bit, Atari ST, ColecoVision, Commodore 64, BBC Micro, ZX Spectrum, Amstrad CPC, Apple II, DOS, Macintosh, and Amiga, through 1988.
Game info: Players control Luke Skywalker as he pilots his X-Wing from a first-person perspective. The arcade edition had both standing and sit-down cabinets available and was one of the top-selling games of the era. Parker Brothers handled the home system ports; Atari ST and Amiga versions are considered to be closest to the arcade experience.
Loose: $25
CIB: $60
New: $150
Arcade cabinet: $1,500+

Star Wars

1987; Namco
Famicom
Game Info: This is a side-scrolling platformer released exclusively in Japan. Luke
appears with black hair here due to technical limitations on the system. Other deviations from the source material include
multiple levels based on scenes from
Empire and *Return* despite the game being
focused on the first film, and the inclusion
of shape-shifting Vader apprentices.
Loose: $15
CIB: $40
New: $120

Star Wars: Attack on the Death Star

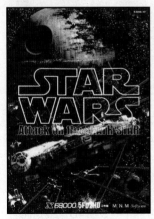

1991; M.N.M. Software
PC-98, Sharp X68000
Game Info: A different port of the 1983
arcade title released exclusively for
Japanese computers. Like many oddball
PC titles released only in Japan, it can be
hard to come by in the U.S.
Price: $30-$70

Star Wars

1991; Beam Software
Nintendo Entertainment System; later
released for Game Boy, Game Gear, and
Master System through 1993.
Game Info: Largely based on the first
film, though Boba Fett appears as an
enemy. Darth Vader's only appearance in
the game is on the "Game Over" screen.
A "hint book" could be purchased exclu-
sively via mail order.
NES edition:
Loose: $15
CIB: $45
New: $175
Game Boy edition:
Loose: $5
CIB: $15
New: $45
Game Gear/Master System edition:
Loose: $10
CIB: $25
New: $40

Super Star Wars

1992; Sculptured Software/LucasArts
Super NES
Game Info: Essentially an upgraded
version of the 1991 NES title; players
mostly control Luke but can play as Han
or Chewie in later levels. A PC port of
this game was in the works, but eventually was canceled despite being near
completion.
Loose: $10
CIB: $25
New: $70

Star Wars Arcade

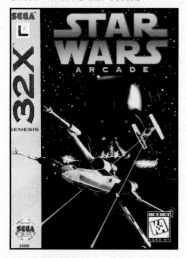

1993; Sega
Arcade cabinet; ported to the Sega 32X in
1994
Game info: Similar to the first *Star Wars*
arcade title, players control a fighter (either
an X or Y-wing) in a battle against imperial
forces, culminating in a run on the Death
Star. The arcade cabinet allowed two people to play cooperatively, with one person
piloting and the other acting as the gunner.
32X edition:
Loose: $5
CIB: $20
New: $45

Episode V: The Empire Strikes Back Games
Star Wars: The Empire Strikes Back

1982; Parker Brothers
Atari 2600; ported to Intellivision in 1983
Game Info: This was the first licensed
Star Wars video game released. Players

controlled Luke, who pilots a snowspeeder
as he took on AT-AT Walkers on Hoth.

Atari 2600 edition:
Loose: $5
CIB: $15
New: $50
Intellivision edition:
Loose: $10
CIB: $25
New: $70

Star Wars: The Empire Strikes Back

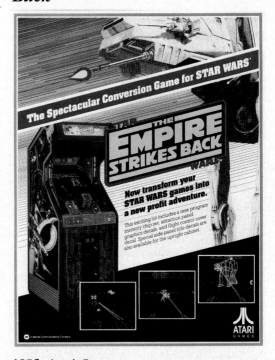

1985; Atari Games
Arcade; later ported to Amstrad CPC, ZX
Spectrum, Atari ST, Commodore 64, and

Amiga
Game Info: Featured similar vector graphics to the first arcade release, but focused on flying around Hoth to take down AT-AT Walkers.
Loose: $10
CIB: $25
New: $50

Star Wars: The Empire Strikes Back

1992; Lucasfilm Games/Sculptured Software
NES; ported to the Game Boy by Ubisoft in 1993
Game Info: While most other *Empire* games are focused solely on Hoth, this instead is an action-adventure title with Luke finishing the Battle of Hoth, going on to meet Yoda and train his Force powers, and rescuing his friends from Cloud City.
NES Edition:
Loose: $20
CIB: $40
New: $200
Game Boy Edition:
Loose: $10
CIB: $25
New: $75

Super Star Wars: The Empire Strikes Back

1993; LucasArts/Sculptured Software
SNES
Game Info: Like the first *Super Star Wars*, this is basically an enhanced port of the NES title. In 1992, a magazine contest was held with the Grand Prize being put into the game. The winner's likeness appears in the "Ice Fields of Hoth" cutscene.
Loose: $10
CIB: $25
New: $50

Episode VI: Return of the Jedi Games

Star Wars: Return of the Jedi – Death Star Battle

1983; Parker Brothers
Atari 2600; ported to the Atari 5200, Atari 8-Bit, and ZX Spectrum through 1984
Game Info: The cover art was done by John Berkey, who produced much of the

original artwork for the film posters. The art for this game was the last bit of *Star Wars* artwork he was officially commissioned to produce.

Atari 2600 edition:
Loose: $15
CIB: $30
New: $70

All other editions:
Loose: $40
CIB: $75
New: $150

Star Wars: Return of the Jedi

1984; Atari, Inc.
Arcade; ported to Amstrad CPC, ZX Spectrum, Atari ST, Commodore 64 and Amiga by Domark in 1988
Game Info: Players control various vehicles from the film in order to complete the story, including a speeder bike, an AT-ST, and the Millennium Falcon itself.
Loose: $10
CIB: $25
New: $50

Super Star Wars: Return of the Jedi

1994; Sculptured Software
SNES; ported to the Game Gear and Game Boy by Realtime Associates in 1995
Game Info: In addition to the run-and-gun 2D platforming gameplay, this game also featured Mode 7 psuedo-3D vehicle levels. The handheld versions are both simplified from the SNES original.

SNES/Game Boy editions:
Loose: $15
CIB: $30
New: $80

Game Gear edition:
Loose: $15
CIB: $25
New: $50

Episode I: The Phantom Menace Games

Star Wars: Episode I – The Phantom Menace

1999; LucasArts
Windows PC, PlayStation
Game Info: This action-adventure title allowed players to control Obi-Wan, Qui-Gon, Amidala, or Captain Panaka.
Loose: $5
CIB: $10
New: $15

Star Wars Episode I: Jedi Power Battles

2000; LucasArts

PlayStation, Dreamcast; ported to the Game Boy Advance in 2001

Game Info: Players could control Obi-Wan, Qui-Gon, Mace Windu, Adi Gallia or Plo Koon. The game was praised for its inclusion of a cooperative two-player mode, but criticized for its high difficulty level.

Dreamcast edition:

Loose: $15

CIB: $20

New: $50

PlayStation edition:

Loose: $5

CIB: $10

New: $45

Game Boy Advance edition:

Loose: $5

CIB: $15

New: $25

Star Wars Episode I: Battle for Naboo

2000; Factor 5/LucasArts

Nintendo 64; ported to Windows PC in 2001

Game Info: The game's main character is Gavyn Sykes, a Naboo lieutenant who appears only briefly in the film.

Loose: $10

CIB: $25

New: $60

Star Wars Episode I: Obi-Wan's Adventures

2000; HotGen

Game Boy Color

Game Info: The game told the story of *Episode I* from Obi-Wan's perspective, and while it received mixed reviews it was praised highly for its sound design.

Loose: $10

CIB: $25

New: $35

Star Wars: Obi-Wan

2001; LucasArts

Xbox

Game Info: Much like the GBC game, this tells the story of *Episode I* from Obi-Wan's point of view. This game includes a multiplayer mode, called Jedi Battle, with two players facing off.

Loose: $5

CIB: $10

New: $30

Star Wars Episode I: Racer

1999; LucasArts
Windows PC, Nintendo 64, Game Boy
Color, Macintosh; ported to Dreamcast in
2000
Game Info: The game focuses on the
podracing aspect of the film, with all of
the racers in the film appearing. Jake Lloyd
and Lewis MacLeod reprise their roles
from the film here. *Racer* is one of the top-
selling racing titles of all time, having sold
more than 3 million copies worldwide.
Nintendo 64 edition:
Loose: $5
CIB: $20
New: $50
Dreamcast edition:
Loose: $20
CIB: $40
New: $60
GBC edition:
Loose: $5
CIB: $15
New: $30

Star Wars: Racer Arcade

2000; Sega-AM5
Arcade cabinet
Game Info: A souped-up version of the
1999 console game made for arcades, this
edition allowed players to essentially sit in
a cockpit of a podracer and steer it using
two throttle controls for an immersive
experience.
Arcade cabinet: $2,500+ for a complete
cab, and individual components can often
cost $150 or more.

Star Wars: Racer Revenge

2002; Rainbow Studios
PlayStation 2
Game Info: The sequel to the 1999 *Racer*
game, the story of this game takes place
eight years after the events of *Episode I*,
with Sebulba seeking revenge on Anakin.
Loose: $5
CIB: $10
New: $30

Episode II: Attack of the Clones Games

Star Wars: The Clone Wars

2002; Pandemic Studios
GameCube, PlayStation 2; Released for
Xbox in 2003
Game Info: Players switch between
piloting one of various vehicles (such as
AT-ATs, AT-XTs, or gunships), and fighting
on-foot as either Anakin or Mace Windu.
Loose: $5
CIB: $10
New: $30

Star Wars: Episode II – Attack of the Clones

2002; THQ
Game Boy Advance
Game Info: A fairly simple action game based on scenes from the movie, with the ability to play as either Obi-Wan, Anakin, or Mace Windu.
Loose: $5
CIB: $10
New: $20

Star Wars: The New Droid Army

2002; THQ
Game Boy Advance
Game Info: The plot follows Anakin throughout many of the events of *Episode II*, though interestingly it also provided an alternate non-canonical storyline for *Revenge of the Sith* in which Anakin defeats Dooku and becomes a Jedi hero, rather than falling to the Dark Side.
Loose: $5
CIB: $10
New: $20

Episode III: Revenge of the Sith Games

Star Wars: Episode III – Revenge of the Sith

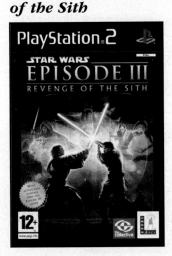

2005; LucasArts (GBA/DS versions handled by Ubisoft)
PlayStation 2, Xbox, Game Boy Advance, Nintendo DS
Game Info: Players controlled Anakin or Obi-Wan throughout various levels that recreated the story of the film; the handheld editions play as a side-scrolling beat-em-up rather than a 3D action game.
Loose: $5
CIB: $10
New: $20

Star Wars: The Clone Wars Games

Star Wars: The Clone Wars - Lightsaber Duels

2008; Krome Studios
Wii
Game Info: This fighting game made use of the Wii remote's motion controls in order to simulate actual lightsaber combat, with the Nunchuk accessory being used to mimic Force powers.
Loose: $5
CIB: $10
New: $15

Star Wars: The Clone Wars - Jedi Alliance

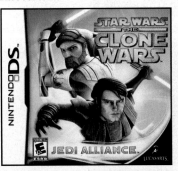

2008; LucasArts
Nintendo DS
Game Info: An adventure game based on the animated series, *Jedi Alliance* follows Obi-Wan and Anakin as they attempt to recover stolen cargo. The game used the DS touch screen for lightsaber combat.
Loose: $5
CIB: $10
New: $15

Star Wars: The Clone Wars – Republic Heroes

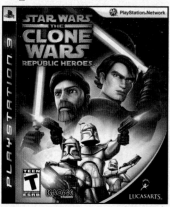

2009; Krome Studios/LucasArts
Windows, Xbox 360, PlayStation 3, Wii, PlayStation Portable, PlayStation 2, Nintendo DS
Game Info: This action-adventure game contains 40 missions and takes place between the first and second seasons of the television series.
Loose: $5
CIB: $10
New: $25

Clone Wars Adventures

2010; Sony Online Entertainment
Windows, OS X
Game Info: This was a massively multi-player online virtual world based on the *Clone Wars* animated series. It permanently shut down in 2014.

X-Wing Series
X-Wing

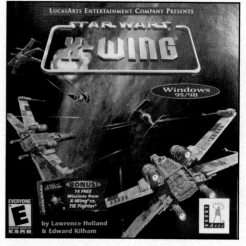

1993; LucasArts
DOS, Windows PC, Macintosh, Linux
Game Info: This flight simulator put players in control of the titular ship as they fought in battles during and immediately preceding the events of *A New Hope*.
The game was a huge hit, winning several awards. It had two expansion packs, *Imperial Pursuit* and *B-Wing*, which continued the storyline.
Loose: $5
CIB: $15
New: $60

TIE Fighter

1994; Totally Games
DOS, Windows PC, Macintosh, Linux
Game Info: Players pilot a TIE fighter
for the Empire, working under Admiral
Thrawn as they try to stop an Imperial
traitor. It too was a huge success, and is
largely considered one of the best flight
simulation games ever made. It saw mul-
tiple expansions, including *Defender of the
Empire* and *Enemies of the Empire*.
Loose: $5
CIB: $15
New: $75

Star Wars: X-Wing vs. TIE Fighter

1997; Totally Games
Windows PC
Game Info: The original release of this
game was multiplayer-focused, with
options for free-for-all or team-based combat, as well as cooperative play. It lacked a
story mode until the release of the *Balance
of Power* expansion, which added one.
Loose: $10
CIB: $25
New: $150

X-Wing Alliance

1999; Totally Games
Windows PC
Game Info: The story focuses on the
Azzameen family, a clan of merchants who
also get into the business of smuggling

items for the Alliance. Ace must defend
his family as well as fight for the Rebellion
over the course of the game.

Loose: $5
CIB: $10
New: $20

Rebel Assault Games
Star Wars: Rebel Assault

1993; LucasArts
DOS, Macintosh, Sega CD, 3DO
Game Info: This was an on-rails shooter
game in which the player controls "Rookie
One" over the course of several missions

based on the original trilogy. The game was one of the earliest to make use of extensive full-motion video sequences on the PC.

Sega CD edition:
Loose: $15
CIB: $20
New: $50
3DO edition:
Loose: $15
CIB: $40
New: $80

Rebel Assault II: The Hidden Empire

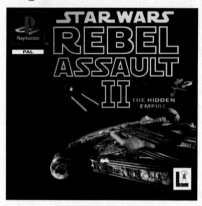

1995; LucasArts
Windows PC, Mac OS, PlayStation
Game Info: This game was notable for being the first piece of media to use new live-action actors and footage within the *Star Wars* franchise since *Return of the Jedi.*
Loose: $5
CIB: $10
New: $30

Jedi Knight series
Star Wars: Dark Forces

1995; LucasArts
MS-DOS, Macintosh; released for PlayStation in 1996
Game Info: The game follows Kyle Katarn, a mercenary who uncovers the Empire's "Dark Trooper Project" which could see the creation of wildly powerful new battle droids.
Loose: $5
CIB: $10
New: $25

Star Wars Jedi Knight: Dark Forces II

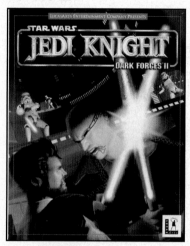

1997; LucasArts
Windows PC
Game Info: This continued the story of Kyle Katarn, who seeks to avenge his father's death. The game introduced multiplayer, and received an expansion in 1998, *Mysteries of the Sith.*
Loose: $5
CIB: $20
New: $60

Star Wars Jedi Knight II: Jedi Outcast

2002; Raven Software/Vicarious Visions
Windows, OS X, GameCube, Xbox
Game Info: Kyle returns for another adventure, this time being joined by Lando Calrissian, Luke Skywalker, and Jan Ors. The story takes place about eight years after *Return of the Jedi*.
GameCube edition:
Loose: $15
CIB: $20
New: $80
Xbox edition:
Loose: $10
CIB: $15
New: $40

Star Wars Jedi Knight: Jedi Academy

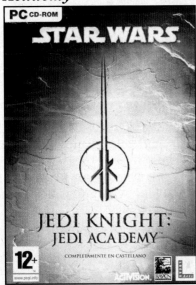

2003; Raven Software
Windows, OS X, Xbox
Game Info: New protagonist Jaden Korr takes over the primary role here, as the student of Kyle at the Jedi Academy. While fulfilling missions for Kyle, Jaden must investigate what happened to his fellow student, Rosh.
Loose: $15
CIB: $25
New: $60

Rogue Squadron series
Star Wars: Rogue Squadron
1998; Factor 5/LucasArts
Windows, Nintendo 64
Game Info: Inspired by the comics of

the same name, this game saw players in control of Luke Skywalker as he led the Rogue Squadron against the Galactic Empire over 16 different missions.

Loose: $10
CIB: $20
New: $60

Star Wars Rogue Squadron II: Rogue Leader

2001; Factor 5/LucasArts
GameCube
Game Info: The player can act as either Luke Skywalker or Wedge Antilles over the course of 10 missions based on the original trilogy of films. This was a launch title for the Nintendo GameCube in America.
Loose: $5
CIB: $10
New: $60

Star Wars Rogue Squadron III: Rebel Strike

2003; Factor 5
GameCube
Game Info: The final game of this trilogy added the ability to leave the vehicle and participate in ground battles, as well as added a cooperative mode for most of the missions.
Loose: $10
CIB: $15
New: $40

Battlefront Series
Star Wars: Battlefront

2004; Pandemic Studios
Windows, PlayStation 2, Xbox; ported to Mac OS in 2005
Game info: This shooter game includes stages and stories from both the original and prequel trilogies and focused on conflicts between the Galactic Republic and the Confederacy of Independent Systems, and between the Rebel Alliance and the Galactic Empire. It proved to be popular for its online multiplayer modes.

Loose: $10
CIB: $15
New: $40

Star Wars: Battlefront 2

2005; Pandemic Studios
PlayStation 2, Xbox, Windows, PlayStation Portable
Game info: Like the first game, this featured both eras of the franchise at the time, with battles taking place during the Clone Wars and during the Galactic Civil War. The campaign (which is not present in the PSP version) focuses on a member of the 501st Legion who begins his journey during the Clone Wars and ends it with the Battle of Hoth.
PlayStation 2/PSP/Windows editions:
Loose: $5
CIB: $10
New: $40
Xbox edition:
Loose: $20
CIB: $25
New: $60

Star Wars Battlefront: Renegade Squadron

2007; Rebellion Developments
PlayStation Portable
Game info: A spin-off from the other *Battlefront* titles, this followed the Renegade Squadron, which was formed shortly before the Battle of Yavin by Han Solo. The story takes place primarily during and between *Empire* and *Return*.
Loose: $5
CIB: $10
New: $20

Star Wars Battlefront: Elite Squadron

2009; Rebellion Developments/N-Space
PlayStation Portable, Nintendo DS
Game Info: Players control the clone trooper X2, who was created by using the DNA of a former Jedi Master. Instead of carrying out Order 66, he betrays the Empire and fights for the Rebellion.
Loose: $5
CIB: $10
New: $30

Star Wars Battlefront

2015; EA DICE
Windows, PlayStation 4, Xbox One
Game Info: A reboot of the *Battlefront* series, this game is primarily focused on online multiplayer battles rather than a story mode. The four game modes are "Walker Assault," "Fighter Squadron," "Blast," and "Supremacy."
Loose: $5
CIB: $10
New: $20

Star Wars Battlefront II

2017; EA DICE
Windows, PlayStation 4, Xbox One
Game Info: Though considered an improvement over the first in the rebooted series from EA, this game is primarily remembered for the criticism and controversy that surrounded its in-game use of microtransactions.
Loose: $10
CIB: $20
New: $30

Knights of the Old Republic Games
Star Wars: Knights of the Old Republic

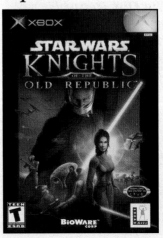

2003; Bioware
Xbox, Windows, OS X
Game Info: This critically-acclaimed role-playing game put players in control of a Jedi, who can travel down either the Dark or Light Side of the force in order to either take control of Darth Malak's forces for themselves, or defeat the Sith and become the hero the galaxy needs.
Loose: $10
CIB: $15
New: $60

Star Wars: Knights of the Old Republic II – The Sith Lords

2004; Obsidian Entertainment
Xbox, Windows, Linux, OS X
Game Info: Taking place five years after the events of the first game, this story followed "The Exile," who had been shunned by the Jedi Order.
Loose: $15
CIB: $20
New: $70

Star Wars: The Old Republic

2011; BioWare Austin
Windows
Game Info: This massively-multiplayer online role-playing game is set in the same time period as the two single-player games in this series. Players can play online together with their characters, who can be one of eight different classes, such as a Jedi, Sith, Smuggler, or Bounty Hunter.

Lego Star Wars Games
Lego Star Wars: The Video Game

2005; Traveller's Games
Windows, GameCube, PlayStation 2, Game Boy Advance, Xbox, OS X
Game Info: This inaugural game in the wacky crossover between Lego toys and the *Star Wars* franchise focused mostly on the prequel trilogy, which had just wrapped up around the time this game released, with a bonus segment focusing on *A New Hope*.
Loose: $5
CIB: $10
New: $30

Lego Star Wars II: The Original Trilogy

2006; Traveller's Tales
GameCube, Game Boy Advance, Nintendo DS, Windows, OS X, PlayStation 2, PlayStation Portable, Xbox, Xbox 360
Game Info: The digital bricks continued to see success with this second game, focused entirely on the original three films. Players could control any one of more than 50 characters from the franchise in this game.
Loose: $5
CIB: $10
New: $25

Lego Star Wars: The Complete Saga

2007; Traveller's Tales
Windows, OS X, PlayStation 3, Xbox 360, Wii, Nintendo DS
Game Info: A compilation containing the first two games in the series, which covered all six films out at the time.
Loose: $5
CIB: $10
New: $25

Lego Star Wars III: The Clone Wars

2011; Traveller's Tales
Nintendo DS, Nintendo 3DS, Wii, PlayStation 3, PlayStation Portable, Xbox 360, Windows, OS X
Game Info: Rather than being based on the films, this is based on the *Clone Wars* animated series.
Loose: $5
CIB: $10
New: $20

Lego Star Wars: The Force Awakens

2016; TT Fusion
PlayStation 3, PlayStation 4, PlayStation Vita, Wii U, Nintendo 3DS, Xbox 360, Xbox One, Windows, OS X, Android devices, iOS devices
Game Info: In addition to covering the events of the film it's based on, this game also includes some content regarding the period between *Return of the Jedi* and *Force Awakens*.
Loose: $10
CIB: $15
New: $30

Other *Star Wars* Games

Star Wars: Jedi Arena

1983; Parker Brothers
Atari 2600
Game Info: This was the first official *Star Wars* game to feature lightsaber action. The goal was to take out the opponent with the use of a Seeker ball, while avoiding and defending from laser blasts.
Loose: $10
CIB: $20
New: $40

Star Wars: Droids

1988; Binary Design
Amstrad CPC, Commodore 64, ZX Spectrum
Game Info: The game followed C-3PO and R2-D2 in a story based roughly on the *Star Wars: Droids* cartoon series.
Loose: $15
CIB: $60

Star Wars: Shadows of the Empire

1996; LucasArts
Nintendo 64; ported to Windows in 1997
Game Info: As part of the larger *Shadows of the Empire* media project that also included novels and comics, the game fol-

lowed mercenary Dash Rendar in a story set between *Empire* and *Return*.
Loose: $10
CIB: $20
New: $75

Star Wars: Masters of Teras Kasi

1997; LucasArts
PlayStation
Game Info: This oddball fighting game had a story focused on the Emperor seeking revenge for the destruction of the Death Star, and also included popular Extended Universe characters like Mara Jade. Though not a popular game, *Solo: A Star Wars Story* referenced the martial art of Teras Kasi, as Qi'ra is apparently skilled at it.
Loose: $10
CIB: $15
New: $60

Star Wars: Yoda Stories

1997; LucasArts
Windows; ported to Game Boy Color in 1999

Game Info: The game is focused on the time Luke Skywalker spends training with Yoda on Dagobah, and features procedurally-generated levels for a unique gameplay experience.

GBC edition:
Loose: $10
CIB: $15
New: $50
PC edition:
Loose: $5
CIB: $10
New: $20

Star Wars Rebellion

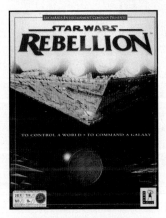

1998; Coolhand Interactive
Windows
Game info: The story takes place immediately after the Battle of Yavin. This game known as *Star Wars Supremacy* in some European markets.
Loose: $5
CIB: $10
New: $20

Star Wars: Force Commander

2000; LucasArts
Windows
This is another real-time strategy title, with a story taking place during the same time as the original trilogy, with certain events in the game intersecting with the film.
Loose: $10
CIB: $15
New: $40

Star Wars: Demolition

2000; Luxoflux
PlayStation, Dreamcast
Game Info: This is a vehicular combat game, based on the premise that, after podracing is outlawed, Jabba the Hutt instead creates a far more deadly vehicle contest.
Loose: $10
CIB: $15
New: $30

Star Wars: Super Bombad Racing

2001; Lucas Learning
PlayStation 2

Game Info: This was a cartoonish, goofy-looking title in which characters from *The Phantom Menace* raced against original trilogy heroes and villains.
Loose: $5
CIB: $10
New: $30

Star Wars: Galactic Battlegrounds

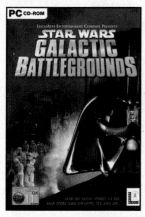

2001; LucasArts/Ensemble Studios
Windows, Mac OS X
Game Info: This was a real-time strategy game with various campaigns based on the different films. It saw an expansion, *Clone Campaigns*, in 2002, to coincide with the release of *Episode II*.
Loose: $5
CIB: $10
New: $40

Star Wars: Starfighter

2001; LucasArts
PlayStation 2, Xbox; ported to PC in 2002
Game Info: The player controls one of various space fighter ships in the leadup to the Battle of Naboo from *Episode I*.

Loose: $5
CIB: $10
New: $15

Star Wars: Jedi Starfighter

2002; LucasArts
PlayStation 2, Xbox
Game Info: A sequel to *Starfighter*, this game takes place during the Battle of Geonosis. The game was written by W. Haden Blackman, who had also written several of the *Star Wars* comic books.
Loose: $5
CIB: $10
New: $25

Star Wars: Bounty Hunter

2002; LucasArts
PlayStation 2, GameCube
Game Info: Players control bounty hunter Jango Fett in the hunt for the Dark Jedi, Komari Vosa. The game reveals why Jango was chosen as the template for the Clone Army and how Boba Fett came to be.
PS2 edition:
Loose: $5

CIB: $10
New: $35
GameCube edition:
Loose: $10
CIB: $15
New: $60

Star Wars Galaxies

2003, Sony Online Entertainment
Windows
Game Info: This MMORPG received critical acclaim and was popular for years. It saw several expansions, including *Jump to Lightspeed, Rage of the Wookies* and *Trials of Obi-Wan*. The official servers shut down in 2011, though many fans have continued to run the game on their own private servers.
Loose: $20
CIB: $50
New: $100
Note: The early "beta disc" releases are considered the most significant for collectors, and regularly see prices of $400 or more in online auctions.

Star Wars: Flight of the Falcon

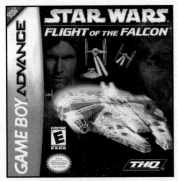

2003; Pocket Studios
Game Boy Advance
Game Info: The game allowed players

to control a variety of spaceships, but was primarily focused on the Millennium Falcon.
Loose: $5
CIB: $10
New: $15

Star Wars Trilogy: Apprentice of the Force

2004; Ubisoft
Game Boy Advance
Game info: The game is focused on the story of the original trilogy, and actually released on the same day as the 2004 DVD box sets. The gameplay is very similar to the GBA version of Ubisoft's *Prince of Persia: The Sands of Time*.
Loose: $10
CIB: $15
New: $25

Star Wars: Republic Commando

2005; LucasArts
Xbox, Windows
Game info: This is a first-person shooter with a focus on tactics that is set during the Clone Wars. Players control a Clone commando team under the command of Delta-38. Thanks to positive reception, a sequel called *Imperial Commando* had been planned, but was ultimately cancelled.

Loose: $15
CIB: $20
New: $50

Star Wars: Lethal Alliance

2006; Ubisoft
PlayStation Portable, Nintendo DS
Game Info: Taking place between *Episode III* and *Episode IV*, the game follows Twi'lek Rianna Saren, who is acting as a mercenary. She is eventually hired by the Rebel Alliance to complete a number of missions in opposition to the Empire.
Loose: $5
CIB: $10
New: $30

Star Wars: Empire at War

2006; Petroglyph Games
Windows, Mac
Game info: This real-time strategy title was set between *Episode III* and *Episode IV*. It saw an expansion, *Forces of Corruption,* in October 2006. Though the online functionality had been shut off in 2014, it was reenabled via Steam in 2017.
Loose: $5
CIB: $10
New: $20

Star Wars: The Force Unleashed

2008; LucasArts
Wii, Nintendo DS, PlayStation 2, PlayStation 3, PlayStation Portable, Windows, OS X, Xbox 360
Game Info: The story followed Darth Vader's secret apprentice, known as Starkiller. Though he works against both the Jedi and the Empire, he soon begins to redeem himself and separate from Vader. The Xbox 360 and PlayStation 3 versions of the game received some downloadable content, which would later be repackaged along with the game for the "Ultimate Sith Edition" release in 2009.
Loose: $5
CIB: $10
New: $20
Ultimate Sith Edition:
Loose: $20
CIB: $30
New: $65

Star Wars: The Force Unleashed II

2010; LucasArts
Wii, Nintendo DS, PlayStation 3, Xbox 360, Windows, iOS
Game Info: Taking place six months after the first *Force Unleashed* and about a year before the events of *A New Hope*, the story follows a clone of the original Starkiller, who can eventually choose between the light and dark side of the force for himself. A third game in this series was planned, but later cancelled.
Loose: $5
CIB: $10
New: $20
Collector's edition:
Loose: $15
CIB: $20
New: $45

GET YOUR GAME ON!

THE HISTORY OF GAMING
- The earliest computers and games
- Early dominance of arcades
- The 1980s industry crash
- Console dominance of today

HOW TO COLLECT
- By company
- By creator
- By character
- By series

CARE & PRESERVATION
- Storing
- Displaying
- Grading
...and more!

MORE THAN JUST GAMES
- Tying gaming into different collections
- Adding promotional materials
- Arcade cabinets and other relics
...and much more!

The Overstreet® Guide To Collecting Video Games

brings our "How To" series inside this exciting hobby, in full color, with so many levels to explore.

CHARLES LIPPINCOTT
THE MAN BEHIND THE STAR WARS MARKETING MACHINE

Today *Star Wars* is known as a gargantuan success, loved by several generations throughout the world. And while George Lucas' works, along with the litany of talented cast and crew, speak for themselves, the movie's initial success was aided significantly by the film's marketing.

The way that *Star Wars* was marketed and merchandized before, during, and after the film's release had a profound impact on how future films would be promoted. Charles Lippincott, who served as advertising/publicity supervisor on *Star Wars: Episode IV – A New Hope*, was the man behind the marketing.

Prior to his work on *Star Wars*, he had been a unit publicist for *Westworld* and a publicist for *Family Plot* and *Fighting Mad* in the early to mid-1970s. After bumping into George Lucas and producer Gary Kurtz on the Universal lot, Lippincott read the *Star Wars* script. Being a science fiction fan,

he enjoyed the script, which led to a meeting with Lucas to discuss the project and possibilities for promotional tie-ins.

Once he joined the film, one of the first things he did was to seek a higher budget for the production. He then worked on copyrighting *Star Wars* intellectual property to protect their rights over the film, its title, and characters, which would prevent other individuals from legally creating their own items. Knowing that they'd need to market directly to science fiction fans, Lippincott publicized the film at science fiction and comic book conventions, in newspapers, and on radio stations throughout 1976. These promotional events and advertisements helped build interest for the upcoming film.

In a key marketing move, Lippincott reached out to Ballantine Books to secure a deal for a novelization of the film. Alan Dean Foster, who had worked on

Lippincott contacted Ballantine Books to initiate a novelization of the movie, which was published before the film's release.

One of his major contributions was pitching the comic book series to Marvel.

other film novelizations, was hired to ghost write the book for Lucas. Foster wrote the novel in the spring of 1976 then he met with Lucas and Lippincott to discuss details and story changes to incorporate in the final draft. *Star Wars: From the Adventures of Luke Skywalker* was in stores by December 1976 – about five months before the movie.

He was able to secure a toy deal with Kenner, which proved extremely successful.

Lippincott also pitched a comic book tie-in to Marvel Comics in the hopes of getting comics in the hands of potential viewers before the film was out. Stan Lee, Marvel's publisher at the time, wasn't initially sold on the idea, but agreed following another meeting. Lippincott gave Marvel a copy of the script, some production stills, and Ralph McQuarrie's designs for the film to guide the comic. After a six-issue adaptation of the film, the comic continued with original stories and adaptations of *The Empire Strikes Back* and *Return of the Jedi*, for a total of 107 issues and 3 annuals during the original run.

Perhaps the biggest success in marketing was the toy line from Kenner. They shopped the toy line before the film as a way to continue building anticipation, but were turned down because movie tie-ins were not proven successes since films were considered to be fleeting in the public consciousness. Lippincott and the marketing department were able to secure a deal with Kenner, and after the movie was released, the toy company was hit with a wave of demand. Because of the shortened timetable and overwhelming interest, they issued an "Early Bird Certificate Package" during the 1977 holiday season as a fill-in until toys could be shipped. The toys continued enticing *Star Wars* fans of all ages through the mid-1980s.

After the film was in theaters, Lippincott and the *Star Wars* crew continued the marketing machine through posters, costumes, clothing, books, albums, and fast food giveaways, as well as licensing to TV shows, including the *Star Wars Holiday Special*, to keep it in the public eye. The merchandise kept audiences connected to the film well after it was out of theaters.

The way Lippincott marketed *Star Wars* became a blueprint goal for how to publicize movies to have audiences both familiar and filled with anticipation before the premiere. His savvy planning protected the film and his ideas were initial steps for many creative people who brought the film to life off-screen. His work before and after the movie was released made Charles Lippincott an integral part of *Star Wars*.

He continued marketing to audiences during and after its theatrical run, including work on the *Star Wars Holiday Special*.

UNIQUE COLLECTIONS
THROUGH ORIGINAL ART

Star Wars #92 by Jan Duursema featuring
Lando Calrissian and Luke in several panels,
plus Princess Leia, Han Solo, and Chewbacca
sold for $1,298 at Hake's Auctions.

One of the main components that propels the success of *Star Wars* is the visual aspect. George Lucas wrote a great adventure script that was realized on film through original designs rather than dipping too often into science fiction tropes of the past. The rich tapestry of glowing lightsabers, immersive space battles, variety of creatures, and natural landscapes resonates with viewers. By extension, the film's success opened new venues for artists to express their creativity as part of the ever-growing series. Through the comics, games, and marketing that followed, *Star Wars* has produced plenty of opportunities for original art collectors.

From the time of the first movie to the present, Marvel Comics and Dark Horse Comics have published hundreds of *Star Wars* comic books. Since the original Marvel run began in 1977, the comics have been readily available on the secondary market at affordable prices. Original art, however, gives fans the chance to own one of a kind pieces from the series.

Original comic art is typically categorized by covers, interior pages (with dialogue and action), and splash pages (a page with one significant image). Covers usually sell for more than pages since they bear the title and depict an image meant to represent the whole issue. Prices vary drastically based on the age of the issue, significance of the story, who appears on the cover, condition, and who provided the cover art. The *Star Wars* #9 cover by Gil Kane and Tony DeZuniga depicting Han Solo and Jaxxon among others, in the first original comic story has sold for $52,580. A cover by Bill Sienkiewicz for the *Return of the Jedi* adaptation sold for $20,315. Covers by Carmine Infantino and Bob Wiacek, who created several covers together, average between $3,000

to $7,250. A Marvel U.K. *Star Wars Weekly* cover sells for $5,000 to $7,000.

Sales of interior pages are based on the same factors as the covers, with a few additions. Pages that feature characters in several panels and action over stationary scenes will be higher sellers.

A page from *Star Wars* #45, depicting Luke Skywalker, R2-D2, and a Star Destroyer in action has sold for $3,825. One from *Star Wars* #92 featuring Lando Calrissian and Luke in several panels, plus Princess Leia, Han Solo, and Chewbacca sold for $1,298. On the other end, pages with less action and fewer characters only clear $200 to $500.

The comic strip, which ran in newspapers from the late '70s to mid-1980s, featured talents like Russ Manning, Rick Hoberg, Alfredo Alcala, and Dave Stevens. Daily comic strips by Manning range from $310 for a basic piece to $6,000 for one featuring Luke Skywalker, C-3PO, and R2-D2. A Sunday strip by Hoberg and Stevens that depicts Boba Fett has sold for over $5,000. Most of the daily strip art sells for $250 to $2,150 and the Sunday strips go for $300 to an average around $2,500.

Animation art can be collected from the 1978 *Star Wars Holiday Special* and the *Star Wars: Ewoks* and *Star Wars: Droids* cartoon shows of the '80s. Production cels for the notorious *Holiday Special* can reach up to $500. Production cels, setups, and background art for *Droids* and *Ewoks* are in the very affordable range of $15 to $60 for

This framed daily comic strip original art by Alfredo Alcala sold at Hake's Auctions for $380.

Sunday strip original art by Russ Manning sold for $2,530 at Hake's Auctions.

character pieces and $130 for full cel set-up with character and background.

Licensing/style guide artwork features some of the most recognizable versions of the characters and ships of *Star Wars*. Style guides are created to provide guidance on licensed material for official Lucasfilm merchandise, like apparel, toys, and other products. This type of art depicts several views of characters, including full-length frontal, back, and profile, as well as closeups and 3/4 views, notable poses, and action shots. These different views have a major impact on the price when the artwork is sold. For instance, a Rick Hoberg full length front view illustration of Darth Vader has sold for $1,135 while a back view of the Sith Lord closed at $285. The ship style guide art typically shows the front and angled views from above or below. Ships range from $185 to $1,200 depending on the vehicle, angle, and size. Similar to style guide material, collectors can find original art for specific packaging that was found on everything from toy cards and boxes like Micromachines, to product boxes like Dixie Cups.

Movie poster fans can expand their collections into rarer territory with movie poster concept art. Before their final images fly off the press and into theaters, artists like Tom Jung, Drew Struzan, Tom Chantrell, Bob Peak, and Roger Kastel created sketches of their poster ideas, which are now worth thousands. A Jung half-sheet concept art in pencil sold alongside a finished half-sheet for $45,410.

Concept art and storyboards for film production can also fetch hefty sums. Art by

This Darth Vader front view licensing/style guide illustration original art by Rick Hoberg sold at Heritage Auctions for $1,135.

The Empire Strikes Back Dixie Cup original box art
sold for $1,265 at Hake's Auctions.

Ralph McQuarrie, who is celebrated for his character and concept designs, is worth upwards of $100,000. Most storyboard art is in the much more affordable range of $200 to $3,000.

Trading cards and games for *Star Wars* embody the creative, adventurous spirit of the series with attractive art. A Greg and Tim Hildebrandt trading card painting featuring Luke, Yoda, Obi-Wan Kenobi, and Vader has sold for $7,765. An uncut card art sheet sells for $430 to $1,500, black and white original art lithograph limited prints average $125. Roleplaying game art, sourcebook original art, and campaign guide page art sell for around $80, while character illustrations can be bought for $30 to $45.

Original art collecting opportunities also include book covers and pages, spoof art from other pop culture properties, pop art, and commissioned paintings for advertising and events, among others.

Typically done in black and white, sometimes even just pencil, original art is not always as flashy and vibrant as finished productions. But what it does is convey the process of a project. It's the point when an idea becomes an incarnation, a guide to final product. Most importantly, original art pieces are unique items that can be proudly displayed as one of a kind.

Greg and Tim Hildebrandt Star Wars Galaxy
series 3 trading cards original painting sold
for $7,767 at Heritage Auctions.

A long
time ago
in a galaxy
far, far away...

MOVIE POSTERS
THEATER LOBBIES TO LIVING ROOM WALLS

Making Films Sound Better

DOLBY SYSTEM
Noise Reduction · High Fidelity

PG PARENTAL GUIDANCE SUGGESTED
SOME MATERIAL MAY NOT BE SUITABLE FOR PRE-TEENAGERS

Before *Star Wars* was established as a beloved film series, the movie relied on advertising campaigns to attract audiences. In the days prior to expansive content sharing on the filmmaking process through the internet, social media, and 24-hour news cycle, movie posters were conduits to film fans. *Star Wars* made the bold move of simply stating the title and tagline on early posters, then followed that with multiple designs to introduce the grandeur of the story and the brave heroes. After the first movie became a hit, poster advertising continued the momentum of enticing viewers through incredible artwork provided by some of the best contemporary poster artists. Since those early releases, *Star Wars* movie posters have become popular series collectibles.

The first promotional poster for *A New Hope* was drawn by Howard Chaykin in comic book style. Depicting the main trio of Luke, Leia, and Han with the epic villain Darth Vader, it introduced viewers to the idea that it would be an adventure, in addition to science fiction. Printed by 20th Century Fox in 1976 in a very limited print run, it was unveiled at the World Science Fiction Convention in Kansas City. The poster is much smaller than the typical one-sheet style, measuring 20" x 29".

The first and second advance posters are similar to each other. The first advance is more reflective with metallic chrome finish, while the second has a duller finish. The other difference is the variance in the letter "W." The first advance is considered more valuable due to the rarity of the finish and different font of the "W," though advance style B is more familiar to the public. It's somewhat basic, but the tagline, "Coming to your galaxy this summer," has become one of the most recognizable of all time.

The style A one-sheet is the one most associated with the film, featuring art by Tom Jung. Luke and Leia appear in heroic white with Darth Vader's dark, menacing

THE FIRST PROMOTIONAL POSTER FOR *A NEW HOPE* WAS AVAILABLE AT THE WORLD SCIENCE FICTION CONVENTION IN KANSAS CITY.

THE STYLE A ONE-SHEET FOR *A NEW HOPE* DEPICTS ART BY TOM JUNG AND IS THE ONE MOST ASSOCIATED WITH THE MOVIE.

helmet looming behind them. They are ready for combat with Luke's lightsaber beaming energy and Leia gripping a blaster while looking out at the viewer. Jung may not have known where the story would go, because it also alludes to a possible romance between the two. With flowing clothing, Luke's shirt is ripped open and Leia's thighs are exposed, akin to images on romance novel covers.

The style C one-sheet depicts an energetic design of the heroes, villains, ships, and the ominous Death Star. Tom Chantrell provided the artwork, contrasting colors of blue and black with red and orange. It cements Han, Luke, and Leia as the leads, with Darth Vader in the background set between Luke and Leia. Style C notably depicts Chewbacca, R2-D2, C-3PO, Obi-Wan Kenobi, and Grand Moff Tarkin for the first time.

The style D, also known as the circus poster, was a collaboration between two artists. Charles White III was commissioned to draw the poster for the 1978 summer rerelease of *Star Wars*. He invited Drew Struzan to contribute to the portraiture while he worked on other aspects. The poster has a '30s and '40s style from concept to font. Luke and Leia are the main image with smaller ones of Han, C-3PO, R2-D2, and Chewbacca. Because there was not enough room to include the necessary credits, White and Struzan made the main image smaller than the poster size. They drew Obi-Wan looking on from the side, making the poster appear to be hanging from a wooden board, creating the circus appearance.

One of the rarest posters is the 1978 one-sheet that commemorated the first anniversary of the release. The poster depicts a large birthday cake surrounded by the original wave of toy figures. Few were printed, making them difficult to find and highly coveted by collectors.

In addition to the one-sheets, which are the standard movie poster size, *Star Wars* also distributed inserts, half-sheets, three-sheets, and six-sheets, among other sizes. They typically utilize the same artwork, though there are variations. For *A New Hope*, those differing sizes primarily depicted the style A art. There are multiple sizes for other films in the series, but the largest variety was made for the first film.

Rerelease posters for *A New Hope* were issued in '79, '81, '82, '92 for the 15th anniversary, and '97 for the 20th anniversary/special edition release. Though in different colors, the posters for '79 and '81 have similar designs of the title and credits, a small image of Luke and Leia from the style A design, and a detail bar in the middle. The '82 rerelease is also similar though the art is slightly larger. Two posters were created for the 15th anniversary in '92. Artists Greg and Tim Hildebrandt interpreted the style A poster art in their own style, using brighter, though still similar color choices; the second was a rerelease of the style D poster. For the 20th anniversary special edition in '97, Struzan drew portraits of Leia, Luke, Han, and Ben in shades of orange and yellow with ships surrounding in blue and black.

The Empire Strikes Back posters began with an advance teaser designed by Bob Peak with a large portrait of

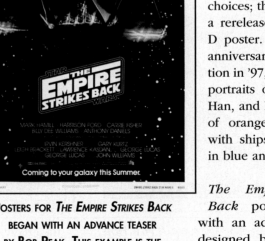

POSTERS FOR *THE EMPIRE STRIKES BACK* BEGAN WITH AN ADVANCE TEASER BY BOB PEAK. THIS EXAMPLE IS THE RARE VERSION WITH THE WHITE LOGO.

Darth Vader's shiny helmet, surrounded by a starfield. The straightforward, albeit menacing, image was used for various poster sizes before more plot details were introduced on later releases.

The style A (also known as the *Gone with the Wind* style) one-sheet was painted by Roger Kastel. It is the most popular of the *Empire* posters, depicting Han and Leia passionately embracing, which parallels Rhett Butler and Scarlett O'Hara, with Luke on his Tauntaun in place of the man on horseback. The comparison between *Gone with the Wind* and *Empire* extends to the vivid colors – the heat of Georgia versus the coolness of space. There was some controversy over the poster not depicting new character Lando Calrissian. It was pulled from distribution, most likely based on this fact.

The style B one-sheet by Jung presents Darth Vader as the major figure with Leia, Han, and Lando on one side, and two images of Luke on the other. Stormtroopers appear to run through the poster and fighters fly from Darth Vader's cape.

Rerelease posters were created in '81, '82, '90 for the 10th anniversary, '95, and '97 for the special edition. Like *A New Hope*, the first two rerelease posters in '81 and '82 were similar designs by Jung, utilizing art from his style B poster, though isolated in smaller portions of the surface. For the 10th anniversary in '90, three posters were commissioned. The Fan Club version by Larry Noble shows the Millennium Falcon soaring through the sky with a giant Darth Vader hovering above. On the foil posters by Dayna Stedry, the first design has a simple commemoration for the film along with a giant close-up of Vader's helmet and the other shows a light and shadow of Luke on a tauntaun and the title over a large "10." The '95 gold foil 15th anniversary is a really neat design of Boba Fett's helmet in bright shades of red, green, and white with black. For the '97 special edition, Struzan focused on the Dark Side, depicting Vader and Emperor Palpatine, plus a Star Destroyer, AT-AT Walkers, and TIE Fighters in shades of black, purple, and sparks of orange.

THE EMPIRE STRIKES BACK STYLE **A** INSERT FEATURES THE *GONE WITH THE WIND* STYLE ARTWORK BY ROGER KASTEL.

Struzan provided the art for the *Return of the Jedi* advance, originally titled *Revenge of the Jedi*. The poster was pulled because it was pointed out that the Jedi did not take revenge, hence the title did not make sense. Few made it to theaters. George Lucas sold the 8,000 to 9,000 that were printed to members of his fan club, which only took three days to sell out. The other interesting fact about this poster was that it had three fold lines instead of the usual four. Adding to the fun of collectability, some were printed with a release date and some weren't. Based on being pulled and the title change, it is one of the most sought after posters for the series.

The replacement style A has art by Tim Reamer, depicting a pair of hands holding a lightsaber with the Death Star in the background. The poster is primarily black with electric blue coming off of the lightsaber as it swings upward.

The style B is more eye-catching, showing a collage of good and evil characters. With artwork by Kazuhiko Sano, it's the one most associated with the movie. Leia, Han, and Luke are in the center with Leia in the iconic gold bikini, Han firing a blaster, and Luke ready to swing his lightsaber. The abhorrent Jabba the Hutt and his minions are on one side while Lando and Wicket are on the other, with Darth Vader at the top.

Return of the Jedi saw rerelease posters in '85, '93 and '94 for the 10th anniversary, and the '97 special edition. The '85 rerelease by Jung features portraits of Han, Leia, Luke, and Lando with C-3PO, R2-D2, Wicket, and Yoda under an exploding Death Star. For the 10th anniversary, Struzan's *Revenge* teaser with the updated title in gold and red foil was reprinted in '93. It was followed closely by Sano's '94 version with portraits of the main cast surrounded by other characters, an explosion at the center, and the Falcon flying below. For the '97 special edition, Struzan drew Chewbacca, Jabba the Hutt, and Yoda – who aren't typically featured on most posters – along with the shadows of Luke and Vader in a lightsaber battle.

FEW ITEMS HAVE THE *REVENGE OF THE JEDI* TITLE, MAKING THIS ADVANCE TEASER PROMO POSTER VERY POPULAR WITH COLLECTORS.

THIS WHITE LOGO STYLE B ONE-SHEET FOR *RETURN OF THE JEDI* IS ALSO A RARITY.

THE 1985 TRIPLE BILL ONE-SHEET WAS MADE FOR
A ONE TIME SHOWING OF ALL THREE FILMS.

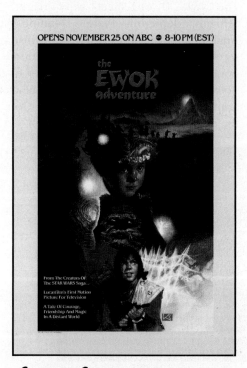

CARAVAN OF COURAGE RECEIVED TWO DESIGNS,
STARTING WITH THIS STYLE A TV POSTER.

After the trilogy was completed, a few commemorative posters were created to incorporate and represent all three movies. The first two were both printed in 1985, starting with the Star Wars Saga American Checklist one-sheet. It depicts the theatrical posters that were released for the original trilogy from Chaykin's comic book style art to the TV movie, *Caravan of Courage* (more on that to follow). There's also a text block where fans could literally check off the posters they had and in what size. The back of the double-sided one-sheet provides details on the posters – the year, the size, the name, and more.

The other '85 poster was the triple bill one-sheet, that was made for a one time showing of all three films. The poster features the trilogy titles along with the "One Performance Only" details in white text over a black background. It is extremely rare and among the most valuable series posters.

Along with '97 special edition posters for the individual films, a trilogy version was created. It appears like a gold plate showing the main characters in poses from earlier posters with the film titles below.

In 1984, two posters were made for *Caravan of Courage: An Ewok Adventure*, the TV movie that sees Wicket helping two children. The style A poster by Sano is a kid-friendly painting of the main characters with imaginative renderings of their adventures in the movie. The style B poster by Struzan funnels the characters from a point at the bottom, spilling them across the top two-thirds in contrasting color tones. When the second TV movie, *Ewoks: The Battle for Endor*, saw rerelease in 1990 a home video poster was made, which looks like a fairy tale adventure with unlikely heroes and scary villains.

Since the prequel trilogy would tell the story of Anakin Skywalker's path to the Dark Side, campaigning for *The Phantom Menace* began with the boy. The style A advance poster, created by Ellen Lee, depicts young Anakin pursued by the shadow of Darth Vader. Creating the illusion of hardship, Tatootine is a desert of bright sand and sky with Anakin isolated in the center. The small initial print run sold out in less than two weeks and over 60,000 were printed to fill backorders.

THE STYLE A ADVANCE ONE-SHEET FOR *THE PHANTOM MENACE* ILLUSTRATES ANAKIN'S FOREBODING FUTURE.

The follow-up style B one-sheet was created by Struzan, displaying a montage of the new characters. Darth Maul has replaced Vader as the menacing background figure with a more precocious looking Anakin in the foreground. The two suns of Tatooine shine through the center of the poster with Queen Amidala appearing regally and Qui-Gon Jinn looking forward wisely.

Along with the regular designs, 30" x 63" double-sided banners were made for Queen Amidala/Obi-Wan, Anakin Skywalker/Jar Jar Binks, Qui-Gon Jinn/Watto, and Darth Maul/battle droid. Each one depicts a photo quality image of the character on two thirds with an action scene below. The 2012 rerelease 3D posters, done in regular and lenticular format, aptly jump off the page. They are focused on the imposing form of Darth Maul, surrounded by Obi-Wan, Yoda, and the podracers.

The style A advance one-sheet for *Attack of the Clones* shows Anakin and Padmé, backs to each other with the doomed romantic tagline "A Jedi shall not know anger. Nor hatred. Nor love." Created by Greg Bell and Paul Venables, Padmé has taken on a softer appearance for her new role as romantic lead. There are serious expressions on their faces with very little lighting. This teaser makes it clear that the central story is about Luke and Leia's parents.

The style B one-sheet was created by Struzan, depicting Padmé leaning into Anakin with his chin tucked against her forehead. Standing in the foreground is bounty hunter Jango Fett, the father of the notorious Boba Fett, and basis for the clone army. Obi-Wan has replaced Qui-Gon as the stern-faced father figure.

THIS *ATTACK OF THE CLONES* STYLE A ADVANCE BANNER CAPITALIZES ON THE DOOMED LOVE AFFAIR.

For the IMAX showings, a very colorful and animated poster was created. Featuring Yoda looking large and ready for battle over city structures, he stands below the tagline "Size Matters Not. Except on an IMAX Screen."

The style A advance for *Revenge of the Sith* displays Anakin at the edge of the poster with his cape turning into Vader's helmet. The way the cape takes up the dominate portion of the poster clearly indicates that Vader is consuming Anakin. It dwarfs him, flowing off of his back representing the fluidity of his transformation into the Sith lord.

On the style B one-sheet, painted by Struzan, Padmé is no longer leaning on Anakin, rather she looks diplomatic and he looks troubled. The foreground image is the battle between Anakin and Obi-Wan. Yoda and Mace Windu are also in action, the emperor appears on his first theatrical one-sheet, and Darth Vader hovers over Anakin.

Homage was paid to *A New Hope* with a style D circus poster by Matt Busch. Almost a mirror image, it has a similar color scheme, Anakin and Padmé replace Luke and Leia, General Grievous in place of Vader, Yoda takes the place of Han and R2-D2 with

C-3PO replace the jawas. A younger Obi-Wan is seen along the side where his older counterpart appears on the original.

Revenge of the Sith also saw character specific posters of Mace Windu, General Grievous, Darth Vader, Anakin and Obi-Wan, Yoda, and a Clone Trooper, each rendered in an action pose and different color scheme. There's also a comical Darth Vader mini poster with the tagline "Who's Your Daddy?" above the release date details for Father's Day 2005.

When the *Star Wars: The Clone Wars* animated film entered the fold in 2008, a poster was made that shows young Anakin, Obi-Wan, Ahsoka Tano, and Yoda fierce and battle-ready with lightsabers ignited, flanked by Clone Troopers.

The Force Awakens had a very big job to do. It was the introduction of a new *Star Wars* trilogy that followed the prequels (which received mixed reviews at best), it would include original series veterans and introduce a slew of new characters, and it was

THE STYLE **A** BANNER FOR *THE CLONE WARS*, INTRODUCED THE FILM BEFORE IT BECAME A HIT TV SHOW.

the first major outing since The Walt Disney Company acquired Lucasfilm. While people would definitely go see the movie no matter what – it is *Star Wars*, after all – savvy marketing was crucial.

With business acumen and play on nostalgia, one of the earliest posters to introduce audiences to *The Force Awakens* was the D23 Expo mini poster with art by Struzan. Newcomers Finn, Rey, and Kylo Ren are focal images with warm sunshine behind Finn and cold, dark space behind Kylo as Rey stands in the middle. Below is the older, grumpier Han Solo beside a strip of the stairs from the powerful carbonite freezing scene of *The Empire Strikes Back*.

Beginning with *The Force Awakens*, the new wave of films has included basic teasers that feature the title over a starfield. There was also a group of bus stop posters known as the One Eye series, each of which depicts a close-up of one of the main characters. In each case, the right eye and a portion of the face is covered by a weapon pertaining to that character.

The main one-sheet is dominated by Rey, Kylo, and Finn, with weapons drawn and ready for a fight. Below them are Han, Leia, Chewbacca, C-3PO, and R2-D2, plus newcomers Poe Dameron, Captain Phasma, BB-8, and Maz Kanata. Ships in flight and Stormtroopers mobilizing complete the busy poster. Once the poster was released it was quickly noted that Luke Skywalker was absent, launching dozens of fan theories and postulations.

The second regular one-sheet shows a pared down version of the cast which is dominated by the imposing form of Kylo Ren. Though it has similar elements to the other poster, it is shrouded in black with fiery focus on Kylo's lightsaber.

IMAX issued four mini posters by Dan Mumford that were given at their screenings. Each one was rendered in a vivid color scheme, with one of Rey and crashed ships from the original trilogy's conflict, one of Poe Dameron and an X-Wing, one

AFTER A FEW TEASERS, *THE FORCE AWAKENS* MAIN ONE-SHEET PRESENTED THE NEW AND RETURNING CAST.

THIS POSTER FOR *THE FORCE AWAKENS* IS ONE OF FIVE KNOWN AS THE ONE EYE SERIES.

THIS SCARIF-DEATH STAR TEASER PROVIDED ONE OF THE EARLIEST LOOKS AT *ROGUE ONE: A STAR WARS STORY.*

SEVERAL SIMILARLY DESIGNED ONE-SHEETS WERE ALSO MADE FOR *ROGUE ONE*, INCLUDING THIS ONE THAT FEATURES THE REBEL SYMBOL.

of Captain Phasma with other First Order Stormtroopers, and one of Finn and Kylo about to cross sabers in the woods.

Rogue One: A Star Wars Story posters began with the black title teaser and a teaser on the beach of Scarif with the ghostly shadow of the Death Star ominously hanging in the sky. As the first standalone film, the teaser separates itself nicely by depicting a beach, blue water, and lush palm trees, much different than the typical space settings on *Star Wars* posters.

The regular one-sheets all feature very similar designs with a blue-black-white color scheme. One poster depicts a large image of Jyn Erso above fellow Rebels and Imperial officer Orson Krennic. Another features the characters over the Death Star with the Scarif battle below. The third shows characters in a triangle pattern over the Death Star with the Rebel symbol in boldly contrasting red.

IMAX created three mini posters with character collages over a plain white background and Regal did an exclusive limited edition art print close-up of a gleaming Death Trooper.

Red is the theme throughout the line of posters for *The Last Jedi*, beginning with the title outlined in red on the first teaser. The second teaser is shrouded in the color with menacing closeups of Luke and Kylo split by the blue beam of Rey's lightsaber. There's also a series of character-specific bus shelters of the main cast all wearing red cloaks and serious expressions.

The regular one-sheet features the principle cast, with Luke and Leia in the center as the only characters looking forward, though both of their faces are slightly obscured. They are surrounded by Rey and Kylo with drawn weapons, plus Poe, Finn, Chewbacca, and others.

A pair of posters complete one contrasting image of the Light and the Dark Sides connected by lightsabers. The Resistance poster is red on white with Rey in the foreground and the First Order poster is black on gray, giving the place of prominence to Kylo. Each is surrounded by allies, like

RED IS A RECURRING THEME IN POSTERS FOR *THE LAST JEDI*, INCLUDING THIS REGULAR ONE-SHEET.

TAKING ON A LIGHTER TONE, THE *SOLO: A STAR WARS STORY* ONE-SHEET IS COLORFUL AND AMUSING.

Leia and Phasma, though interestingly Luke appears on both, symbolizing his call to the Resistance and his impact on Kylo's story.

The artwork for *Solo: A Star Wars Story* is much lighter and lighthearted in contrast. The initial release was another basic title teaser on solid black. The cast teaser depicts the younger iterations of Han, Lando, and Chewie with new characters Qi'ra and Beckett all contained in the letters of "Solo" with the Millennium Falcon flying below.

The regular poster expanded on that image with full-length renderings of the characters in orange and white in front of the outline of the Falcon's cockpit windows. Han poses ready to shoot, Chewbacca is by his side, Lando appears appropriately cocky, and Qi'ra looks like a space-gunslinger.

The large format wilding posters depict individual characters in poses that are similarly self-assured and amusing, embodying the tone of the film.

THIS CINEMARK XD EXCLUSIVE POSTER SHOWS ALL SIX OF THE BUS SHELTER IMAGES FOR *THE LAST JEDI*.

MOVIE POSTERS
KEY FACTORS AND PRICING TRENDS

When collecting *Star Wars* movie posters there are a few important factors to keep in mind that will help identify versions and possible price differences.

Posters made in the U.S. for domestic and international audiences typically depict the same artwork, but there are a few ways to notate the differences. U.S.-released international versions usually don't include the MPAA rating (a U.S. system) or release dates. For the international versions that do include the date, they can often be recognized by a different date than when the movie premiered in the U.S. or the date written with the day before the month. Another sign is that the date will use the word "cinema" instead of "theater" or the British spelling "theatre."

Most poster auctions will denote if the poster was made by NSS or studio-made. The National Screen Service (NSS) was a poster distributor that was hired by studios to distribute to movie theaters for advertising campaigns. NSS posters are designated with a number block on the bottom of the poster. Studio style are simply posters that were printed by the studio, typically given to employees, handed out at advance screenings, or used as prize giveaways. Usually they don't see much difference in price, though NSS are more often folded because they were shipped to movie theaters.

The terms "advance" and "teaser" are used interchangeably in some poster auctions. It's important to remember that a teaser typically has less specific artwork, which might just be one character or the title, without the credits. Advance posters can have the regular release artwork or teaser images that are issued prior to the movie.

Prices for *Star Wars* posters range from $1 to over $20,000. Higher prices are achieved for larger format posters, rarer or limited print runs, those with better artwork, examples from the original trilogy, and original releases over reissues.

The prices have gone up across the board since the third trilogy started coming out in 2015. Since then, older posters saw a boost in prices for both original and prequel trilogies. Posters for the new movies see high prices before the movie enters theaters, which lasts for about a year, then drops a bit.

The following price list for *Star Wars* posters is based on those released in the United States. They include theatrical releases and later reissues as well as popular specialty posters. Prices are listed based on conditions of Poor/Good, Very Good, and Near Mint.

Movie posters are printed in a variety of sizes to fill the needs of available advertising spaces and opportunities. Here is a short list of popular sizes and their dimensions referenced in the price list.

One-sheet = 27" x 40"
    or 27" x 41"
Insert = 14" x 36"
Half-sheet = 22" x 28"
Three-sheet = 41" x 81"
Six-sheet = 81" x 81"
Seven-sheet = 84" x 91"
24-sheet = 246" x 108"

Poster 1 1st Edition Artist: Howard Chaykin **Luke Skywalker** c The Star Wars Corporation 1976

**1976 World Science Fiction Convention
poster (20" x 29")
$1,000 $2,000 $2,800**

Advance teaser style A (variant "W")
foil one-sheet
$275 $1,200 $2,000

Advance teaser style B (regular "W")
one-sheet
$400 $900 $1,800

Teaser banner (105" x 24")
$2,200 $3,500 $4,200

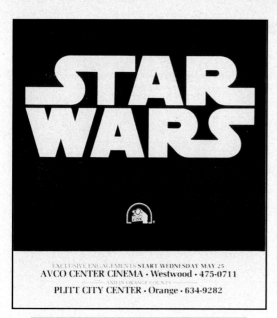

Advance logo herald (7" x 8")
$65 $130 $200

Advance "Entertainment Odyssey"
herald (7" x 9")
$40 $110 $185

Advance "A long time ago…" tagline
herald (8" x 10")
$30 $100 $175

Style B advance teaser (blue) one-sheet
$150 $700 $1,500

Style B advance seven-sheet
$3,000 $8,800 $13,000

Style A one-sheet
First printing
$100 $1,000 $3,000

Second printing
$80 $360 $1,200

Third printing
$60 $350 $650

Fourth printing
$40 $320 $600

Style A international one-sheet
$240 $900 $1,950

Style A insert
$70 $350 $700

Style A international insert
$50 $200 $400

Style A half-sheet
$150 $500 $1,200

Style A international half-sheet
$100 $300 $540

Style A 30" x 40"
$150 $700 $1,000

Style A three-sheet
$175 $550 $1,100

Style A 40" x 60"
$50 $550 $825

Style A six-sheet
$900 $2,500 $4,200

Style A seven-sheet
$3,500 $7,750 $12,000

Style A 24-sheet
$3,900 $8,000 $15,500

Style C one-sheet
$200 $1,000 $2,300

Style C international one-sheet
$400 $900 $1,800

Style D/circus poster one-sheet
$60 $400 $1,000

Style D 30" x 40"
$150 $400 $1,000

Style D 40" x 60"
$140 $800 $1,500

Star Wars Happy Birthday One Sheet

Happy Birthday/style E one-sheet
$625 $1,800 $4,750

1978 concert poster (24" x 37")
$2,000 $4,500 $7,800

1979 rerelease one-sheet
$25 $150 $280

1981 rerelease one-sheet
$20 $75 $155

1981 rerelease insert
$20 $90 $150

1981 rerelease half-sheet
$20 $30 $50

1982 rerelease one-sheet
$15 $80 $170

1982 rerelease insert
$40 $70 $100

1982 rerelease half-sheet
$15 $40 $65

1982 rerelease 30" x 40"
$15 $40 $80

1982 rerelease 40" x 60"
$40 $80 $105

1982 rerelease style A video one-sheet
$60 $85 $150

1982 rerelease style A video insert
$40 $60 $75

1992 style B 15th anniversary one-sheet
$10 $80 $175

1992 style D 15th anniversary one-sheet
$15 $75 $150

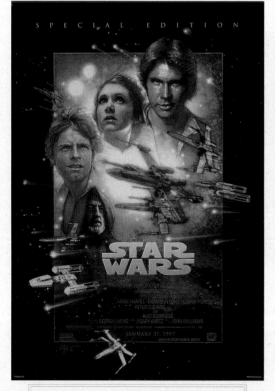

1997 Special Edition trilogy style B
one-sheet
$2 $25 $60

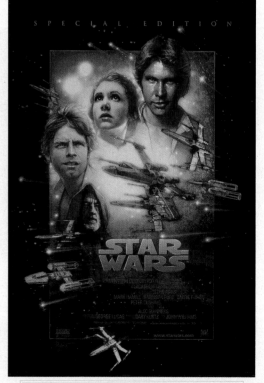

1997 Special Edition trilogy style B
international one-sheet
$3 $20 $55

Advance teaser one-sheet
$50 $400 $800

Advance teaser white logo one-sheet
$425 $1,500 $2,770

Advance teaser subway poster (58" x 45")
$200 $400 $600

Advance teaser three-sheet
$150 $375 $700

Advance teaser six-sheet
$400 $900 $1,600

Advance teaser 24-sheet
$1,000 $5,500 $10,000

Style A/*Gone with the Wind*
one-sheet test poster
$1,800 $6,000 $26,400

Style A/*Gone with the Wind*
one-sheet
$100 $800 $1,550

Style A international one-sheet
$100 $250 $450

Style A insert
$150 $400 $775

Style A international insert
$150 $320 $535

Style A half-sheet
$45 $155 $305

Style A international half-sheet
$45 $120 $215

Style A 30" x 40"
$130 $600 $1,100

Style A 40" x 60"
$250 $700 $1,200

Style A subway poster (45" x 58")
$200 $300 $450

Style B one-sheet
$75 $300 $600

EMPIRE STRIKES BACK   ONE SHEET B

Style B purple version one-sheet
$100 $525 $900

Style B dark blue insert
$75 $225 $450

Style B light blue insert
$65 $210 $385

Style B
half-sheet
$70 $150 $300

Style B dark blue half-sheet
$70 $210 $350

Style B 30" x 40"
$70 $200 $310

Style B 40" x 60"
$140 $325 $500

1981 rerelease one-sheet
$30 $240 $450

1981 rerelease insert
$35 $120 $250

1981 rerelease
half-sheet
$40 $100 $180

1981 rerelease 30" x 40"
$25 $105 $220

1981 rerelease 40" x 60"
$35 $150 $275

1982 rerelease dark blue one-sheet
$50 $125 $250

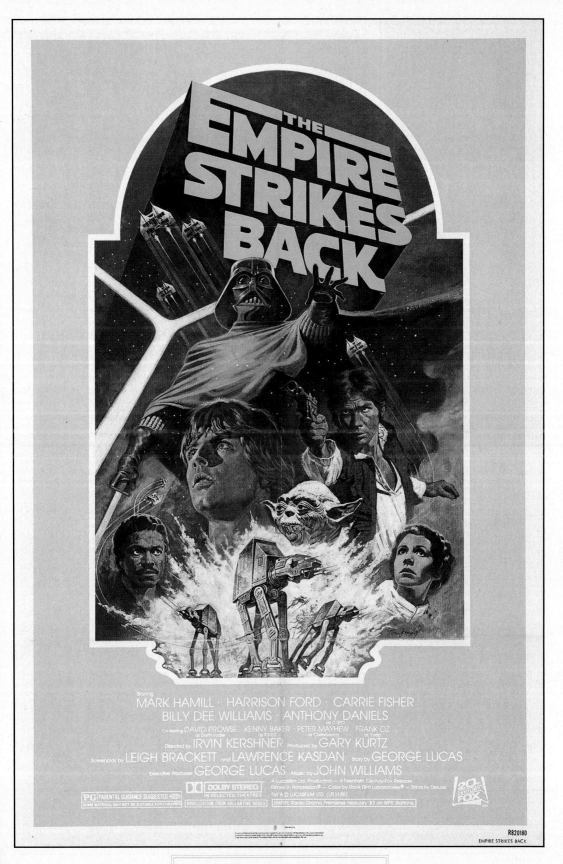

1982 rerelease light blue one-sheet
$275 $750 $1,200

1982 rerelease half-sheet
$20 $60 $100

1982 rerelease insert
$40 $80 $140

1982 rerelease 30" x 40"
$25 $55 $80

1982 rerelease 40" x 60"
$35 $70 $105

1990 10th anniversary
fan club one-sheet
$15 $45 $70

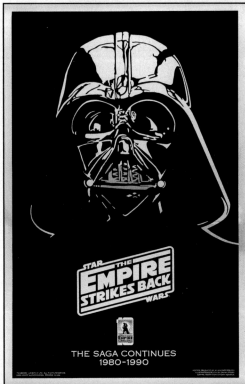

1990 10th anniversary foil one-sheet
$50 $290 $535

1990 10th anniversary foil style B one-sheet
$50 $200 $350

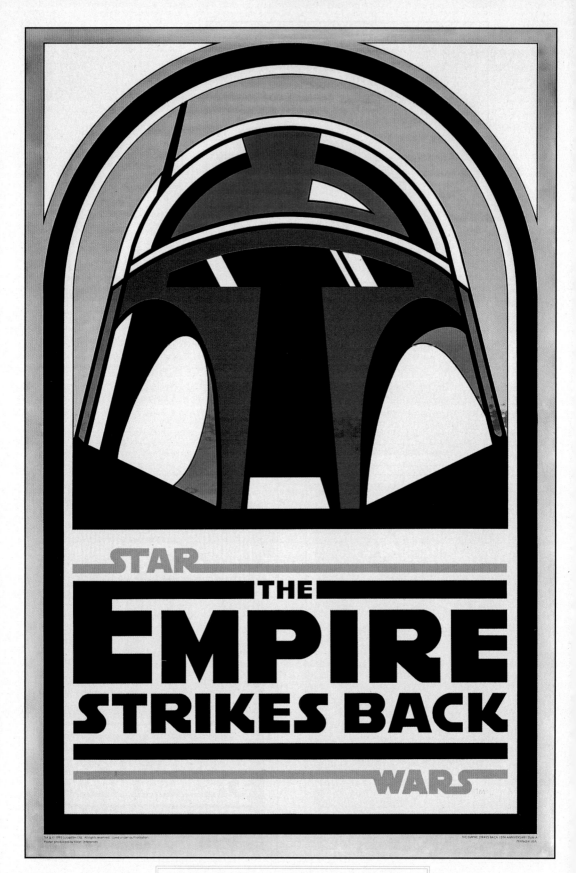

1995 gold foil 15th anniversary one-sheet
$150 $375 $600

1997 Special Edition
style C one-sheet
$10 $45 $90

1997 Special Edition style C
international one-sheet
$5 $25 $50

The next chapter in the STAR WARS saga...

Revenge of the Jedi advance teaser
promo poster (40" x 44")
$170 $350 $550

Revenge of the Jedi advance dated one-sheet
$275 $1,300 $2,500

Revenge of the Jedi advance undated one-sheet
$650 $1,950 $3,500

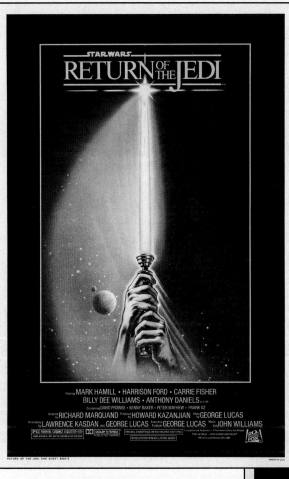

Style A one-sheet
$30 $200 $430

Style A international one-sheet
$20 $155 $300

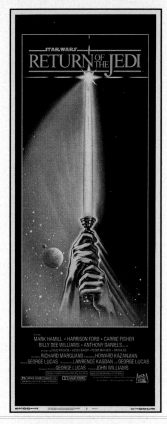

Style A insert
$50 $240 $500

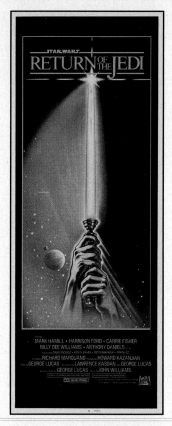

Style A international insert
$30 $230 $425

Style A half-sheet
$50 $175 $300

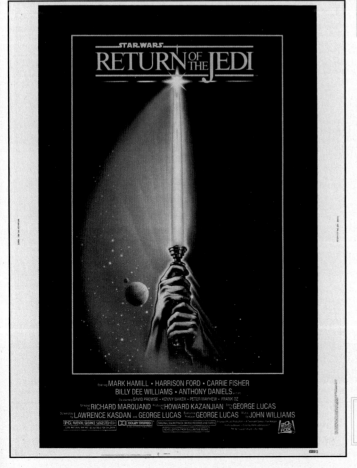

Style A international half-sheet
$30 $110 $200

Style A 30" x 40"
$45 $130 $280

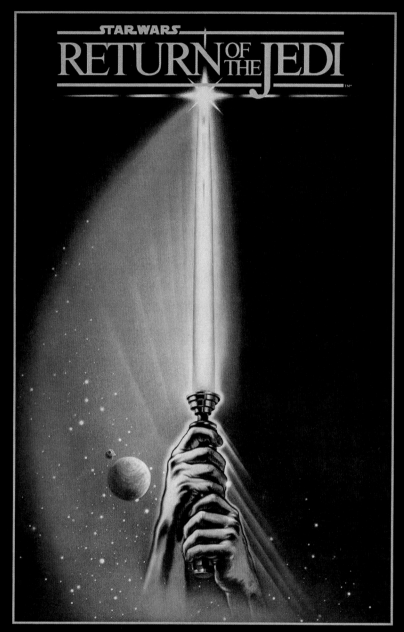

Style A 40" x 60"
$60 $200 $350

Style B one-sheet
$30 $275 $575

Style B white logo one-sheet
$280 $590 $900

Style B international one-sheet
$50 $180 $300

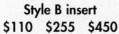

Style B insert
$110 $255 $450

Style B international insert
$100 $230 $400

Style B half-sheet
$75 $130 $200

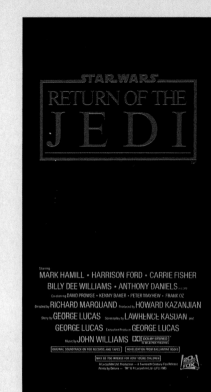

Style B international half-sheet
$60 $100 $180

Style B 30" x 40"
$125 $310 $500

Style B 40" x 60"
$160 $325 $600

Style B three-sheet
$420 $875 $1,300

Style B six-sheet
$2,175 $5,800 $9,450

Style B 24-sheet
$1,000 $4,650 $8,320

1985 rerelease style one-sheet
$20 $90 $175

1985 rerelease half-sheet
$5 $45 $80

1985 rerelease insert
$20 $80 $160

1993 gold foil logo 10th anniversary
one-sheet
$15 $70 $130

1993 red foil logo 10th anniversary
one-sheet
$15 $60 $100

1994 10th anniversary one-sheet
$10 $40 $70

1997 Special Edition style D one-sheet
$4 $20 $55

1997 Special Edition style D
international one-sheet
$5 $20 $50

1997 Special Edition style E one-sheet
$5 $40 $70

1985 Star Wars Saga
American Checklist one-sheet
$10 $70 $130

For the first time in America, The Star Wars Trilogy

STAR WARS
RETURN OF THE JEDI

ONE PERFORMANCE ONLY

The Northpark West Cinema is proud to present, one complete, uncut showing of the Star Wars Trilogy, in 70 Millimeter, Dolby Stereo and THX Lucasfilm Sound. Thursday, March 28, at 4:00 PM. All seats $10.

Tickets on sale at the boxoffice 12:00 Noon on Thursday, March 28. Boxoffice located at 1100 Northpark Ctr. (214) 363-7542

A Lucasfilm Ltd. Production   A Twentieth Century Fox Release
© 1985 Twentieth Century Fox   TM* & © Lucasfilm Ltd. (LFL) 1985

PG PARENTAL GUIDANCE SUGGESTED
SOME MATERIAL MAY NOT BE SUITABLE FOR CHILDREN

PRESENTED IN **70MM**   DOLBY STEREO   THX

This special performance will benefit The Corporation For Public Broadcasting.

1985 Triple Bill one-sheet
$8,000 $12,500 $20,500

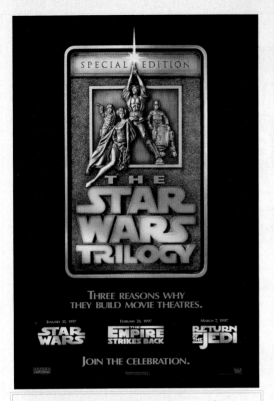

1997 Special Edition trilogy style A
advance one-sheet (original dates)
$5 $25 $50

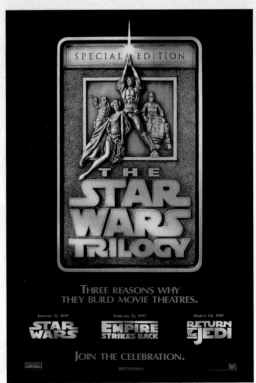

1997 Special Edition trilogy style F
advance one-sheet (new Return date)
$5 $15 $30

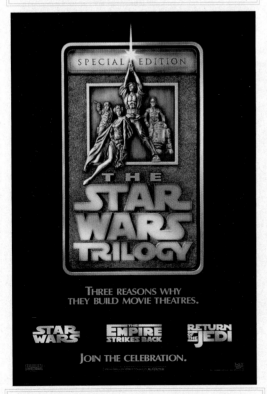

1997 Special Edition trilogy style A advance
international one-sheet
(Three Reasons Why... tagline)
$3 $12 $25

1997 Special Edition trilogy style A
advance international 2 one-sheet
(Join the Celebration tagline)
$2 $8 $15

Caravan of Courage: An Ewok Adventure
Style A TV poster (26" x 33")
$20 $45 $75

Style A one-sheet
$1 $20 $45

Style B one-sheet
$5 $30 $55

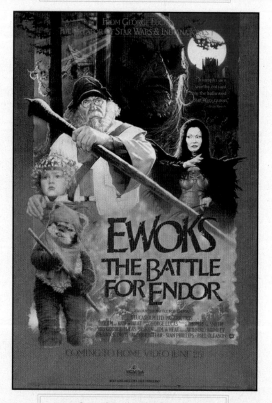

Ewoks: The Battle for Endor
1990 video poster
$1 $4 $9

1998 style A advance one-sheet
$5 $25 $65

1998 style A advance banner (93" x 47")
$10 $45 $90

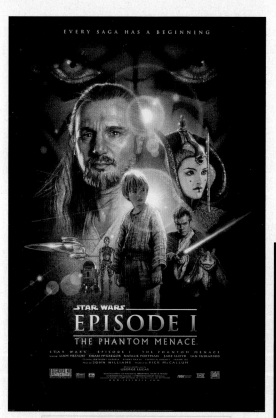

Style B one-sheet
$5 $20 $50

Style B vertical banner (47" x 68")
$10 $45 $90

Style C one-sheet
$4 $18 $35

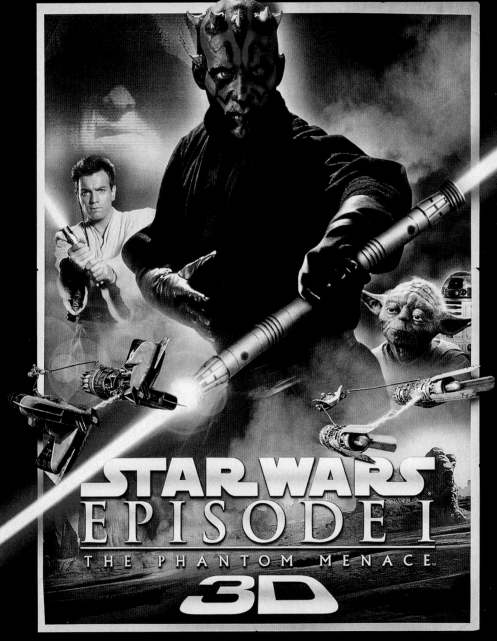

2012 style A 3D one-sheet
$3 $20 $45

2012 style A 3D international one-sheet
$1 $15 $30

2012 style A 3D lenticular one-sheet
$300 $640 $975

2012 style A 3D mini poster (13" x 20")
$1 $8 $15

2012 style A 3D banner (48" x 70")
$15 $30 $45

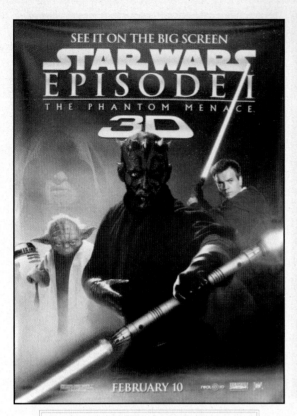

2012 style A 3D secondary banner
(48" x 70")
$15 $30 $45

2012 style A 3D international banner
(48" x 70")
$20 $40 $65

2012 Digital Print Media
3D giclée poster (17" x 22")
$10 $20 $30

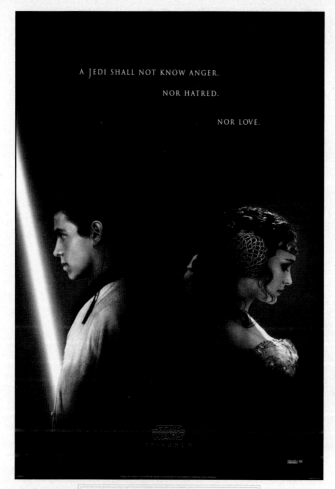

Style A advance one-sheet
$3 $15 $27

Style A advance banner (108" x 59")
$10 $30 $50

Style B one-sheet
$1 $17 $30

Style C one-sheet
$1 $15 $27

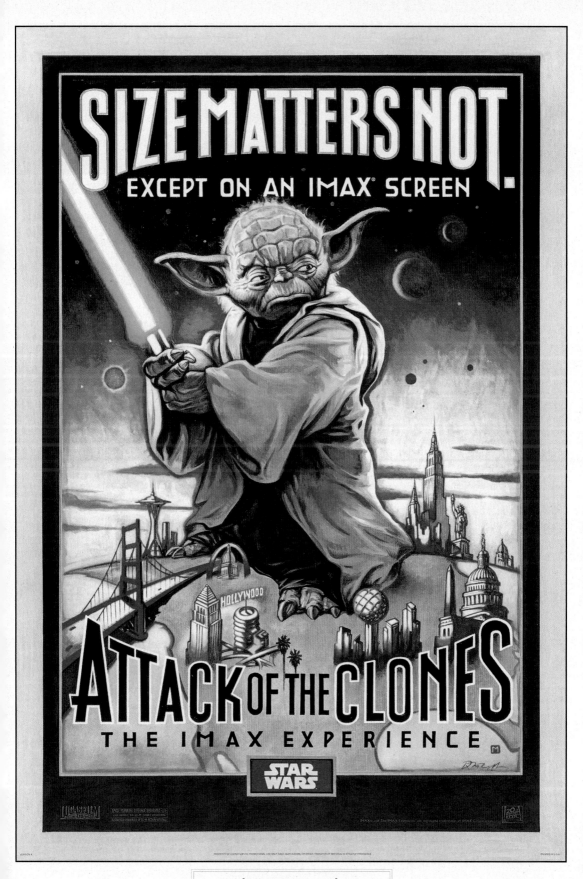

Style A IMAX one-sheet
$25 $55 $75

Style A IMAX uncut printer's proof poster (25" x 38")
$15 $30 $55

Style A IMAX banner (48" x 72")
$40 $90 $140

Style B bus stop (48" x 70")
$5 $20 $35

Style A one-sheet
$1 $13 $25

Style A advance vertical banner
(60" x 96")
$5 $20 $40

"Who's Your Daddy" teaser mini poster
(11" x 17")
$1 $12 $25

Style B one-sheet
$3 $20 $40

Style C one-sheet (ratings box)
$5 $25 $45

Fan Club style D one-sheet
$50 $170 $285

Style A one-sheet
$3 $14 $25

Style A mini poster (11" x 17")
$1 $4 $8

Style A banner (94" x 60")
$5 $12 $20

Advance Celebration 7 mini poster
(13" x 19")
$20 $105 $190

D23 Expo mini poster (13" x 19")
$15 $80 $175

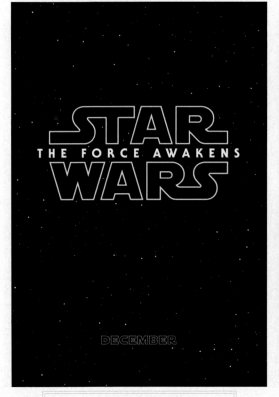

Title teaser one-sheet
$10 $40 $70

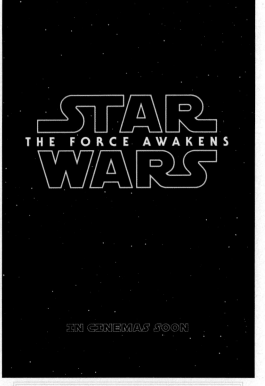

Title teaser international one-sheet
$10 $30 $50

Main cast regular one-sheet
$15 $60 $100

Main cast regular international one-sheet
$10 $50 $80

Kylo Ren over cast international one-sheet
$35 $135 $250

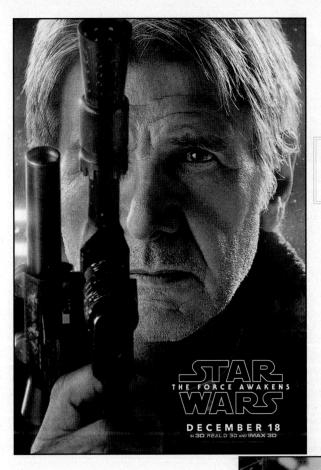

One Eye Series Han Solo
bus stop (48" x 70")
$15 $70 $120

One Eye Series Leia
bus stop (48" x 70")
$15 $70 $120

One Eye Series Rey bus stop (48" x 70")
$10 $55 $100

One Eye Series Kylo Ren
bus stop (48" x 70")
$20 $70 $125

One Eye Series Finn
bus stop (48" x 70")
$10 $55 $100

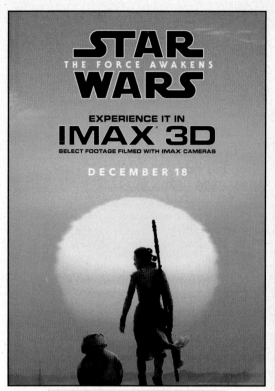

IMAX banner (48" x 70")
$50 $200 $350

AMC IMAX Theaters exclusive Rey,
crashed ships poster (10" x 13")
$5 $12 $20

AMC IMAX Theaters exclusive
Poe Dameron, X-Wing (10" x 13")
$5 $12 $20

AMC IMAX Theaters exclusive
Captain Phasma (10" x 13")
$5 $12 $20

AMC IMAX Theaters exclusive
Finn and Kylo (10" x 13")
$5 $12 $20

Red Pegasus Comics / Texas Theater poster (13" x 19")
$20 $110 $200

Title teaser one-sheet
$17 $35 $60

Scarif/Death Star one-sheet
$20 $55 $105

Scarif/Death Star international one-sheet
$15 $45 $80

Rebel crew one-sheet
$30 $65 $100

Rebel crew international one-sheet
$25 $50 $75

Rebels/Empire over Death Star
international one-sheet
$40 $82 $125

Cast with Rebel symbol
international one-sheet
$60 $105 $150

"Hope" exclusive mini poster (13" x 19")
$15 $60 $100

Cinemark XD exclusive mini poster (9" x 13")
$1 $10 $20

AMC Dolby commemorative mini poster
(13" x 19")
$1 $10 $20

IMAX banner (48" x 72")
$15 $65 $100

Rebel crew bus stop (48" x 72")
$20 $70 $125

AMC IMAX Theatres exclusive poster of
cast over Vader helmet (13" x 19")
$5 $20 $35

AMC IMAX Theatres exclusive
poster of Jyn and cast (13" x 19")
$5 $20 $35

AMC IMAX Theatres exclusive poster
cast over Death Star (13" x 19")
$5 $20 $35

"Deathtrooper" Regal Exclusive art print
poster (13" x 19")
$5 $17 $30

Title teaser one-sheet
$14 $55 $90

Luke/Kylo teaser one-sheet
$35 $85 $130

Luke/Kylo teaser international one-sheet
$15 $45 $80

Cast regular one-sheet
$40 $80 $120

Cast regular international one-sheet
$15 $50 $85

Resistance international one-sheet
$40 $85 $130

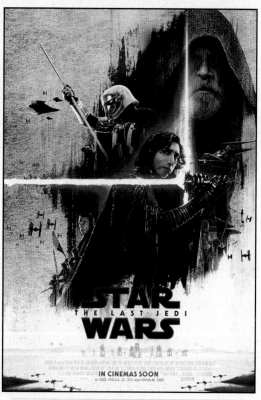

First Order international one-sheet
$40 $85 $130

Light/Dark Fandango exclusive poster (11" x 17")
$5 $12 $20

Cinemark XD exclusive poster (8" x 24")
$5 $18 $30

Red Cloak Leia
bus shelter
(48" x 72")
$20 $60 $100

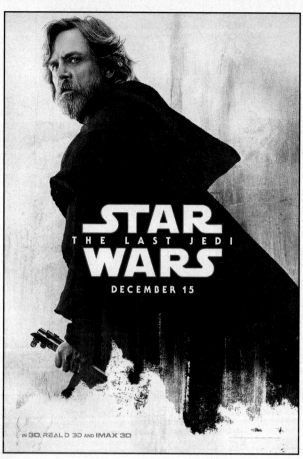

Red Cloak Luke bus shelter
(48" x 72")
$20 $60 $100

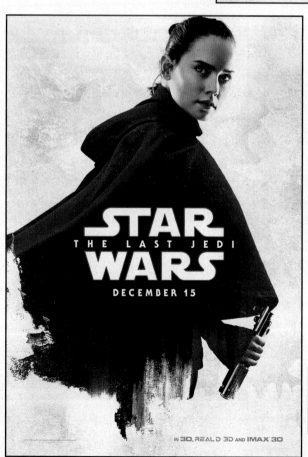

Red Cloak Rey bus shelter
(48" x 72")
$20 $55 $85

Red Cloak Kylo Ren bus shelter (48" x 72")
$20 $40 $65

Red Cloak Finn bus shelter (48" x 72")
$20 $40 $65

Red Cloak Poe bus shelter (48" x 72")
$20 $35 $55

IMAX banner (48" x 72")
$50 $90 $130

AMC IMAX Theatres exclusive poster
Luke training Rey (10" x 13")
$1 $5 $10

AMC IMAX Theatres exclusive poster
Battle of Crait (10" x 13")
$1 $5 $10

AMC IMAX Theatres exclusive poster
Finn and Captain Phasma battle (10" x 13")
$1 $5 $10

AMC IMAX Theatres exclusive poster
Snoke and Kylo Ren in throne room (10" x 13")
$1 $5 $10

Title teaser one-sheet
$20 $65 $110

Cast style one-sheet
$30 $75 $125

Regular one-sheet
$35 $80 $130

ADVANCED POSTER DESIGN WITH STAR WARS MOVIE POSTER ARTISTS

Good movie posters can be subtle teasers, capture a specific moment, or convey an entire plot. It's a challenging task for any artist, yet some talented individuals produce beautiful, memorable renderings that are forever tied to a film. In the case of *Star Wars*, artists who specialize in graphic design, advertising, book covers, fine art, and even comics have created dozens of designs to entice movie audiences. Some of the most popular posters in the series were created by Tom Jung, Roger Kastel, Kazuhiko Sano, and Drew Struzan.

TOM JUNG

Tom Jung is a multitalented artist who specializes in art direction, graphic design, storyboard art, and advertising. A Boston native, he attended the School of the Museum of Fine Arts after high school. Once he was drafted into the Army, he contributed to the local newspaper, providing editorial car-

toons along with designing and illustrating public service communications. Following his military service, he became a freelance illustrator and art director in New York.

In 1958 he started redesigning ad campaigns of foreign films for American theaters and created pressbooks and one-sheets for distribution at independent theaters. Early in his career, Jung favored the caricature style akin to *MAD* magazine, which can be seen on the movie posters for *School of Scoundrels* and *The Golden Age of Comedy*.

He worked for MGM as an art director, designing posters for films like *Grand Prix* and overseeing designs for other posters. In one of his most memorable assignments, Jung chose Howard Terpning to illustrate the 1967 rerelease poster for *Gone with the Wind*, which was later imitated by Roger Kastel for *The Empire Strikes Back*. In the late '60s he worked for Cinema Center Films as art director on a group of nearly 30 movies.

By the mid-1970s he was regarded as an art director and designer who could develop a concept, design, and illustrate a poster with complete confidence and little need for oversight. Some of his work at that point included posters for dramatic war movies like *The Deer Hunter* and *Apocalypse Now*.

In 1977, Jung was chosen to create the style A design for *Star Wars*. At this point, most people had only seen text-based advanced teasers, so his poster would largely serve as an introduction to the movie. Working off the theme of good versus evil, he put the heroic Luke Skywalker and Princess Leia in the foreground with Darth Vader's helmet behind them. The poster is split by the cross section beam from Luke's lightsaber, further suggesting his significance. Jung also notably drew the title in the famous *Star Wars* crawl style, which was repeated on many other series posters.

Jung returned to the series in 1980, providing the art for *The Empire Strikes Back* style B design, which saw several more characters, including Lando Calrissian who did not appear on the style A version. The movie's title is reinforced by the large image of Darth Vader, standing like a giant over the rest of the cast. The characters are all gathered in a shape that mimics the villain's helmet, down to the angle of Vader's leg and a running Stormtrooper which appear similar to the helmet's mouth area.

Rounding out the trilogy, he drew a fresh poster for the *Return of the Jedi* 1985 rerelease. Keeping with the blue color scheme of both the style A and B posters, Jung painted portraits of the main cast above the credits and below an exploding Death Star. Unlike his more serious earlier *Star Wars* entries, this one takes on a whimsical tone, going so far as to put smirks on Han, Lando, and Yoda.

Tom Jung gave many fans their first look at the cast on his *Star Wars* style A poster.

On *The Empire Strikes Back* style B design, Jung painted the cast in a shape similar to that of Darth Vader's helmet.

ROGER KASTEL

Readers can certainly judge a book by its cover when Roger Kastel painted it. Originally from White Plains, New York, Kastel became an artist during his teen years. He commuted to Manhattan during high school to study at The Art Students League of New York, and became a professional artist after serving in the Navy during the Korean War.

Kastel did freelance work for different studios and ad agencies in New York, providing storyboards and layouts while continuing to train at The Art Students League. In 1960 he scored his first paperback cover for Simon & Schuster, which was followed by hundreds more for various publishers.

Among those was his iconic paperback cover for Peter Benchley's *Jaws*. His cover was based on the original design by Paul Bacon, with the same shark and swimmer poses. Kastel's version is far more detailed, giving the shark a more accurate depiction from the snout to its rows of sharp teeth. The art is so frightening and thrilling that Universal Studios purchased the right to use the image for the movie poster. The image has become synonymous with both the movie and its source material.

His entry into the *Star Wars* canon came in 1980 with *The Empire Strikes Back* style A design. Also known as the *Gone with the Wind* style, it mirrors the popular 1960s rerelease poster for the 1939 epic film. The beautiful artwork takes on a dramatic tone with Luke bundled against the harsh environment of Hoth while Han and Leia share a romantic embrace. It is one of the most popular posters from the entire film series.

Roger Kastel's *The Empire Strikes Back* style A pays homage to the *Gone with the Wind* rerelease poster with dramatic renderings of Leia, Han, and Luke.

KAZUHIKO SANO

Before becoming a fine artist, Kazuhiko Sano was more interested in music, particularly acts like The Beatles, James Brown, The Drifters, and Elvis Presley. As the musical styling of acid rock and counterculture surfaced in the 1960s, he started noticing color more, and became interested in painting and illustration.

After failing to get into an art school in Japan, the Tokyo native moved to the U.S. to study at San Francisco's Academy of

Art University, in the mid-1970s. It wasn't long after he started that a professor recognized the particular skill in his work and guided him out of graphic design and into illustration.

He worked on advertising campaigns for several prominent companies and created popular fine art paintings. In the '70s and early '80s he created book cover art for over a dozen *Star Trek* paperback novels that featured accurate portraits of the cast, along with creatures, ships, and planets within their pages.

Jumping from the Enterprise to the Millennium Falcon, he provided the style B poster art for *Return of the Jedi* in 1983. The poster showcases his cleanly detailed portraiture with depictions of Luke, Han, Lando, and Leia in the famous gold bikini. As it represents all three arcs of the film, the infamous Jabba the Hutt with some of his minions and Wicket also make appearances. Darth Vader is shown in what became his customary spot, hovering at the top of the poster, cloaked in darkness.

Sano returned to *Star Wars* in '94 to create a *Return of the Jedi* rerelease poster. This one focused more on shadowed closeups of the characters, expressing their dismay and resolve for the coming battle. The base color in shades of blue accentuates the explosion at the poster's center. Once again, Sano included Jabba and Ewoks, adding in R2-D2 and C-3PO.

Kazuhiko Sano created two designs
for *Return of the Jedi*: the style B in 1983
and the rerelease in 1994.
Both feature realistic portraits
of multiple characters
over blue backgrounds.

DREW STRUZAN

Throughout his extensive career, Drew Struzan has illustrated more than 150 movie posters and is known as a favored artist of George Lucas and Steven Spielberg. His realism-focused style can be seen on memorable posters for *Star Wars*, *Indiana Jones*, *Back to the Future*, *Harry Potter*, *Hook*, and *The Thing*, among many others.

A native of Oregon City, Oregon, he attended the Art Center College of Design in Los Angeles. While working his way through school, Struzan sold art and accepted small commission work. Following graduation, he stayed in Los Angeles to work as a staff artist for the design studio Pacific Eye & Ear, creating album covers for musicians like Black Sabbath, Glenn Miller, and Earth, Wind and Fire.

The next step in his journey was the beginning of his movie career. He started Pencil Pushers, a small company with a friend who had a background in the movie industry, which lasted eight years. During this time, he honed his skills, providing artwork for one-sheets with an airbrush style, which would become his signature. Things took

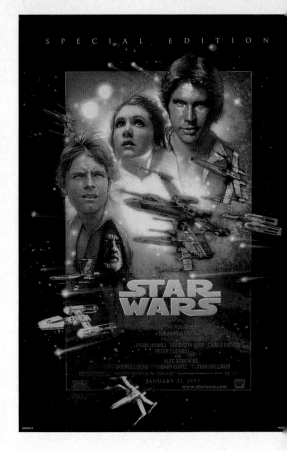

a dramatic turn for the best in 1977 when George Lucas hired artist Charles White III to design a *Star Wars* poster for the '78 rerelease.

White, who was well known for his airbrush style, asked Struzan to help with the portraits of the characters on the poster. White focused on the ships, Darth Vader, C-3PO and mechanical details, while Struzan worked on the human characters. Together they painted several action moments before realizing that there wasn't enough room to list the film's credits. They manipulated the image to make it appear to be a torn bill posted on plywood and added Obi-Wan on the lower left side to make it look wider and deeper. The *Star Wars* style D poster became popularly known as the circus poster.

The advance teaser he painted for *Return of the Jedi* is one of only a few items to feature

Drew Struzan's first entry into *Star Wars* was the 1978 style D rerelease that he did with Charles White III. It has become popularly known as the circus poster.

Struzan's 1997 special edition posters share thematic similarities and the ships appear to fly off the images in a continuous line.

the original title, *Revenge of the Jedi*. The art is composed primarily of Darth Vader's helmet with a smaller image of Luke and Vader engaged in a lightsaber battle. The dominantly red and black poster creates a foreboding ambiance leading into the film.

Struzan returned to the franchise in 1997 to create new posters for the special edition releases of the original trilogy. Thematically, each poster depicts character portraits, ships flying through the sky, and two main color tones. Luke, Leia, Han, and Darth Vader are on the posters as expected, but Struzan also created portraits of Obi-Wan, Emperor Palpatine, Chewbacca, and Jabba the Hutt – who rarely saw prominent placement on the posters. Set side by side, the three posters have a directional flow with ships flying to the left on *A New Hope*, straightforward on *The Empire Strikes Back*, and flying to the right on *Return of the Jedi*.

Struzan was also the artist behind the regular one-sheets for all three prequel films. Once again, he captured the tone of each installment, illustrating the personalities of both new and younger versions of characters. The personal journeys of the three new leads – young Obi-Wan, Padmé Amidala, and Anakin Skywalker – are accurately depicted from one poster to the next.

With the third trilogy on the way in 2015, Struzan came out of retirement to design a special poster for *The Force Awakens*. The D23 Expo mini poster introduces newcomers Finn, Rey, and Kylo Ren, featured along with Han Solo. It contrasts warm and cool colors with his signature realistic depictions.

These four artists, along with other talented designers, have attracted movie fans with promises of adventure, action, suspense, and a little romance. Through different styles and interpretations, they capture the essence of *Star Wars* with wonderful detail and creativity. Whether with one entry or several, they have become an important part of the *Star Wars* artistic experience.

MAKING THE GRADE
AFA'S CEO CHAD THOMPSON
TALKS TOY GRADING

Star Wars toy collecting is a thriving market enjoyed by fans all over the world. As such, it can be challenging to purchase an item with confidence without a unified agreement on condition. Since 2000, Action Figure Authority, a division of the Collectible Grading Authority, has provided toy grading and encapsulation for collectors. AFA grades action figures and toys through a system similar to ones that have been successful in comic books.

Here, AFA's CEO Chad Thompson provides some background on the company and the larger Collectible Grading Authority organization. He presents a detailed look at the complexities of their grading process, how items are encapsulated and protected from any damage, and the important information found on their labels. He also touches on subjects like memorable toys, conventions, and how grading has impacted the hobby.

Overstreet: Can you give me a brief company history of Collectible Grading Authority, and specifically of Action Figure Authority?

Chad Thompson (CT): Action Figure Authority (AFA), a division of Collectible Grading Authority (CGA) was founded in 2000 as a way to provide toy collectors throughout the world with added peace of mind when making purchases sight unseen. Until the formation of AFA, dealers, collectors, and investors had no universal standard by which to judge an item's condition. Virtually everyone had their own ideas, criteria, and definitions by which to rate any given item.

AFA has worked diligently for the past 18 years to develop the standard we use to accurately convey the condition of original and un-tampered with collectibles, thereby creating a safer collecting environment, and helping to ensure your investment is protected for years to come. You can be certain that each AFA-graded item was carefully examined by well-trained, unbiased professionals, which allows for a more relaxing and safer collecting experience.

Overstreet: What types of items do you grade?

CT: CGA has four different grading divisions.

AFA for packaged, loose, and prototype action figures and related toys: Modern Grading Scale recommended for sealed in package toys produced from 2000-present; Standard Grading Scale for sealed/new in package toys and new in mailer box toys from all years; Loose Grading Scale for loose, complete toys from all years; and Qualified Grading Scale (items are accompanied with documentation) for opened package toys with new contents, handmade prototype toys, incomplete rare and pre-production loose toys, and autographed toys.

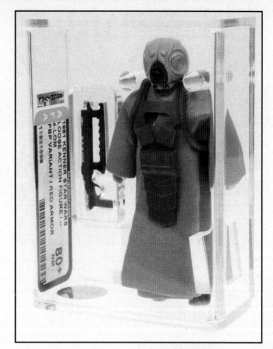

Collectible Doll Authority is for packaged collectible dolls and related toys, Die-Cast Authority for packaged die-cast vehicles and related toys, and Video Game Authority for packaged video games and related items.

Overstreet: What's the most common type of toy that you grade?

CT: Over the past 18 years, *Star Wars* toys have been the most popular toy line submitted to AFA for grading.

Overstreet: What's the most memorable toy that you've graded?

CT: Prototype rocket-firing Boba Fett J-slot V2 sealed in bag with test mailer.

Overstreet: Start to finish what does the grading/encapsulation process entail?

CT: When items arrive at AFA, they are carefully unpacked, photographed immediately, and placed in the grading queue. Our professional graders will then carefully identify and examine each item to verify it's both original and untampered with. Each item is

then assigned a grade, a unique serial number, and sealed inside a high quality acrylic display case.

Overstreet: How many people determine the actual grade?

CT: Each item is typically examined by several graders with at least one senior grader confirming the final grade and details.

Overstreet: What are important things you note to determine the grade?

CT: When an item is graded, AFA's experienced team of graders go through a detailed process to assess flaws and look for any signs of restoration or tampering. Any damage, deterioration, discoloration, and even factory flaws to the cardboard, blister, or action figure are factored into the final grade. In addition to the final grade, sub-grades for card, blister, and figure are provided to help provide additional insight into the final grade assigned.

Overstreet: How long does the process take?

CT: Depending on the type of item,

our grading process can take anywhere from five minutes to multiple hours per item.

Overstreet: How many types of cases do you have?

CT: For graded items, we offer two different case and label styles. Our classic label is a smaller label and hologram placed on the inner side of the case which is not directly visible from the front. Our clear view label is a larger label and hologram placed inside the case above a graded item which is directly visible from the front. In addition to case styles for graded items, we offer a full line of standard and custom size sliding display cases which can be opened and closed. Sliding display cases can be ordered directly on our website without ever mailing your item to AFA.

Overstreet: What archival properties do your cases have?

CT: All of our acrylic cases are manufactured in-house from the highest quality acrylic under the guidance of an acrylic fabrication master with over 35 years of experience as an artisan. While all of our acrylic cases offer some UV resistance, our archival material case options offer approximately 99% UV-resistance. Each case is custom designed by AFA to fit each specific item and to properly protect an item from the damage that can come from excessive handling. Other features include special holders to secure each item in place and a very thin seam across the bottom back case edge to allow for minimal circulation of air.

Overstreet: What kind of information appears on your labels? Do you note releases, variations, if something is signed, etc.?

CT: Each graded item comes with a label that contains specific information about that item. This information includes year of manufacture, company, series, title, toy name, and any variations. The label also includes a unique serial number which can be verified on AFA's website.

Overstreet: Once things are encased can they be opened?

CT: Once an item is graded and sealed, the case cannot be opened without breaking the bottom. This is because the adhesive used to bond our acrylic is stronger than the material itself. A case must remain sealed in order to preserve the integrity of the AFA grade.

Overstreet: Do you set up at conventions or events to take submissions?

CT: Yes, AFA sets up at conventions all over the U.S. and other countries and takes submissions on-site. In addition to many smaller conventions, we attend [Comic-Con International: San Diego] in July of each year where we offer discounts on both grading and sliding bottom acrylic cases.

Overstreet: From your perspective, how has grading toys affected the toy collecting hobby?

CT: Grading within the toy hobby provides a much safer environment for collectors and has helped the hobby mature into a true investment market similar to comic books, sports cards, etc.

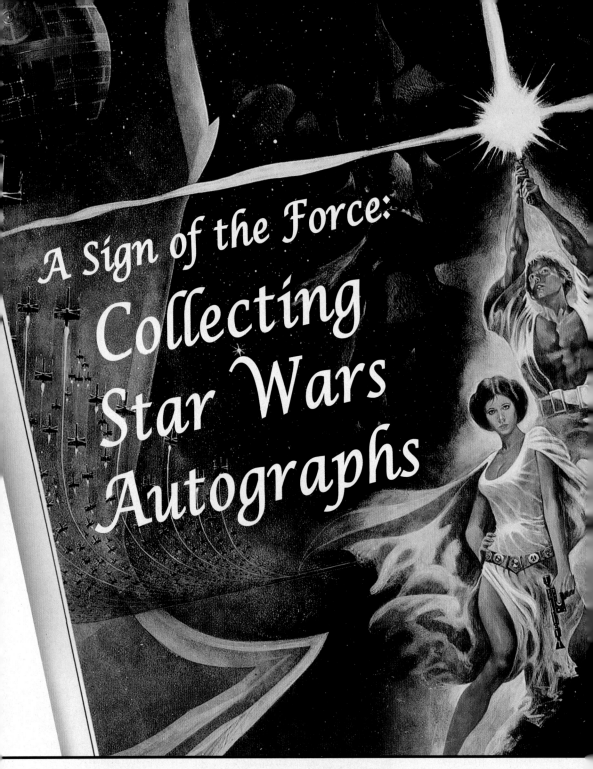

A Sign of the Force:
Collecting Star Wars Autographs

Collecting *Star Wars* autographs is a facet of the hobby that could keep collectors busy and entertained for a long time. By invoking a feeling of connection with filmmakers and actors, they enhance the existing joy of collecting. Autographs are also easy to collect, as they are consistently sold in auctions and can also be procured at pop culture conventions.

There's no shortage of options when collecting *Star Wars* autographs. By just considering George Lucas, the principal and supporting cast, directors, and screenwriters, there's potential to collect autographs from at least 70 people. Then there are the score composers, puppeteers, creature designers, makeup artists, prop masters, set designers, poster artists, and actors who

George Lucas is the most popular autograph from the series. His signature sells in a wide range from $30 to $4,500, depending on what he signed.

played bit parts as creatures, Rebels, or Imperial officers. Factor them in and the list grows into the hundreds.

Because *Star Wars* is such a large, creative film series, autographs can be found on many types of memorabilia. Most commonly, they appear on movie posters, lobby cards, and actors' head shots or movie stills. Toys, action figures, and other collectibles are often autographed at conventions while documents like scripts, contracts, checks, film notes, and letters come up in auctions. The variety of autographed material also includes magazines, props, shirts and hats, even index cards.

Items signed by George Lucas sell in a large price range that is affordable for most fans. High value material includes rarities like the concert poster, which reaches $4,500, or documents related to the movies that can go for

$1,500. Original one-sheets from the first trilogy signed by Lucas sell for $500. On the other end of the spectrum, Lucas-signed movie stills and behind the scenes photos average about $70 and less glamorous material, like signed notecards, will only hit $30.

Carrie Fisher, Mark Hamill, Harrison Ford, and Peter Mayhew are priority autographs for collectors. Their signatures sell for $50 up to thousands, depending on the item and who else has signed it.

When it comes to the actors, autograph prices vary significantly from a few dollars to a few hundred. Key factors that determine prices are screen time in the series, whether the character was popular, and what else the actor has done.

Mark Hamill, Carrie Fisher, and Harrison Ford are the trio most closely associated with the movies, but their autograph prices aren't strictly even. Ford's career has been more expansive with the *Indiana Jones* series and other high profile action films. Plus, he's known to be reclusive, which makes his autograph a harder commodity to attain.

Typically, more screen time is synonymous with higher autograph value, but that isn't a strict rule. In regard to character popularity, Boba Fett didn't have a lot of screen time, but people love the character, so items signed by Jeremy Bulloch sell fairly well. However, autographs of actors who played characters with larger screen time who weren't received well won't make as much.

Some actors will achieve high prices regardless of character likeability or screen time. Peter Cushing had a small part as Grand Moff Tarkin, but he was a celebrated actor in Hammer Film Productions' horror movies, so his autograph will sell more than those of other Imperial officers. The prequel trilogy featured celebrities like Liam Neeson, Natalie Portman, Ewan McGregor, and Samuel L. Jackson, who are known for a large variety of films, and are therefore more expensive autographs than some of their costars.

After someone involved in the series dies, that person's autograph will typically become more valuable. This is due to the fact that those deaths can strike an emotional chord with fans who feel a sudden sense of urgency to acquire a signature. It also happens because there is now a finite number of autographs, making them rarer commodities. Typically, the prices will spike immediately following the person's passing, then they will decrease a bit and level out after a few months.

Another facet of *Star Wars* autograph collecting is for the movie poster artists. A Charles White III signature on his popular style D/circus poster averages $400.

The price also depends on the specific material being signed. For instance, original movie posters versus reproductions, rare cast-owned items versus mass produced toys, vintage collectibles versus newly released memorabilia. In those cases, collectors will be paying for the autograph *and* the value of the item. One of Mark Hamill's contracts sold for over $15,500, a true rarity, while script pages might sell for $100 to $300. An original version of the *New Hope* style D poster signed by Charles White III averages $400, whereas a repro of the *Return of the Jedi* advance signed by Drew Struzan sells for around $50.

Certain material is more likely to be signed by several people when enough surface space is available. This usually includes movie posters, scripts, magazine covers, and blank comic covers. Photo stills can get multiple signatures, though usually only of the people pictured. Material signed by several cast/crew members range from $200 to $11,000 – depending on how many people have signed and which ones. The averages are settled between $3,000 to $5,000 for multiple signatures on an original trilogy poster, and slightly less for the prequel and third trilogies.

PRE-AUTOGRAPHED MEMORABILIA

When collecting photos, posters, props, and other items that are already autographed, verifying authenticity is the most important part of the process. Unfortunately, anyone can start a website or join sales platforms, and claim that their autographs are authentic. Doing just a brief search on one celebrity yields results that are clearly not signed by the same person, but also some that could be real. Buying from a website or seller that is unfamiliar is a gamble.

Organizations such as Professional Sports Authenticator (PSA/DNA) and James Spence Authentication (JSA) are dedicated to authenticating autographs by studying and compiling examples. Once verified, these agencies will give the autographed item a letter or certificate of authenticity – commonly called an LOA or COA.

Another helpful tool when it comes to collecting pre-signed autographs are online forums. These online message boards – whether they are dedicated to a type of collectible, genre, or series – are filled with collectors and dealers willing and ready to share their knowledge and experiences. If an autographed item hasn't been verified by an authentication agency, forum members can assist by offering guidance and sometimes examples of the autograph in question for comparison. While it is not a foolproof method, it can be very helpful.

PURCHASING AUTOGRAPHS AT CONVENTIONS

Many *Star Wars* autographs can be purchased first hand at conventions for $40 to $150, depending on the person, item size/type, and convention size (sometimes actors will charge more at larger shows and less at smaller ones).

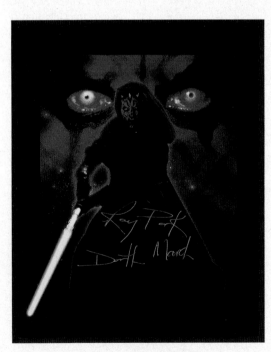

Ray Park's portrayal of Darth Maul is a favored performance in *The Phantom Menace*. His autograph goes for $20 to $70.

Samuel L. Jackson's role in the *Star Wars* series, combined with his Hollywood star caliber puts his autograph at $60 to $400, depending on the item.

An *Attack of the Clones* photo signed by Ewan McGregor and Hayden Christensen can sell for about $150.

Convention guests are always armed with 8" x 10" photos to sign for attendees. Some will have a half-dozen different images, while others come with binders full of options. This is the easiest collecting option since attendees don't need to bring their own item and they are fairly easy to keep safe during the remainder of the con. After getting an 8" x 10" signed, always make sure the signature is dry before putting it away. Easy options for safe storage include thick cardboard envelopes or a padded folio case, which can be purchased at an office supply store or post office.

A slightly larger, though still manageable alternative is the 11" x 17" print. These are typically either mini versions

Toys and figures are also popular collectibles for signatures. A Rey bobble head from *The Force Awakens* averages $60 to $90.

of movie posters or stills from the movie. If the plan is to get multiple signatures on one image, an 11" x 17" is much better option than an 8" x 10" photo. Again, make sure the signature is dry before putting it away. The easiest option is a small plastic sleeve in a short, thick plastic or cardboard tube.

For movie posters, the first thing collectors should do is study the artwork. Is it the kind of poster that will make a signature pop or might the signature get lost in the art? Most *Star Wars* posters depict detailed art, though to different degrees, and most of the movies offer more than one design. A comparison of *The Empire Strikes Back* style A and style B posters shows that the latter has more surface space in which signatures will display vibrantly.

Carry rolled posters in an acid-free plastic sleeve, then inside either a 3-ply thick cardboard or hard plastic tube. If using cardboard, do not use the kind with a snap seal because it can damage the ends of the poster. Use one with a cap that can easily be removed and replaced. The cardboard tubes are thinner and less cumbersome, however, plastic tubes generally come with a strap that can be worn, leaving hands free.

For folded posters, carry them in an acid-free Mylar sleeve then in some kind of binder or folio that will protect them from damage during the rest of the con.

Do not roll or fold the poster immediately after it has been signed. Give it a minute to dry, especially if the person signed with a paint pen. Examine the autograph area to make sure the person didn't accidentally leave any smudges from food or beverage debris. Unfortunately, this does happen. If something was transferred onto the poster use a paper towel to clean the soiled area and do not roll or fold if it is wet. If the stain persists, the ink in that area may need to be restored.

Action figures and other toy collectibles can be signed loose or still packaged. Since newer figures are mass produced on a high level, this can make them stand out. Use a felt tip or paint pen for the signature and do not store with signature facing other items because it can rub off.

Whether buying pre-signed items from auctions or getting things signed in-person at conventions, autograph collecting is an entertaining category in any *Star Wars* collection. It's a personalized way to express fandom and fosters a feeling of connection to those involved in the series.

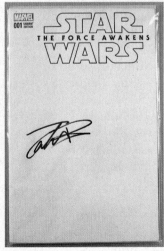

Fans also get actors to sign comic books based on the series. This blank cover signed by John Boyega sold for $45.

For the first time in America, The Star Wars Trilogy

STAR WARS

™

THE EMPIRE STRIKES BACK

™

STAR WARS RETURN OF THE JEDI

™

PLITT CARNEGIE THEATRE
ONE PERFORMANCE ONLY

The Carnegie Theatre is proud to present
one complete, uncut showing of the Star Wars Trilogy, in 70 Millimeter and Dolby Stereo.
Thursday, March 28, at 5:30 PM. All seats $10.

Tickets on sale at the boxoffice 12:00 Noon on Thursday, March 28.
Boxoffice located at 1026 N. Rush Street.   (312) 944-2966

A Lucasfilm Ltd. Production — A Twentieth Century Fox Release
Prints by Deluxe — TM* & © Lucasfilm Ltd. (LFL) 1985

PG PARENTAL GUIDANCE SUGGESTED
SOME MATERIAL MAY NOT BE SUITABLE FOR CHILDREN

PRESENTED IN **70MM** ☐☐ DOLBY STEREO

*This special performance will benefit
The Corporation For Public Broadcasting.*

Posters depicting multiple signatures can go for $3,000
or more in auctions. Ones with fewer signatures
like this one can sell for as low as $100.

Buckle Up
for the Ultimate Adventure

Star Wars
Stories
& Collectibles
at
Disney Parks

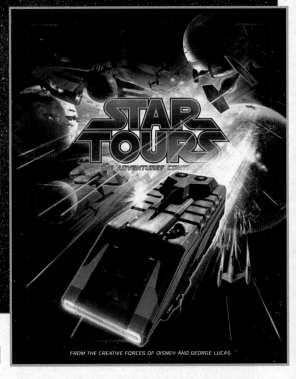

FROM THE CREATIVE FORCES OF DISNEY AND GEORGE LUCAS

By Carrie Wood

Long before the Walt Disney Company purchased Lucasfilm and gained the rights to produce new *Star Wars* content, the franchise and its characters had a strong presence at Disney theme parks around the world. *Star Tours*, a thrill ride that takes its riders to a galaxy far, far away by use of motion simulation technology, first debuted at Disneyland Park in California in late 1986, and was followed by the ride's opening at Tokyo Disneyland and Disney's Hollywood Studios (then Disney-MGM Studios) in 1989, and Disneyland Park in Paris in 1992.

The opening of *Star Tours* across the Disney parks was the result of a previous partnership between Disney and George Lucas, with Lucas having written *Captain EO*, a

3D sci-fi short film that starred Michael Jackson and was directed by Francis Ford Coppola. *Captain EO* proved to be popular after its 1986 opening, and Disney – originally wanting to make a motion-simulation ride based on the 1979 film *The Black Hole* before shelving that idea due to the lack of interest in the film – went to Lucas again to collaborate on *Star Tours*.

Star Tours, in its original iteration, put its riders inside a Starspeeder 3000, piloted by the less-than-competent RX-24, or simply Rex (voiced by Paul Reubens). Rex intended to take his passengers on a smooth, unexciting trip to Endor – however, after bumbling his way through the maintenance bay, his jump to lightspeed is miscalculated, and the ship instead gets caught inside a cluster of comets. Rex is able to escape from the comet, but is caught in the tractor beam of an Imperial Star Destroyer. An X-wing arrives to free the tour passengers from certain doom, and Rex pilots the Starspeeder to help assist the Rebels in their assault on the Death Star, making one final jump to lightspeed to escape the explosion caused in its destruction. Rex manages to get the passengers back to the spaceport, though he nearly collides with a truck in the process, and the poor pilot droid is cut off before he is able to apologize for the rough ride.

The original ride proved to be a massive success for Disney, though after more than 20 years in operation, *Star Tours* began to be shut down at the four parks it occupied in favor of an updated edition. The discussion of a "*Star Tours II*" was first mentioned by Lucas himself in 2005 during Star Wars Celebration, though it wouldn't be until the 2009 D23 Expo that Disney confirmed that it was indeed happening. The California and Florida rides both closed in 2010 in order for the refurbishment to take place, while the Tokyo version of *Star Tours* remained open until 2012, and the Paris iteration continued to operate in its original format well into 2016.

The updated version of the ride, called *Star Tours: The Adventures Continue*, first opened in both American parks in mid-2011 before making its way overseas. The new attraction features an updated ride system, new high-definition audio, additional audio-animatronics, and 3D visuals for a fully immersive experience.

Despite having the subtitle of *The Adventures Continue*, the updated *Star Tours* was initially envisioned as a prequel to the original attraction; while riders are still treated as space tourists looking to hitch a ride through the galaxy, they board a Starspeeder 1000 (instead of a 3000 model) and the ride's plot was intended to take place between the original and prequel trilogies. The pilot for the updated ride is none other than C-3PO, though Rex can still be found in the queue – he's been labeled as "defective" and marked to be sent back to the factory, but will sometimes experience a power surge and say something from the ride's original script.

While the original *Star Tours* was the same ride experience every time, *The Adventures Continue* instead has four different story chunks that are randomized on each ride-through. There are, as of this book's publication, four different opening segments, four different primary destination segments, six different hologram messages, and four different final destination segments that could possibly be chosen from during a single ride. All told, it means that there are more than 300 possible routes that could be taken – which encourages fans to go back and ride it multiple times.

Despite being a somewhat random experience every time, *The Adventures Continue* does feature a core plot that stays consistent – though disguised as a regular tour, this particular Starspeeder 1000 carries a Rebel spy (chosen at random from the riders on board) and must be delivered to a secure location.

The Adventures Continue, when it first opened, was clearly set between the two trilogies that had been released at that time. However, in the years since, characters have been added from the sequel trilogy, such as Kylo Ren, Rey, Maz Kanata, BB-8, and Poe Dameron – which kind of throws a bit of a wrench into when exactly the ride's story takes place. But as a non-canonical experience, being able to fully immerse oneself into the *Star Wars* universe at large has entertained the throngs of Disney park-goers for the last several years and will likely continue to do so, especially with the entire themed land of *Star Wars:* Galaxy's Edge opening in California and Florida by the end of 2019.

Galaxy's Edge will be a land within both Disneyland Park and Disney's Hollywood Studios; both lands are expected to be nearly identical to each other. The area will be the "Black Spire Outpost," set on the planet of Batuu. Guests will be able to enjoy drinks at a cantina, interact with various characters, and browse a marketplace. New rides will include one in which guests can pilot the Millennium Falcon, and another where they will face off against First Order troops. The story of the new area is set between the original trilogy and the sequel trilogy, and is meant to depict the rising threat of the First Order across the galaxy.

Other *Star Wars* attractions that have been present at various Disney parks have included *Star Wars: Path of the Jedi*, a short film screening that recaps the events of the theatrical releases, and Jedi Training: Trials of the Temple, where parents can sign up their young Padawans to receive instruction from a Jedi Master and face off against the likes of Darth Vader and Kylo Ren in a short

stage show. The *Star Wars* Launch Bay is a walkthrough attraction seen at the parks, which features memorabilia displays, interactive games, meet-and-greets with popular characters like Chewbacca, and a large gift shop. *Star Wars* has even taken over other attractions – in California, a *Star Wars* overlay transformed Space Mountain into Hyperspace Mountain for a limited time.

Disney has also hosted various *Star Wars*-themed events over the years, the most notably being *Star Wars* Weekends, which was held in the summers of 1997, 2000, 2001, and 2003-2015. The festival event would include special stage shows and other attractions, as well as guest appearances by many franchise actors. In addition, many of the classic Disney characters could be found sporting *Star Wars*-themed outfits for these events.

So – what does all of this mean in terms of collectibles?

Like any good theme park ride, the Disney *Star Wars* attractions often direct their riders into a gift shop after the conclusion of the ride. While these shops tend to carry a bunch of things that can be found at any other toy store (lightsabers, plush toys, shirts, kids' costumes, action figures, and so on), they also carry a large amount of things that can't be found outside of a Disney park. These theme park exclusives range from the obvious to the bizarre, and are often desirable to both hardcore *Star Wars* collectors as much as they are to Disney park fans.

What is a trip to a Disney park without a proper pair of Mickey ears? Exclusive to the Disney resorts are the various themed

Mickey caps, including ones themed to C-3PO, R2-D2, BB-8, and even the Death Star itself. There's also a light-up headband that uses clear plastic and flashing LED lights to depict X-wings taking on a TIE fighter squad. In the parks themselves these are going to run about $15-$20 each. Thanks to how common they are to the parks, they're pretty easy to find secondhand online, too – though the Death Star and C-3PO caps tend to run about $5 to $10 more than the others.

Pin trading is a key part of the Disney park experience for many, and *Star Wars* is definitely a part of that. There's a trading pin for just about every character, ship, and catchphrase in the franchise at this point – when it comes to *Star Wars,* if it exists, there's a Disney trading pin of it at this point. There's droid pins, ship pins, trooper pins, emoji pins, spinning pins, Ewok pins, logo pins, and even Goofy-as-Vader on multiple pins.

Oddly enough, when it comes to pins, sometimes you can find them cheaper on online auction sites than you can at the parks themselves. Even individual pins within the parks can run $10 to upwards of $20 depending on the size, complexity, and print run (most pins made are limited to a couple thousand or so, though some are limited to just a few hundred). But thanks to how Disney pin trading is such a huge deal on its own – we could really do a whole other book on just *Star Wars* Disney pins due to how many of them there really are – it's actually pretty easy to find entire lots of pins containing a bunch of *Star Wars* ones for just a few bucks each.

There's always standouts, though; pins exclusively sold at the *Star Wars* Celebration events can often go for $50 or more for an individual pin, or several hundreds of dollars for a complete set of them. Disney has also released very limited pins only sold on May the Fourth, or at their D23 events – these also carry a far higher price online than what their face value would've been in-person. It's certainly not difficult to find some really great-looking *Star Wars* Disney trading pins, but it can be quite hard to locate event-exclusive releases.

Some of the most sought-after park exclusives when it comes to *Star Wars* are the various popcorn buckets. These refillable plastic buckets are usually crafted with a pretty high level of detail, making them a worthwhile display piece in addition to a simple snack container. Some standouts have included the TIE Fighter bucket, the "Han Solo Frozen in Carbonite" bucket (which was exclusive to Star Wars Weekend), and the AT-AT bucket with poseable legs, to name a few. These usually run anywhere from $25 to $75 in online auctions, depending on the exact bucket as well as the condition of the item itself.

Thanks to Disney's online shop, a lot of the merchandise that's sold at the park gift shops can be found at the same price fairly easily. With the Galaxy's Edge lands opening in 2019, it's likely to bring in a slew of new (and likely exclusive) must-have merchandise for the discerning *Star Wars* collector as well, making the Disney park collectible market one worth paying close attention to in the coming years.

Holiday Cheer with Star Wars Hallmark Ornaments

Collecting Hallmark ornaments has been a yearly tradition for decades, turning simple decoration into beloved keepsakes. Through their ornaments and other products, Hallmark has developed a community of family and friends who belong to clubs, attend events where new products are revealed, and present each other with annual gifts to mark holiday occasions. The high quality ornaments are given significant detail and creativity that has expanded into several pop culture properties, series, and companies. Naturally, *Star Wars* became a part of that tradition.

HALLMARK COMPANY HISTORY

Hallmark began long before *Star Wars* entered the fold. The company's roots trace back to January 1910 when 18-year-old Joyce Clyde Hall left Nebraska for Kansas City, Missouri. He was armed with two shoeboxes of picture postcards and the intent to create a sales endeavor. Joyce, often referred to as J.C., was then joined by his brother Rollie, and they established Hall Brothers.

Initially, J.C. wholesaled products created and manufactured by others, but five years later when a fire destroyed the

The Millennium Falcon, the first *Star Wars* ornament by Hallmark, sells for $60.

Luke Skywalker in Bespin outfit was the first in the Star Wars Collector's Series. It typically sells for $20 to $35.

The Tusken Raider ornament averages $70 to $85.

inventory, the Hall Brothers purchased printing presses and began producing their own greeting cards. By 1928 they started marketing as Hallmark, capitalizing on a term that had been used by goldsmiths to signify quality (the company name officially changed to Hallmark Cards, Inc. in 1954).

By the middle of the 20th century, Hallmark expanded into products like gift wrapping, signed a licensing deal with Walt Disney, innovated the modern method of displaying greeting cards in stores, and established the Hallmark Hall of Fame presentations. They introduced Hallmark Keepsake Ornaments in 1973, upping the ante on ornament quality and style, while also instigating the hobby of collecting ornaments. The Hallmark Gold Crown store program began in '86, creating a network of retailers that sold Hallmark products. In the past two decades Hallmark created a website and e-cards, branched further into entertainment with the Hallmark Channel and original programming, and have continued creating greeting cards, distributed around the world to over 100 countries, printed in 30 languages.

STAR WARS ORNAMENTS

Issued in 1996, the first *Star Wars* ornament was "the fastest hunk of junk in the galaxy." Not only was the Millennium Falcon ornament detailed, it could be plugged into a mini light socket to light up the cockpit and activate the blue-lighted engines. That year it was joined by The Vehicles of Star Wars miniature ornaments, containing an AT-AT, X-Wing, and TIE Fighter.

Since then, Hallmark has issued a bevy of *Star Wars* ornaments. Taking on the likenesses of characters and vehicles, they portray outfits, isolated moments, and scenes from the series. Several main characters have seen multiple ornament editions, with secondary, and even tertiary characters and spacecraft getting the Hallmark treatment. Most are around 3-4" tall, though there are some miniatures and some multi-piece versions. Some of the more fun ornaments feature light and/or sound and a few festive examples even come with Santa hats.

As the original film celebrated its 20th anniversary and special edition versions were being released, Hallmark introduced the official *Star Wars* series of ornaments in '97.

A New York Comic Con R2-Q5 and
R2-A3 ornament reaches $500.

The Wampa ornament from
Comic-Con International: San Diego
sells between $275 and $325.

The first Luke Skywalker ornament, in his Bespin outfit, was distinguished as number one for the yearly Star Wars Collector's Series of collectible ornaments. Others issued in '97 were Darth Vader (with voice and light-up capabilities), Yoda, and a miniature set of C-3PO and R2-D2. Each year since has yielded a handful of new ornaments based on the original trilogy. In '99 prequel trilogy characters and ships were added to the line, and the third trilogy followed in 2015. The ornaments are almost exclusively movie characters, though there are a few from the animated series, including the miniatures set of Asajj Ventress, Anakin Skywalker, and Yoda from *Clone Wars*.

As far as the annual Star Wars Collector's Series, it continued after Bespin Luke with Princess Leia #2, Han Solo #3, Obi-Wan Kenobi #4, R2-D2 #5, Darth Vader #6, C-3PO #7, Chewbacca carrying C-3PO #8, Slave Leia #9, Luke carrying Yoda #10, R2-D2 and Jawa #11, Emperor Palpatine #12, Han in Stormtrooper uniform #13, Luke in Rebel pilot uniform #14, Jedi Master Yoda #15, General Grievous #16, Wicket and Teebo #17, Scout Trooper #18, C-3PO and R2-D2 #19, Force Awakens Han #20, and Force Awakens Luke #21 (the most recent number when this book was published).

In addition to the Collector's Series, there are other special ornaments with some created in limited quantities, Comic-Con International: San Diego or New York Comic Con exclusives, and Star Wars Celebration special editions. Some have been crossed with other properties like LEGO, some appear as lunchboxes, and at least one depicts a series movie poster.

PRICING STAR WARS ORNAMENTS

Star Wars ornaments are often popular sellers as soon as the new yearly editions are available. In addition to *Star Wars* fans, they appeal to Hallmark collectors and ornament collectors, driving collectability and prices. Individual pieces in the series typically average $20-$50, if they are in Very Good condition and the boxes are undamaged. Some, however, can be found for under $10.

The Death Star tree topper realizes $150.

Despite the distinction of being in the Star Wars Collector's Series, those numbered ornaments match the averages of the rest of the line, as most are priced at $25-$45. A select few are below the $20 mark (General Grevious, Scout Trooper), while some others sell for $60 or more (see below).

Ornaments for convention exclusives, Star Wars Celebration, or labeled as limited edition achieve high-dollar sales, into the hundreds. On the opposite end of the spectrum, the LEGO-based ornaments are valued at $15-$25. One notable pricing disparity is that the '98 X-Wing lunchbox ornament sells for under $10 while the 2001 *Empire Strikes Back* lunchbox version hits over $30. As far as the films themselves, the prequel trilogy ornaments typically achieve lower prices than the other movies, particularly *The Phantom Menace*.

NOTEWORTHY SALES:

- 1996 Millennium Falcon $60
- 2001 R2-D2 Star Wars Collector's Series #5 $60
- 2002 Death Star $75-$90
- 2003 TIE Fighter $60-$70
- 2004 Star Destroyer $65-$75

- 2006 Imperial AT-AT and Rebel Snowspeeder $60-$75
- 2007 Tusken Raider $70-$85
- 2008 Imperial Shuttle $60-$70
- 2009 Greedo limited edition $60-$80
- 2009 Shock Trooper and Shadow Trooper Comic-Con International: San Diego $550
- 2010 K-3PO and R-3PO Comic-Con International: San Diego $400
- 2010 Rebel Snowspeeder $60-$75
- 2011 IG-88 and Dengar Comic-Con International: San Diego $500
- 2011 R2-Q5 and R2-A3 New York Comic Con $500
- 2012 4-Lom and Zuckuss Comic-Con International: San Diego $200
- 2012 Obi-Wan Kenobi and Ponda Baba Star Wars Celebration $200
- 2013 Wrath of Rancor Comic-Con International: San Diego $300
- 2014 Cantina Band $60
- 2014 Wampa Comic-Con International: San Diego $275-$325
- 2015 An Epic Vision Star Wars Celebration $175
- 2015 C-3PO and R2-D2 Star Wars #19 $60-$70
- 2015 U-3PO and R5-D4 Comic-Con International: San Diego $125-$150
- 2016 Beginnings: Boba Fett Comic-Con International: San Diego $100
- 2016 Death Star tree topper $150
- 2017 Beginnings: Stormtrooper Star Wars Celebration $100
- 2017 Jedi Master set $150-$175
- 2017 T-70 X-Wing Fighter Comic-Con International: San Diego $100

AFTERWORD

With 40 years of stories told through thousands of titles, *Star Wars* is still propelling forward with new content. *Episode IX*, the last chapter in the third trilogy, is, as of this book's publication, set for theatrical release on December 20, 2019. Though concrete announcements regarding other films have not been made, there could be more movies in the works.

In July 2018, Marvel Comics reached the 50th issue of their current *Star Wars* comic book series, which continues the adventures of Luke, Leia, and Han. Marvel is also publishing monthly series for Darth Vader and other characters, along with miniseries connected to the new movies. IDW Publishing is running the *Star Wars Adventures* comic, as well as limited series.

Future events like Star Wars Celebration and D23 Expo are being planned and *Star Wars* will likely continue to have a presence at large comics and pop culture conventions. The Star Wars: Galaxy's Edge themed land will be added to Disney parks in both California and Florida by the end of 2019.

New books, video games, and TV series are also planned for the future, as are more toys and collectibles, along with apparel and costumes for kids and adults and product tie-ins with a variety of brands.

As vintage toys reach astounding new prices and more projects continue to be announced, the collecting market is packed with *Star Wars* memorabilia for hungry collectors – ourselves included. We hope that our passion for this iconic franchise has come through over the course of this book, and that it has been as much of a joy for you to read as it was for us to put together. It's a great time to be a *Star Wars* fan, and we can't wait to see what's next.

AMANDA SHERIFF
AUTHOR/ASSOCIATE EDITOR

BOB OVERSTREET
AUTHOR/PUBLISHER

STEPHEN A. GEPPI
PRESIDENT AND CEO

J.C. VAUGHN
VICE-PRESIDENT OF PUBLISHING

MARK HUESMAN
CREATIVE DIRECTOR

CARRIE WOOD
ASSISTANT EDITOR

BRAELYNN BOWERSOX
STAFF WRITER

GEMSTONE
PUBLISHING

WWW.GEMSTONEPUB.COM